THE SPONTANEOUS SELF

THE SPONTANEOUS SELF

VIABLE ALTERNATIVES TO FREE WILL

PAUL BREER

Original printing, Institute for Naturalistic Philosophy, Cambridge, MA, 1989
Second printing, Xlibris Corporation, Bloomington, Indiana, 2012

Library of Congress Control Number: 2012914695
ISBN: Hardcover   978-1-4771-5969-9
                 Softcover   978-1-4771-5968-2
                 Ebook   978-1-4771-5970-5

Grateful acknowledgment is made for permission to use copyrighted material from the following sources:

Dylan Thomas: *Poems of Dylan Thomas*. Copyright c 1952 by Dylan Thomas, 1967 by the Trustees for the Copyrights of Dylan Thomas. Reprinted by permission of New Directions Publishing Corporation.

Transformations of Consciousness by Ken Wilber, Jack Engler and Daniel P. Brown. Selection c 1986 by *The Journal of Transpersonal Psychology*. Reprinted by arrangement with Shambhala Publications, Inc., 300 Massachusetts Ave., Boston, MA 02115.

The Wisdom of Insecurity by Alan W. Watts. Copyright c 1951 by Pantheon Books, Inc.; *The Way of Zen* by Alan W. Watts, copyright c 1957 by Pantheon Books, Inc. Both reprinted by permission of Pantheon Books, a Division of Random House, Inc.

On the Genealogy of Morals by Friedrich Nietzsche, trans. by Walter Kaufmann and R.J. Hollingdale, and edited, with commentary, by Walter Kaufmann. Copyright c 1967 by Random House, Inc.; *The Will To Power* by Friedrich Nietzsche, trans. by Walter Kaufmann and R.J. Hollingdale and edited, with commentary, by Walter Kaufmann. Copyright c 1967 by Walter Kaufmann. Reprinted by permission of Random House, Inc.

Beyond Freedom and Dignity by B.F. Skinner. Copyright c 1971 by B.F. Skinner. Reprinted by permission of Alfred A. Knopf, Inc.

To order additional copies of this book, contact:
Xlibris Corporation
1-888-795-4274
www.Xlibris.com
Orders@Xlibris.com
90191

TABLE OF CONTENTS

PREFACE

Eight years ago I met Tom Clark at a meeting of the Alan Watts Fellowship in Boston. At the time, he was working on a monograph called "Buddhism, Behaviorism, and the Myth of the Autonomous Self." I was in the process of sketching out a book on the illusion of self based on thinking I had done since leaving the Rochester Zen Center. We were delighted to discover that we shared a basic conviction that the "I" most Westerners take as their real self was no more than a conceptual fiction. At the same time we were intrigued by the differences in our approach to that fiction. While Tom was concerned with demonstrating how it had surfaced in traditions as disparate as Buddhism and behaviorism, I was more concerned with spelling out what it implied for our everyday lives. In the months that followed, we met often to clarify the meaning of what we then called "non-ego".

After a year or more of discussion I set down my own thoughts about the self in a manuscript entitled "Letting Go of Ego." Fortunately, it was never published. While I was eager to share how the gradual giving up of a belief in ego had changed my own life, I lacked the conceptual tools for explaining how such a life was even possible. By this time Tom was immersed in Western philosophy and began introducing me to the ideas of contemporary thinkers like Dennett, Hofstadter, Searle, Nagel, and Parfit. With his help I began to recast my own thinking about ego in more traditional Western terms. What had originated as an attempt to clarify the meaning of the Buddhist concept of "no-self" gradually became an inquiry into free agency and its psychological implications. While the conceptual shift made little difference in how I experienced non-agency in my personal life, it made it easier for me to explain that experience to other Westerners. It also allowed me to use philosophers like Hume and Nietzsche to support my argument that the agent/I is an illusion.

Another five years passed before I felt ready to try writing again. *The Spontaneous Self* is a result of this second effort. During the year or so that it took to finish the manuscript, Tom and I met often to discuss the philosophical and psychological implications of non-agency. His clarity of mind and unflagging support helped to make it one of the most productive years of my life. Throughout an editing process that spanned at least seven separate readings, he demonstrated equal facility in detecting flaws in my logic and correcting aesthetic lapses in my prose. Given the fact that I adopted almost all of his recommendations, it follows that the final version reflects much of his own philosophical thinking and literary taste.

There were others who helped. Professor Eli Hirsch offered both analytic and stylistic criticisms of many chapters and wrote a summary comment from which I have extracted the paragraph on the back cover. Besides pointing out logical problems in some of the early chapters, he provided me with a new perspective from which to view the book as a whole. Through the eyes of a professional philosopher, my personal account of what it was like to give up a belief in free agency became reframed as an essay in the "phenomenology of hard determinism."

Gary Rancourt, who has remained steadfastly enthusiastic about this project ever since we met in my "Letting Go of Ego" class, recommended several important changes, including the writing of a separate chapter on the origins of free agency. He also made me aware how repetitive some of the text was, a problem I have only partially solved. Professor Amelie Rorty helped me to see that I had underestimated the role of socio-economic factors in the growth and persistence of the agency concept. A satisfactory response to her objection will have to wait for a later book on the social implications of non-agency.

Kurt Halliday, Jo Procter, and Dr. Henry White all read parts of the manuscript and recommended a variety of changes, most of which I was happy to take.

INTRODUCTION

I have divided *The Spontaneous Self* into four sections, each with a function of its own. *In Search of the Homunculus* begins by defining the overall scope of the book and then proceeds to question the evidence for our conventional view of self. I argue, with Hume, that when we go looking for the "I" we imagine ourselves to be, we find nothing but a stream of thoughts and feelings. The section closes with speculations on why the concept of free agency has persisted primarily in the Western world.

A Question of Survival addresses the problem of how individuals and societies maintain their stability. In chapter five, I examine the self-correcting process by which organisms learn to govern themselves without benefit of an inner psychic supervisor. In chapter six, I explore the hypothesis that neither free will nor its correlate, moral responsibility, is necessary for maintaining social control.

The eight chapters which comprise *The Psychological Implications of Giving up Free Will* explore those dimensions of life most likely to be affected by a change in beliefs about agency. Using my own experience as a guide, I examine the implications of non-agency for blame, credit, achievement, acceptance, power, emotion, love, and identity. Because the eight chapters draw on a common logical structure, they are most profitably read one or two at a time rather than in a single sitting.

In *Dispelling the Free Will Illusion*, I describe and illustrate the techniques I have developed for uprooting the illusion of agency in my own personal life. The last chapter attempts to answer the question of why we cling so desperately to the idea of free agency if it is, in fact, only an illusion.

In Search of
the
Homunculus

1

AN OVERVIEW OF THE AGENCY PROBLEM

Of all the beliefs that shape our thinking, feeling, and acting, few are more pivotal than those that define what it means to be a self. Like our basic assumptions about time, space, purpose, and truth, the assumptions we make about personal identity are instilled early in childhood and almost universally taken for granted from that point on. Despite the work of generations of philosophers and psychologists, we rarely question the validity of such fundamental premises – even when there is good reason to suspect they may be distorted.

There is good reason to suspect that our Western notion of what it means to be a self *is* distorted. It may be unrealistic enough, in fact, to qualify as a delusion, i.e., "a false belief regarding the self or persons or objects outside the self that persists despite the facts . . ." (Merriam-Webster). Neither the facts of private introspection nor those of public observation support our traditional concept of who we are. If we go on clinging to our belief despite the evidence, it is perhaps because we find that belief flattering. What may be less obvious – and this will become the focus of later chapters – is the price we pay for that flattery.

The same belief that prevents us from seeing ourselves accurately has the effect of distorting the way other people see us and the way we perceive them. Those distortions, by altering our most common thoughts and feelings, ultimately find their way into every detail of our personal and interpersonal lives. Because the basic distortion comes out of a cultural belief, it affects people from all ethnic, class, and religious groups. While the delusion is most

1

fully developed in modern Western societies, rudimentary signs of it can be found in every culture of which we have some record.

In the societies of Europe and North America where the delusion holds sway over educated and uneducated alike, it is protected by what Alan Watts called "an unrecognized but mighty taboo – [namely] our tacit conspiracy to ignore who, or what, we really are."[1] The term *taboo* reminds us that our way of defining ourselves is supported by every institution in society – the church, law, family, schools and colleges, government, the media – even by the language we speak. In daring to violate that taboo, we risk more than censure. We risk exposing ourselves to the truth of who we really are. That truth, if and when we ever awaken to it, threatens to trigger an upheaval in consciousness and, in the process, to transform our most fundamental ideas about what it means to be human.

When I say that we have a distorted idea of who we are, I am not referring to the way we perceive and judge ourselves as individual personalities, although it is obvious that those idiosyncratic self-images have a powerful effect on how we feel and act. Nor am I referring to the Buddhist notion that we are deluded when we fail to see that our true Self transcends our particular body and mind. While the Eastern notion of the Self as the undifferentiated ground of being avoids the error I have in mind, it does so only by denying the reality of the individual personality.

In suggesting that we do not know who we are, I mean simply that the inner spirit or soul we take to be our real self is an illusion. Most of us automatically assume that there exists within each of us an agent or force that serves as stage director – overseeing our personal drama from the wings, ready to feed us our lines, cue our entrances, and in general see to it that we play our parts well. There are good reasons, however, for doubting that any such entity exists. When David Hume, the eighteenth century Scottish philosopher, looked into his own mind for such an agent, all he found was a stream of thoughts and sensations, but no self creating or even having those experiences.

Hume was only twenty-eight at the time he published his discovery in *A Treatise of Human Nature*. The critical passage has been quoted many times before but is important enough to be quoted again:

> For my part, when I enter most intimately into what I call *my-self*, I always stumble on some particular perception or other, of heat or cold, light or shade, love or hatred, pain or pleasure.

I never can catch *myself* at any time without a perception, and never can observe any thing but the perception.[2]

Despite Hume's inability to explain to his own satisfaction what he had found, the suspicion that the self may be no more than an illusion has survived two hundred and fifty years of debate in the West. With the dawn of artificial intelligence and the recent explosion of discoveries in the neurosciences, that suspicion is more alive now than ever before.

What I mean by agent is what writers of a more spiritual age called the soul and what modern psychologists refer to as ego. Despite the difference in coloring, all three terms refer to a common animating principle or entity that stands at the center of our being, directing our thoughts, decisions and moral judgments. More than any feature of personality or physical appearance, it is this soul-ego-agent that we conventionally think of as our real self. It is that which ultimately distinguishes us from each other. When we get right down to it, you are you and I am I because of a difference in agency. We may resemble each other in behavior or looks. We could even be identical twins, but because the animating force within us is unique, we as individuals are unique.

That, at any rate, is what most of us have been brought up to believe. Starting early in childhood, we are taught that our true self resides not in our bodies or even in our minds, but in our souls. As soul-agents, we are not only unique but, unlike all other creatures on earth, endowed with the power and freedom to cause our own behavior. We are more than bodies, more than minds. In our essence, we are spiritual beings. That conception of homo sapiens is rarely challenged even by those who profess a materialist philosophy. The broad acceptance of free will among the religious and non-religious alike obscures the fact that the concept of agency rests on the same dualistic assumptions as our belief in God, the Devil, heaven, hell, the Holy Ghost, salvation, and divine judgment. What makes free agency a specifically spiritual concept is the assumption that the agent's choices are not caused by antecedent conditions. They are mysterious, inexplicable – unconnected to the chain of cause and effect which links all events in the material world. The agent is free, in other words, because of its power to cause behavior without itself being the effect of other causes. To the extent that we humans possess that power, we qualify as Unmoved Movers. We are god-like, divine, and not fully of this material world.

There is reason to suspect, however, that the little man or woman inside of us (the homunculus) is no more real than any of the other spiritual entities with which we have traditionally populated the unseen world. From that perspective, it is questionable how much longer a culture committed to a rational-empirical world view can sustain the notion of an inner agent creating thoughts and actions *ex nihilo*. Historically, free agency was probably conceived 3500-4000 years ago by warrior herdsmen in what is now northern Iraq and Iran. As ideology, the concept of the "freely willing historically effective hero" served to rationalize the overthrow of an oppressive, hieratically-structured world in which individual autonomy was subordinated to the cyclical order of nature.[3] As it spread from Mesopotamia into the Levant, Greece, and ultimately Europe, the image of man as semi-divine prompted its own mythology and religion and, in time, its own peculiarly Western brand of civilization. While that civilization has changed dramatically over the course of our millennia, the belief in free agency which inspired much of its religion and philosophy remains intact. Now, in the waning decades of the twentieth century, the concept of an inner homunculus self is being threatened by a resurgence of naturalistic thinking fed by neurological research and computer simulation of mental processes. The view of ourselves as half angel, half beast may be losing its grip.

If it should turn out that we are not souls or agents after all, what else is there for us to be? The answer is almost too obvious. If we are not the prime movers of our thoughts, feelings, and actions, must we not be the thoughts, feelings, and actions themselves – as well as the physical bodies in which those experiences arise? This much is certain: if we are not free agents, we cannot be the authors of our own experience and behavior. Nor can we be the internal managers who organize and process that experience; the experience organizes and processes itself. It is not even appropriate to say that we are subjects *having* the experience. We *are* the experience. We are that which is happening here in these bodies. We are constellations of experience and behavior arising spontaneously out of genetic and environmental circumstance. We are also the physical structures in which those events are taking place.

A WORLD WITHOUT AGENCY

A shift in the way we define ourselves has implications for practically everything we do. One way to clarify the meaning of agency while demonstrating its relevance to other areas of life is to imagine what life would be like without it. Consider the following scenario as presented in John Martin Fischer's *Moral Responsibility*.[4] You have just discovered that your best friend is being electronically controlled by scientists in California who secretly implanted a mechanical device in his brain when he was a child. For years the device has allowed the scientists to manipulate his behavior and thoughts without either his or your knowing about it. Only now do you realize that all the gestures, habits, nuances of feelings, and twists of mind you thought to be your friend's own doing are the result of scientific manipulation.

In Fischer's fantasy, the scientists and their device serve as remote and proximate causes of your friend's experience and behavior. Together, they symbolize the environmental, genetic, and biochemical factors that determinists have traditionally called upon to account for what we think and do. The heuristic value of the fantasy lies in its ability to elicit the very kind of feelings we might have toward each other in a world where people no longer believed in free agency.

If you find that in attempting to figure out how you might feel toward your friend, you are distracted by the thought of all those California scientists hovering in the background, trying to agree on how to manipulate your friend (while listening in on his most personal conversations with you), it might be helpful to change the scenario slightly. Assume that when the device was implanted years ago, it was programmed to do all the things the scientists have been doing by remote control. The scientists are no longer necessary. The device itself is fully capable of controlling your friend's every thought and feeling. In any given situation, the device can induce desires, access thoughts, trigger memories, coordinate sensory input, review any pertinent cultural norms, consider the consequences of alternative actions according to a programmed hierarchy of values – and send a signal to the motor system initiating appropriate forms of behavior. Once implanted, the device needs no supervision. It is capable of rational, appropriate action under a wide variety of conditions. It even has the ability to revise its own programs in response to changes either in the environment or in the body/mind of the host organism.

Let us assume that your friend is still unaware of this device buried in his brain. It is only you who have awakened to the truth. As far as he is concerned, he is in control of his choices and actions. The thought has simply never occurred to him that what he experiences as the exercise of free will is really the work of a tiny machine. At this point, rather than trying to convince him of his error, it might be more productive to consider how your own feelings have been affected by this discovery.

Can you continue, Fischer asks, to respect him for being such a creative thinker when you know that mechanical device is responsible for generating all his thoughts? Does it make sense to feel grateful toward him for his kindness or resentful toward him for his insensitivity when you know that both are the product of a machine? How much does his caring for you mean now that you realize how little *he* has to do with it. And if everything he thinks and feels is controlled by that device, is there really anyone there for you to love? When you come right down to it, is he anything more than a robot? According to Fischer,

> . . . Once you had been convinced that direct manipulation exists, a striking thing would occur; many of your most basic *attitudes* toward your friend would change. Your friend would no longer seem to be an appropriate object of such attitudes as respect, gratitude, love, indignation, and resentment. Furthermore, it would seem somehow out of place to praise or blame your friend on the basis of his behavior. . . . These responses, it is quite clear, are of central importance to our lives. Imagine a life without gratitude, respect, love, indignation, resentment, and so on. Such a life would be very thin and radically different from the lives we now lead. We care very deeply about these attitudes and about the activities of praising and blaming that are bound up with them.[5]

We do not have to accept all of Fischer's speculations to agree that our beliefs about agency make a difference in our attitudes toward each other. Praising and blaming, gratitude and resentment usually imply that there exists within the other person some kind of agent (soul, spirit, Self) that is instrumental in causing him or her to think, feel, and eventually act in a certain way. When, in our fantasy, we substitute a mechanical device for that agent, our attitudes change. The fantasy provides a glimpse of what might follow if we were to give up our belief in agency, i.e., if we were to accept that we were not the causes of our own experience but the experience itself.

But there is another side to this coin. Fischer is so worried about what we might lose in giving up our belief in agency that he hesitates to look at what might be gained by doing so. Like most philosophers who have written about the subject, Fischer assumes that resentment, indignation, moral credit and moral blame all represent quintessential and desirable aspects of human life. There is no indication in anything he says that he has considered the possibility that we might be better off without them.

Just how desirable are those responses? Are they as desirable as Fischer makes them out to be when he says life would be "thin" without them? Is that really true, for example, of resentment and indignation? Would we really feel deprived if we never felt either again? What about bitterness, scorn, and vindictiveness? Or, when the tables are turned, humiliation, shame, and defensiveness? Are these feelings essential to our existence or to our nature? Would we be less human without them?

To help you answer such questions for yourself, we can make the concept of agency even more concrete. Change the scenario again so that it is no longer your friend in whom the implanted device has been discovered – but you. Assume that every thought you are having right now, every image competing for your attention, every itch, sigh, yawn, and breath you are experiencing as you read this book, is being dictated by a tiny machine in your brain. Contrary to what you have always believed, it is the machine that is responsible for what you feel and do, not some autonomous agent or soul (not *you*). There is no longer any *you* in the traditional sense; you are (and always have been) a unique, self-regulating system of mental and physical processes arising spontaneously out of the workings of a device planted in your brain.

Now, how does all of this affect your feelings about yourself? Do you still feel guilty for all the pain *you* have caused others? How about all the things *you* have failed to do that others had a right to expect from you? Do you still feel like punishing yourself for all the mistakes you have made – the bad career choices, the bad marriages, or all the havoc you have wreaked on your body with smoking, drinking, and overeating? If all your actions have been determined not by you-as-agent but by a device in your brain, can we really say that you are morally responsible for what has happened? If all your desires, as well as all your failures to inhibit those desires, have arisen out of the workings of this machine, is it appropriate for you to go on feeling guilty or remorseful about anything?

The answer would seem to be no. You might wish strongly that certain decisions had not arisen. You might lament the consequences of those decisions for both yourself and others, but you would not hold yourself accountable for making them happen. Self-punishment (e.g., guilt or remorse) presupposes an inner agent that is free to choose otherwise at the time the choice is made. If there is no you-as-agent to cause the decision – if you are the decision itself (among other things) – there is no reason to feel guilt or remorse about anything. But can we say (following Fischer) that those feelings are "extremely important to us?" Would we find it wrenching to give them up? Are they, as we have assumed for so long, an essential part of what it means to be human?

The same questions need to be asked of other feelings equally colored by the belief that we as agents cause our own behavior and can thus be judged for what we do. One of the most pervasive of such feelings is anxiety, especially what psychologists call evaluation anxiety or anxiety arising out of the fear of being judged adversely. Our belief in agency leads us to anticipate judgment not only of our behavior but of ourselves as authors of that behavior. The fear that others will disapprove of us, be disappointed in us, or stop respecting us has the power to make our hearts pound and our voices quaver. But what if there were no author/agent inside of us creating our behavior? How anxious would we be if we knew that all our thoughts and actions were determined by a device in our brain or, as they are in fact, by a combination of genetic and environmental circumstances?

Some will argue that a willingness to be judged and, thus, made anxious may be the price we have to pay for the privilege of living in a civilized world. Ever since Freud adduced that argument in *Civilization and Its Discontents*, it has become popular to rationalize our anxiety as a by-product of society's efforts to protect itself against runaway sex and violence.[6] We seem so convinced of his argument that we rarely question whether the price may be too steep. It may be time to ask whether anxiety has to be part of that price at all.

Depression and anxiety often go together. While anticipating negative judgment, we often put ourselves (i.e., our agents) down for failing. We blame ourselves for not being intelligent, skillful, or determined enough to succeed. We respond to rejection by blaming ourselves for not being lovable. While mourning the death of a loved one, we exacerbate our grief by blaming ourselves for not having done more. Under the right circumstances, our self-loathing (i.e., our agent-loathing) can become so extreme as to drive us to suicide.

In light of the possibility that much of our anxiety and depression are based on an illusion, it seems appropriate to pose a question that Fischer never got around to asking: Are the satisfactions of being a free agent, i.e., power, dignity, and a feeling of being special in the universe, worth the grief that goes with judging and being judged? There are many who would say yes. It will be argued, for example, that the positive consequences of believing in agency more than compensate for the pain such a belief entails. After all, pride is as much a part of the agency syndrome as is guilt. Being praised for our achievements is just as common as being blamed for our failures. Without a belief that our achievements are to some degree caused by a free agent operating within us, there would be nothing for which we could take moral credit.

While Fischer is quick to point out the loss of ego gratification implied by non-agency, he fails to consider the gain in peace of mind that might come with shedding our identity as free-willing souls. He shows no sign of having considered the feeling of lightness and buoyant joy that can arise when we realize that we do not have to *make* our lives happen. My own experience of the last eight years has made it clear that this is precisely the sensation that arises. It is the sensation of effortless flowing, of moving with the stream, of being *in* the stream – as opposed to standing on the bank struggling to redirect its course. It is an exquisite sensation which, in my own life, has replaced most of the tension I felt as an agent straining to bend the world to my will.

A Necessary Illusion?

Arguing in terms of the consequences of how we define ourselves, of course, begs the question of who we really are. If our first obligation is to discover the truth, shouldn't we be talking about the validity of our beliefs rather than what might happen if we substitute one view of ourselves for another? Wouldn't it be wiser to go looking for the truth first and then turn our attention to learning how to live with that truth, whatever it might be?

As plausible as that might sound, it is certainly not a universal opinion. Consider what Marvin Minsky has to say about free will in *The Society of Mind*:

> Does this mean that we must embrace the modern scientific view and put aside the ancient myth of voluntary choice? No. We *can't* do that: too much of what we think and do revolves around those old beliefs. Consider how our social lives depend upon the notion of *responsibility* and how little that idea would mean without our belief that personal actions are voluntary. Without that belief, no praise or shame could accrue to actions that were caused by Cause, nor could we assign any credit or blame to deeds that came about by Chance. What could we make our children learn if neither they nor we perceived some fault or virtue anywhere? ... No matter that the physical world provides no room for freedom of will: that concept is essential to our models of the mental realm. Too much of our psychology is based on it for us to ever give it up. We're virtually forced to maintain that belief, even though we

know it's false – except, of course, when we're inspired to find the flaws in *all* our beliefs, whatever may be the consequence to cheerfulness and mental peace.[7] (original italics)

Free will plays such a pivotal role in our lives, Minsky is arguing, that we have no choice but to believe in it. He agrees that the notion is false, but insists that we cannot survive without it. Our notions of responsibility, fault, and virtue demand that we act *as if* we were free, even though we aren't. For Minsky the issue is no longer whether or not we are free, but how to maintain the illusion that we are free when it is clear that we are not.

Pretending that things are other than what we know them to be is certainly not unheard of in human affairs. The delight we experience in an effective metaphor resides in its power to equate events or objects we know to be different (e.g., Shakespeare's equating of life and theater in, "Life's but a walking shadow, a poor player that struts and frets his hour upon the stage, and then is heard no more . . ."). Without a similar suspension of disbelief, the dramatic arts themselves would be reduced to a bizarre and tedious affair in which an assortment of hired help move about on a large wooden floor talking or singing about other people's business.

But is the illusion that we are free agents really of a piece with metaphors and the theater? Free agency is a concept which permeates practically every corner of our conscious and unconscious lives. How long can we go on pretending about something so central? What kind of mental gymnastics will be required to continue acting as if we were the cause of our thoughts and actions as evidence mounts that we are really the thoughts and actions themselves?

The wish to sustain the illusion is predicated on the assumption that society would collapse without it. That is a common enough assumption among philosophers, but few have really examined it closely. Almost everyone who sees fit to mention the subject starts by assuming that the only way to make people behave responsibly and productively is to convince them that they are the causes of their own behavior. Pride, guilt, remorse, and regret can then be used to keep them in line. But guilt, remorse, and regret can be extremely painful experiences, as can the anxiety, anger, and despair that so often accompany them. They can be so painful that, instead of preventing deviance, they often inspire it, as in the case of the youth whose humiliating failure at school arouses the need for violent retaliation against the system he perceives to have cheated him.

By exaggerating the negative consequences of non-agency and overlooking its benefits, we have frightened ourselves away from any critical analysis of the concept. Most of us cannot even imagine life without an inner self that does our intending and choosing for us. If we can bring ourselves to examine that notion closely, we may discover just how illusory it is. In the process we may realize just how much the assumption of agency has contributed to the misery we accept as part of the human condition. If we pursue the inquiry long enough, we may also discover how easy life can be without that assumption.

The idea that free will may be an illusion is hardly a new one. Many philosophers, both dead and living, have rejected the notion that an inner agent can serve as a necessary or sufficient cause of behavior without itself being caused by previous events. But it is not in the tradition of Western philosophy to apply such conclusions to real life situations outside the classroom. With few exceptions, the free will debate has played itself out in an academic vacuum. Only rarely (e.g., in the realm of law) have philosophers thought through the implications of what they appear to believe so strongly. What we never hear about is whether they act on their beliefs in personal matters – and, if so, with what consequences.

My own interest in non-agency has evolved out of a five-year immersion in the chilly waters of Rinzai Zen. While I have long since given up what Alan Watts called "aching-legs Zen" for the comforts of reading and thinking, I have retained the Easterner's concern with integrating philosophy into everyday life. It strikes me as little more than a game, fascinating perhaps but still a game, to embrace the idea of non-agency without taking steps to incorporate that idea into the way one deals with work, love, pain, death and all the other dimensions of human existence. Because the idea is so central, taking it in deeply has the potential for transforming the way we feel about almost everything we do.

That taking in process started in my own life about eight years ago. A re-reading of Alan Watt's *The Way of Zen* opened my eyes to the paradoxical truth that even the most deliberate or violent effort arises on its own without the help of an interior agent.[8] Many months passed before I could appreciate the implications of that insight. When applied to my own behavior, it set in motion a lengthy process during which I gradually came to experience more and more of my feelings, thoughts, and behavior as arising spontaneously.

In the beginning that understanding was almost purely intellectual. While I could claim that I no longer believed in agency, my feelings and behavior continued to belie the point. Occasional bouts of anxiety, defensiveness, pride, bragging, and anger indicated a persisting belief that I (as agent) was responsible for causing my own behavior. In the years that followed, those feelings became the focus of a systematic attempt to uproot all traces of agency and to rid myself of the emotional life that seemed to go with that belief.

Although eight years of constant self-scrutiny have failed to complete the job, enough has happened to give me hope that the experiment is working. I use the term "experiment" guardedly. With a sample population of one, some may question whether results of this personal exercise in cognitive bootstrapping are even worth reporting. Beyond sample size, there are problems with reliability and validity. I serve not only as the subject in the experiment, but the author of the ideas to be tested, the trainer who instructs the subject in those ideas, the observer who records changes in the subject's behavior, and the analyst who writes up the results. While proceeding in this manner has served to keep study costs down, there are reasonable grounds for concern about objectivity and generalizability of findings.

The lack of a control group makes an already dubious enterprise even more suspect. Personality changes that I have experienced over the last eight years may have been due not to a shift in beliefs about agency but to aging or some other process. Without others of similar age and circumstance with whom to compare myself, there is no way for me to be certain about the source of those changes. It is also possible that a shift in belief away from agency has played a causal role in my changing, but only because of something unique in my personal history or genetic makeup that has sensitized me to the process. If others were to try the same thing, they might be disappointed to find that it accomplished nothing.

What justifies my sharing the results of this exploration with you is the possibility that at least some of the changes I have undergone are generalizable to anyone who experiences a similar shift in belief. If there is any danger here, it is probably the temptation to claim too much for ideas and too little for processes like aging. I hope that temptation will be constrained by the need to demonstrate a logical connection between my beliefs about agency and any personality changes I have observed. Some of the changes I have experienced over the past eight years, e.g., a growing preference for eighteenth century chamber music, have no obvious connection to the way I define myself. Others, like the gradual dropping away of anxiety, seem to be a direct outgrowth of a shift in my beliefs about personal responsibility.

The book is both an argument and a strategy for replacing the illusion of agency with a view of ourselves as constellations of experience and behavior arising spontaneously out of circumstance. If there is any originality here, it does not lie with the argument against free will. That argument has evolved in a variety of places and constitutes a major chapter in the history of both Eastern and Western philosophy. What may be new is the spelling out of how the illusion of agency adds to the pain of life and, paradoxically, how much freer we would feel if we were to begin defining ourselves as that which is arising here.

Ever since the Iron Age, free will has held sway over Western culture. Like other tacit premises which have shaped our uniquely Western style of thinking, our belief in free agency is deeply embedded in the social order and is thus highly resistant to change. We should not infer from that resistance, however, that it is unchangeable. Other equally central beliefs about creation, immortality, the position of the earth in the solar system, inevitable progress, and the origins of life have been exposed as logically inconsistent or empirically untenable. Our belief in an eternal and causally autonomous soul is vulnerable to the same scientific and naturalistic critique that has led to the gradual rejection of those other beliefs. Current developments in the neurosciences and in artificial intelligence have already compromised our faith in a homunculus-soul. Future brain research and advances in robotics can only deepen that skepticism.

It is possible, of course, to dispel the illusion of free agency in one's own life without waiting for the culture-at-large to change. At the individual level, learning to see ourselves not as soul-agents but as constellations of body and experience is a cognitive problem that requires a cognitive solution. The strategy I have personally followed over the last eight years can be thought of as a form of cognitive therapy in which the distortion being treated is an insistence on defining myself as a causally autonomous agent. In my own case, that process has involved a combination of didactic argument, self-scrutiny, and experimentation with a language devoid of references to agency.

The techniques described later in the book (see chapter fifteen) should make it easier to accept life just as it is and to enjoy all the emotional and behavioral benefits that go with that perspective. Straining, blaming, craving, defending and protesting are all implicated in the agency syndrome. Their emotional counterparts – anxiety, guilt, despair, pride, and anger – can be expected to change as behavior itself changes. For anyone patient enough to see the process through, the end result is a transformation of personality. The more thorough the uprooting of agency, the more radical will be that transformation.

REFERENCES

1. Watts, A., *The Book*, New York: Vintage, 1966, p. ix.
2. Hume, D., *A Treatise of Human Nature*, Middlesex: Penguin Books, 1969, p. 300. First published in 1739-40.
3. Campbell, J., *Occidental Mythology*, New York: Penguin Books, 1964, p. 24.
4. Fischer, J., *Moral Responsibility*, Ithaca: Cornell University Press, 1986, Introduction.
5. Fischer, J., *Moral Responsibility*, p. 9.
6. Freud, S., *Civilization and Its Discontents*, New York: W.W. Norton, 1961.
7. Minsky, M., *The Society of Mind*, New York: Simon and Schuster, 1985, p. 307.
8. Watts, A., *The Way of Zen*, New York: Vintage Books 1957.

2

WHAT DOES IT MEAN TO SAY I?

Some questions never arise because we are convinced that we already know the answers. Everyone, for example, knows what it means to say *I*. The answer is so obvious that only psychologists and philosophers bother asking it. For most of us, it is sufficient to know that *I* means *me*, the person who is speaking – in this case Paul Breer, the person sitting at this computer writing this book. But, simple as that sounds, it is not immediately clear what is meant by the term "person." Do we mean body? Can we say that my body is doing the writing? Or is it my mind? Or, if both body and mind belong to *me*, does it follow that *I* am something other than either?

Psychologist William James was one of the first to pursue the question of what it means to say *I*. He called attention to the fact that, in its simplest sense, *I* designates a location. It tells others that the action is taking place here, where *here* refers to the physical body of the speaker. We experience the world, he said,

> with our body as its center, center of vision, center of action, center of interest. Where the body is is "here"; when the body acts is "now"; what the body touches is "this"; all other things are "there" and "then" and "that". . . The body is the storm center, the origin of coordinates, the constant place of stress in all the experience-train. Everything circles round it, and is felt from its point of view. The word "I," then, is primarily a noun of position, just like "this" and "here."[1]

This positional *I* that James talks about is anchored to the physical body but includes the mind as well. When I say that I went to the store, I am referring to both this body and all the physio-chemical processes, thoughts, unconscious and conscious feelings, aches, pains, perceptions, memories, and movements contained or taking place in this body. In this sense, *I* means *here*, where here implies the body of the speaker and everything going on either inside or on the surface of that body. The term we ordinarily use for that unique configuration of body, behavior, thoughts, feelings, and perceptions is *person*. "I went to the store" and "This person went to the store" represent alternative ways of designating which body/mind was involved in the going. It was this person that was involved; it was I.

But there is another equally important way we use the pronoun *I*. When we say, "I like my body", or "I have a good mind", we are no longer referring to the body/mind complex itself, but to some inner entity to which these attributes belong. The *I* retains a positional meaning (the *I* that likes its body is still located here in this particular body/mind complex), but now appears to refer to something within or behind that complex. The *I* of "I like my body" or "I have a good mind" is more than a signpost telling us where the experience is taking place. It points to an inner being that serves as owner/author of that experience.

This entity is more apparent in some uses of *I* than in others. When we say, "I went to the store" or "I picked up a pencil," there is little suggestion of anything beyond the constellation of body, thoughts, feelings, and behavior that make up what I have called the person. We begin to sense the presence of an inner entity separate from the body-mind when we say, "I just got a great idea," or "I forgot to water the plants." This *I* tells us not only that the thinking and forgetting happened *here*, but that an entity located somewhere deep inside this body/mind is responsible for those experiences.

We get an unmistakable sense of that inner entity in the statement, "I have made a mess of my life." The *I* is still positional in that the making of a mess happened here and not somewhere else, but it is clear that the speaker is simultaneously alluding to an inner agent that is responsible for making the mess happen. The *I* is now the author of the action, rather than simply the place where it happened. Unlike the positional *I* which plays an adverbial role in defining where the action took place, the inner *I* has all the earmarks of a subject causally related to a predicate. To distinguish it from the purely positional *I*, I am going to call this inner, subjective *I* the *agent*. If the positional *I* is equivalent to the person, this subjective *I* is equivalent to the soul or ego.

At the very least, the pronoun *I* always has a positional meaning; it tells us in what body/mind the action is taking place. The question is whether that meaning is merely positional or both positional and subjective. One way to determine whether we are using the term subjectively as well as positionally is to replace the *I* in whatever statement we are making with a purely positional phrase indicating that the thought or feeling *is arising here* (e.g., replace "I feel hot" with "Feeling hot is arising here"). If nothing is lost in the translation (as in the example I just gave), chances are we are using *I* positionally to refer to ourselves as persons but not subjectively to refer to ourselves as agents.

Try another example where *I* clearly alludes to the inner agent. Replace "I forgot your birthday" with "Forgetting your birthday arose here." The implication of personal responsibility which is so clear in the first statement is missing altogether in the second. It would seem safe to conclude, then, that the *I* in "I forgot your birthday" was serving a dual function. It denoted where the forgetting took place (here in this body), while simultaneously identifying the agent responsible for making that forgetting happen. If the distinction seems academic, have patience. Later on, I will try to show how changes in language based on this distinction can be used to dispel the illusion of agency and all the feelings that go with identifying ourselves as agents rather than persons.

The agent/I, then, is the initiator of action, the thinker of thoughts, the subject that chooses, decides, wills, and intends. Because it has the power to make things happen (or keep them from happening), it is accountable for its actions; it is the locus of moral responsibility. Traditionally we have identified this agent as the soul – the force or entity that dwells deep within the body/mind and serves as its ultimate pilot. In our more secular age, we are more apt to refer to it as the ego. Either way, it is the essential self, the real me, the person I really am.

In its guise as soul, the agent has sometimes been thought to dwell "about half way between the ears, and a little behind the eyes. . . ."[2] Writers of a less intellectual disposition have placed it closer to the heart. Descartes had no hesitation in assigning it to the pineal gland.

> Let us then conceive here that the soul has its principal seat in the little gland which exists in the middle of the brain, from whence it radiates forth through all the remainder of the body by means of the animal spirits, nerves, and even the blood, which, participating in the impressions of the spirits, can carry them by the arteries into all the members.[3]

Whatever might be said of its location, the soul is commonly seen as a non-physical entity that serves as the ultimate source of both physical and non-physical actions. Most of us, James said, think of the soul as

> the *active* element in all consciousness; . . . whatever qualities a man's feelings may possess, or whatever something in him may include, there is a spiritual something in him which seems to *go out* to meet these qualities and contents, whilst they seem to *come in* to be received by it. It is what welcomes or rejects. It presides over the perception of sensations, and by giving or withholding its assent it influences the movements they tend to arouse. . . . It is the source of effort and attention, and the place from which appear to emanate the fiats of the will.[4] (original italics)

In his *Society of Mind*, Minsky gives us a definition of the agent/I (which he calls *Self*) with which most people today would probably agree. It is

> the part of mind that's really me, or rather, it's the part of me – that is, part of my mind – that actually does the thinking and wanting and deciding and enjoying and suffering. It's the part that's most important to me because it's that which stays the same through all experience – the *identity* which ties everything together. And whether you can treat it scientifically or not, I know it's there, because it's me. Perhaps it's the sort of thing that Science can't explain.[5] (original italics).

Science may not be able to explain the Self, of course, for the simple reason that it is an illusion. Real or not, the Self (soul, agent) is generally thought to be that which makes decisions and moral choices, and serves as control center of the body/mind complex. From the myths of the early Iron Age to twentieth century theology, the Western world has conceived of the agent/I as a separate substance or force, sometimes material, more often immaterial. Those who have written about this agent see it not as a process or pattern of thought but as an entity that *engages* in thinking, a subject that initiates and controls. If the person is *that which is going on here* or even *that which usually goes on here*, the agent is the entity responsible for making that *going on* happen, the doer of the action.

A major difference between the agent and the person is their susceptibility to change. As our individual essence, the agent remains the same throughout life while the person changes with every thought or feeling. We are the same souls at ages five and seventy-five, but, to some degree, different persons from moment to moment. Descartes, from whom we have inherited much of our confusion about agency, stated that

> For though all the accidents of the mind [soul] suffer change, though, for instance, it thinks of others things, wills others, and senses others, it is yet always the same mind.[6]

According to conventional belief, the agent/I is not only unchanging but eternal. When it leaves the body at death, it can no longer be said to occupy a particular place in time and space, and thereby loses all meaning as a term of position. If disembodied souls have the capacity to communicate with each other, we must presume their use of *I* to be purely subjective and no longer positional.

While the agent remains the same forever, the person is constantly changing. Our thoughts and feelings are different from moment to moment. Our bodies deteriorate with age. With exposure to new experiences, new books, and new friends, our beliefs often change. Knowledge and skills expand and contract; behavior patterns shift or harden, depending on circumstances. We even have formalized procedures such as education and psychotherapy for making such changes. By contrast, there is no force on earth or in heaven that can alter our souls. We are stuck (or blessed) with whatever spiritual essence we entered this world.

As I have been using the term, the *person* includes all empirical attributes of the body/mind – but not the Self (soul) thought to possess that body/mind and its contents. This means that the person can be described in ordinary language (e.g., as strong or weak, warm, cold, active, passive etc.), while the soul/agent cannot. The soul has no attributes; when we speak of someone as having a good or kind soul, we usually mean that he or she is a good or kind person. The soul is pure, devoid of all empirical trappings. It is an activating force – spiritual substance – but not a palpable thing.

In the Cartesian world, body and mind are thought to occupy totally separate domains. As even defenders of dualism testify, this bifurcation of the physical and mental poses serious problems for explaining how thoughts manage to influence behavior. It makes even more mysterious how our souls (being pure and undifferentiatable) are able to activate our sensory-motor systems from within. While the neurons in our brain play an important mediating role, it is the soul according to Western tradition that constitutes the ultimate cause of what we do. We are left with the question, then, of how an entity as ethereal as the soul can affect something as material as one's feet or hands.

The same question arises when we consider how individuals manage to change themselves. According to traditional thinking, the agent plays a creative role in shaping the person. When we refer to someone as a self-made man, we really mean (in the terminology used here) an agent-made person. Through its intentions and decisions, the agent is responsible for generating some of the behavior that makes each of us a unique person. Other aspects of the person, however, are shaped by genes (body height and weight, eye and skin color, etc.), and by cultural training (language, dress, table manners etc.). Within the limits imposed by genes and culture, however, the agent is considered free to choose the kind of person it wants. Sartre, in fact, insists that the person is wholly plastic, that is, capable of becoming anything the agent wants it to be.

> What do we mean by saying that existence precedes essence?
> We mean that man first of all exists, encounters himself, surges
> up in the world - and defines himself afterwards. If man as the
> existentialist sees him is not definable, it is because to begin
> with he is nothing. He will not be anything until later, and
> *then he will be what he makes of himself.*[7] (my italics)

To most of us, however, this implies an unrealistic assessment of the constraints imposed by heredity and environment. A more common view takes the person to be a product of many forces, of which the agent is but one.

In its role as creator of the person, the agent plays the part of subject: it initiates thought and behavior, exercises control over feelings, changes opinions ("I changed my mind"), changes personality (e.g., by deciding to enter therapy), and even effects changes in the body (by choosing to diet or exercise). As mentioned earlier, the agent also stands in a possessive relationship to the person. I *have* a body. I *have* feelings. I *have* a bad temper. These are *my* thoughts, *my* intuitions, *my* dreams.

It should not be surprising, then, to find that the agent sometimes takes the role of object as well. We say, "A great idea just occurred to *me*," or "My temper often gets the better of *me*," or "This pain in my back is driving *me* crazy." In each of these, the inner agent, instead of initiating action, serves, as the affected object of events arising in the body/mind. Collectively, then, the agent/I is capable of playing all three grammatical roles – subject, possessor, object – vis-à-vis the person.

FREUD AND AGENCY

While Freud occasionally referred to the soul, he was too much of a materialist to take the concept seriously. However, the tripartite partitioning of id, ego, and superego he offered in its place has had the effect of perpetuating our centuries-old habit of explaining human behavior in terms of agency. In the history of the individual, Freud tells us, it is the id that comes first, emerging at birth as a pool of instinctual desire governed by the "pleasure principle." That part of the id which is modified by the perceptual system is later differentiated as ego; with the repressing of the Oedipus complex, the superego emerges as a further differentiation within the ego. Together, ego and superego serve very much the same function as the more traditional soul – with the important exception that the latter has the capacity to survive indefinitely without a host body.

As Freud has formulated them, each of the three entities constitutes an *I*, a point of view that can be either conscious or unconscious. There can be no question that Freud thought of all three as causal agents – a strategy clearly at odds with his oft-cited claim that all psychic phenomena are *determined*. That contradiction is most obvious in his treatment of ego. While he starts by conceptualizing ego as an integrated set of processes, he quickly gives in to the temptation to convert processes to agents. In his own words,

> We have formed the idea that in each individual there is a coherent organization of mental processes; and we call this his *ego*. It is to this ego that consciousness is attached; the ego controls the approaches to motility – that is, to the discharge of excitations into the external world; it is the mental agency which supervises all its own constituent processes, and which goes to sleep at night, though even then it exercises the censorship on dreams.[8]

We see how quickly an "organization of mental processes" becomes a "mental agency." Any doubt that Freud saw ego not as a process but as an agent should be dispelled by the following analogy:

Thus in its relation to the id, it [ego] is like a man on horseback, who has to hold in check the superior strength of the horse; with this difference, that the rider tries to do so with his own strength while the ego uses borrowed forces. The analogy may be carried a little further. Often a rider, if he is not to be parted from his horse, is obliged to guide it where it wants to go; so in the same way the ego is in the habit of transforming the id's will into action as if it were its own.[9]

While ego may have begun as a heuristic fiction in Freud's thinking, it quickly grew into a substantive entity. In summarizing that evolution, one critic states that in Freud's later writings,

the ego emerged as that agency which is turned out toward reality, and theorists who followed him, among them and perhaps most importantly his daughter, began to focus their attention on its vicissitudes. To them, the ego seemed almost a psychic hero as it battled off id and superego at the same time that it tried to cope with the world of the everyday. Anna Freud wrote of its powerful artillery, the mechanisms of defense, which helped the ego in its struggles but whose overtly rigid use caused it new problems. And Heinz Hartmann gave the ego a property that was to prove decisive for psychoanalytic technique when he asserted that the ego had an aspect that was not tied up with the individual's neurotic conflicts. . . . This "unhampered" aspect of the ego seemed free to act and choose, independent of constraints, including social constraints. It almost seemed the psychic locus for a notion of the "Will" or for the seat of moral responsibility.[10]

The psychic world we have inherited from Freud is a world inhabited by three ghostly agents locked in a struggle for control of the mind. All three represent sub-divisions of what I have been calling the agent. While that tie to the agent/I seems clearest with respect to ego, it is equally true of id and superego. When we say *I*, we sometimes mean the id/I, (as in "I want a drink –– now."). At other times *I* represents the voice of the superego ("I don't think that would be a good idea"). Most frequently *I* means the ego/I, the one that says, "I think I'll wait until later."

Wanting, moralizing, and choosing are all processes. As I shall argue in later chapters, there is no need to assume an entity *doing* any of them. The workings of all three can be explained without populating our psyches with quarrelsome homunculi. Freud's insistence on doing so reflects his acceptance of the traditional assumption that every action must have a *doer*. According to this rarely questioned premise, processes are incapable of functioning, especially in conjunction with each other, without the help of some kind of supervisor agent. Freud not only accepted this assumption but extended it to include unconscious processes as well – a decision that allowed him to

> cling to at least a pale version of the Lockean creed by imagin-ing that these "unconscious" thoughts, desires, and schemes *belonged to* other selves within the psyche. Just as I can keep my schemes secret from you, my id can keep secrets from my ego. By splitting the subject into many subjects, one could preserve the axiom that *every mental state must be someone's conscious mental state* and explain the inaccessibility of some of these states to their putative owners by postulating other interior owners for them.[11] (original italics)

The assumption that all thoughts, desires, and schemes *belong* to an agent within us or, worse yet, that all such experiences are *controlled* by one of these ghostly entities, points to the heart of our cultural delusion. We are persons who insist on seeing ourselves as agents. As I hope to show later on, persons and agents are responsible for their actions in very different ways and that difference in responsibility has implications for much of what we think, feel, and do. At the center of our delusion stands an insistence that, as agents, we have the power to create ourselves and, thus, must take moral responsibility for what we have created.

The first step in dispelling that delusion is learning to recognize when we are acting on the false assumption of agency. Concretely, this means learning to identify signs of agency as they emerge in thought and speech. Once we have learned to distinguish the agent from the person, we can take up our detective work in earnest. As with the ghost in the attic that keeps us awake at night, dispelling the illusion of agency requires that we be willing to look carefully and to keep looking until we are convinced that there is no one there.

REFERENCES

1. Kallen, H., *The Philosophy of William James*, New York: The Modern Library, 1925, p. 151.
2. Watts, A., *The Essence of Alan Watts*, Millbrae: Celestial Arts, 1974, p. 3.
3. Beardsley, M. (ed.), *The European Philosophers from Descartes to Nietzsche*, New York: Modern Library, 1960, p. 93.
4. James, W., *The Principles of Psychology*, Cambridge: Harvard University Press, p. 285. First published in 1890.
5. Minsky, M., *The Society of Mind*, New York: Simon and Schuster, 1985, p. 39.
6. Beardsley, M. (ed.), *The European Philosophers from Descartes to Nietzsche*, p. 95.
7. Sartre, J., "Existentialism Is A Humanism," in Kaufmann, W. (ed.), *Existentialism from Dostoevsky to Sartre*, New York: Meridian Books, 1975, p. 349.
8. Freud, S., *The Ego and the Id*, New York: W.W. Norton, 1960, p. 7. First published in 1923.
9. Freud, S., *The Ego and the Id*, p. 15.
10. Turkle, S., *Psychoanalytic Politics*, London: Burnett Books, 1979, pp. 52-53.
11. Hofstadter, D., and Dennett, D., *The Mind's I*, New York: Basic Books, 1981, p. 12.

3

HOW DO I KNOW THAT I EXIST?
AN EXPERIMENT

Imagine that tonight you have a very convincing dream in which you evaporate into the atmosphere. Upon awakening tomorrow morning, how might you reassure yourself that you still existed? Before answering, you might want to consider whether I am referring to you as person or you as agent. For the former, there are many obvious answers. You could pinch yourself and the pain would tell you what you wanted to know. If there were a mirror handy, you could look into it. You could even raise your arm or shake your head in order to confirm that the movements which you felt proprioceptively were reflected in the glass. You could also listen to your heartbeat, check your breathing, clear your throat, or, depending on your living arrangement, shout.

If none of these seemed to work, you might consider getting dressed and going into the street where others would see you. Any gesture aimed in your general direction would carry the implication that at the very least someone was there taking up space. Being recognized by name would suggest that you were not only a "someone", but the specific person you thought you were.

As commonsensical as these measures seem, they wouldn't have satisfied Descartes whose search for something he could be certain of led him to reject the necessary reality of all physical objects on the grounds that we might only be dreaming of them. Descartes said that

> you have no right to make the inference: *I walk, hence I exist,*
> except in so far as your awareness of walking is a thought;

it is of this alone that the inference holds good, not of the motion of the body, which sometimes does not exist, as in dreams, when nevertheless I appear to walk. Hence from the fact that I think that I walk I can very well infer the existence of the mind which so thinks, but not that of the body which walks.[1]

The only thing we know is real, he concluded, is our thinking. Because we think, we know that we exist. Any doubts we might have about that fact simply represent another kind of thinking. In the end, it is those doubts that prove our existence.

But whose existence does this thinking prove? Is it you as person (the constellation of physical and mental processes making up that body/mind) or is it you as agent (the inner entity responsible for *doing* the thinking, feeling, and behaving)? The following paragraph leaves little doubt that he meant the latter:

What then is it that I am? A thinking thing. What is a thinking thing? It is a thing that doubts, understands, affirms, denies, wills, abstains from willing, that also can be aware of images and sensations. Assuredly if all these things pertain to me, I am indeed a something.[2]

From the brute datum of thinking Descartes concludes that he as thinker exists. But in and of itself thinking offers no support for that conclusion. Like most people then and now Descartes simply assumed that for every thought there must be a thinker (a "thinking thing"), for every feeling, a feeler, etc. By itself, the sheer fact of thinking tells us simply that there is consciousness *arising*. To the extent that I identify with that consciousness, it means that I exist as a person. There is no evidence in the fact of thinking, however, for the existence of an autonomous agent standing apart from and serving as the author of those thoughts. Descartes' cogito represents one of many ways of confirming that I exist as a person; it says nothing about my existence as an agent.

If thinking per se cannot substantiate my existence at an agent, is there anything that can? Is there any evidence at all to support the claim that somewhere inside of me there exists an entity that creates my thoughts, feels my pain, and makes my decisions? My ability to remember events from the past may suggest an autonomous entity of some sort, but that inference is unwarranted. My memories are critical for confirming that I exist as a person and that my existence as an ever-changing constellation of body and mind is continuous over time, but they say nothing at all about my existence as an agent. Remembering does not prove the existence of a rememberer separate from the remembering itself any more than thinking proves the existence of a thinker separate from its thoughts.*

Perhaps the answer is as simple as philosopher John Searle maintains:

> In normal behavior, each thing we do carries the conviction, valid or invalid, that we could be doing something else right here and now, that is, all other conditions remaining the same. This, I submit, is the source of our unshakable conviction of our own free will.[3]

And if it is the source of our belief in free will, it is presumably the source of our belief in a causally autonomous agent, since, one clearly implies the other. The feeling that I "could be doing something else right here and now" implies that there is an entity inside of me with the power to impose its will on whatever wishes or thoughts may be competing for expression. There can be no disputing that most of us have that feeling most of the time. The lack of such feeling, in fact, especially if it persists, is unusual enough to arouse our clinical concern. If experience is to be our guide, we must take that feeling seriously. But what exactly is this feeling of being free to choose otherwise, and what does our having the feeling prove? The sensation that "I could be doing something else right here and now" certainly does not prove that there is an agent inside of me exercising free will. If it proves anything at all, it is more likely to be that I am unaware of all the genetic and environmental

---

* Vatsiputriya: If there is no Soul, who is it that remembers? Vasubandhu: What is the meaning of the word "to remember"? Vatsiputriya: It means to grasp an object by memory. Vasubandhu: Is this "grasping by memory" something different from memory?" Vatsiputriya: It is an agent who acts through memory. Vasubandhu: The agency by which memory is produced we have just explained. The cause producive of a recollection is a suitable state of mind, nothing more. Vatsiputriya: But when we use the expression "Caitra remembers," what does it mean? Vasubandhu: In the current of phenomena which is designated by the name Caitra, a recollection appears. Stcherbatsky, T., "The Soul Theory of the Buddhists," *Bulletin de l'Academie des Sciences de Russie*, quoted in Parfit, D., *Reasons and Persons*, Oxford: Clarendon Press, 1984, p. 503.

forces operating upon my thoughts and behavior at any given moment. It is not that I am free of such forces, but simply that I am ignorant of what they are. Skinner puts the same point in behavioral terms.

> As the experimental analysis has shown, behavior is shaped and maintained by its consequences, but only by consequences that lie in the past. We do what we do because of what *has* happened, not what *will* happen. Unfortunately, what has happened leaves few observable traces, and why we do what we do and how likely we are to do it are therefore largely beyond the reach of introspection. Perhaps that is why . . . behavior has so often been attributed to an initiating, originating, or creative act of will.[4] (original italics)

We attribute our choices to an autonomous will rather than circumstance, Minsky adds, because it fosters the illusion that we understand what is going on in our minds.

> Every action we perform stems from a host of processes inside our minds We sometimes understand a few of them, but most lie far beyond our ken. But none of us enjoys the thought that what we do depends on processes we do not know; we prefer to attribute our choices to *volition, will, or self-control.* We like to give names to what we do not know, and instead of wondering how we work, we simply talk of being "free." Perhaps it would be more honest to say, *"My decision was determined by internal forces I do not understand."* But no one likes to feel controlled by something else.[5] (original italics)

For both William James and Alan Watts the feeling of agency is tied to physical sensations. James argued that, when the "Self of selves" (what we are calling the agent) is examined carefully, it is found

> to consist mainly of the collection of these peculiar motions in the head or between the head and throat. I do not for a moment say that this is *all* it consists of, for I fully realize how desperately hard is introspection in this field. But I feel quite sure that these cephalic motions are the portions of

my innermost activity of which I am *most distinctly aware*. If the dim portions which I cannot yet define should prove to be like unto these distinct portions in me, . . . it would follow that our entire feeling of spiritual activity, or what commonly passes by that name, is really a feeling of bodily activities whose exact nature is by most men overlooked.[6] (original italics)

James is suggesting here that the agent/I reveals itself most clearly in physical experience. Watts goes further and claims that the feeling of being an agent is *nothing more* than a set of physical sensations which we have learned to associate with the concept of will.

But what is this thing that we feel in ourselves when we say, "That is the concrete, material me?" . . . Supposing somebody says, "O.K., now you've got to use your will, you've got to exercise strong will." That's the ego, isn't it. What do you do when you exercise your will? You grit your teeth, you clench your fists. If you want to stop wayward emotions you go uptight. You pull your stomach in, or hold your breath, or contract your rectal muscles. But all these activities have absolutely nothing to do with the efficient functioning of your nervous system. . . . And so, in exactly the same way, all these muscular strains we do and have been taught to do all our lives long, to look as if we're paying attention, to look as if we're trying, all this is futile. But the chronic sensation of strain is the sensation to which we are referring as I.[7]

While James is content to point out that we know the workings of the putative agent only through its physical manifestations (e.g., knitting of the brow), Watts insists that there really is no agent and that the sensation of straining is only a charade. Watts goes so far as to define the relationship between agency and straining as "an illusion married to a futility." The ego (agent), he continues, is "the image of ourselves, which is incorrect, false, and only a caricature, married to, combined with, a futile muscular effort to will our effectiveness."[8] If Watts is right, the muscular straining and tightness we take to be signs of our inner agent at work cannot be accepted as evidence that such an entity actually exists. If they represent proof of anything at all, it is proof of our *belief* in agency. We strain because we are convinced of our freedom – not because we really are free.

LANGUAGE AND FREE AGENCY

Throughout Western culture, the belief that we are the causes of our own behavior is implanted early in life and reinforced by every institution in society. That belief is supported, above all, by the language we use. We rarely speak without affirming agency: *I* think, *I* know, *I* have decided, *I* am sorry – the words force us to assume the existence of an agent separate from and responsible for the thought or feeling in which it is *engaged*. And yet, behavior can be separated from its agent, Nietzsche said,

> only owing to the seduction of language (and of the fundamental errors of reason that are petrified in it) which conceives and misconceives all effects as conditioned by something that causes effects, by a "subject." . . . But there is no such substratum; there is no "being" behind doing, effecting, becoming; the "doer" is merely a fiction added to the deed – the deed is everything.[9]

It is built into the metaphysics of our language that every action must have a doer, that every choice is made by an inner agent. The more forceful the action and the more difficult the choice, the more clearly we seem to feel the presence of the doer, but that presence is very likely no more than an artifact of the way we have defined our relationship to the world.

In describing French psychoanalyst Lacan's theory of mind, social commentator Sherry Turkle says that it is

> impossible to express such a radically "anti-ego" theory in ordinary language: the language's pronoun structure reflects our culturally embedded notions about subjectivity. From the moment that we begin to write or speak, we are trapped in formulations such as "I want," "I do," "I desire."[10]

The problem is not limited to psychology. At the root of the agency assumption is a cognitive distortion, the effects of which extend throughout much of scientific inquiry. As Nietzsche put it a hundred years ago,

All its coolness, its freedom from emotion notwithstanding, our entire science still lies under the misleading influence of language and has not disposed of that little changeling, the "subject" (the atom, for example, is such a changeling, as is the Kantian "thing-in-itself").[11]

The test I employed in the last chapter to differentiate between person and agent can be used to illustrate how language reinforces the illusion that the agent is real. Consider for a moment how you feel when you say, "I made a great decision today." Do you feel anything different when you substitute, "A great decision arose here today"? The second way of saying it removes all traces of agency. It is now the person talking. The decision took place here, in this body, on its own. There is no inner agent that can be credited with having made it happen, hence no pride to be taken in *your* having done it. Any shift in feeling you might have experienced as a result of the change in wording confirms the importance of language. It suggests that your sensation of being an agent owes much to the words you use and to the assumptions implicit in those words; by itself, however, that sensation proves nothing about the reality of an agent/I.

If we cannot use the common sensation of agency to substantiate the existence of the agent/I, might we not be better off looking for the entity itself – not in the physical realm, of course, since no one claims to have seen, heard, smelled, tasted, or touched any such agent – but in the realm of thoughts and feelings? If it is possible to know our thoughts and feelings through introspection, i.e., by becoming aware of the contents of consciousness, should we not be able to gain a similar experience of the agent/I in the act of creating those thoughts or feeling those feelings?

When David Hume conducted such an experiment on himself 250 years ago, he came across an unending series of perceptions, but no agent creating or even *having* them.

> For my part, when I enter most intimately into what I call *myself*, I always stumble on some particular perception or other, of heat or cold, light or shade, love or hatred, pain or pleasure. I never can catch *myself* at any time without a perception and never can observe any thing but the perception. When my perceptions are remov'd for any time, as by sound-sleep; so long am I insensible of *myself*, and may truly

be said not to exist. And were all my perceptions remov'd by death, and cou'd I neither think, nor feel, nor love, nor hate after the dissolution of my body, I shou'd be entirely annihilated, nor do I conceive what is farther requisite to make me a perfect non-entity. If any one upon serious and unprejudic'd reflection, thinks he has a different notion of *himself*, I must confess I can no longer reason with him."[12] (original italics)

Hume did not conclude, as had Descartes, that because thoughts were present, there must be a self (agent) thinking them. He insisted that, if such an agent really existed, it should be accessible to experience through introspection. When he failed to uncover any such entity, he was forced to the uncomfortable conclusion that it did not exist.

Many years later, after trying to describe the "Self within the self" in terms of a central nucleus of "palpitating inward life," William James confessed that:

when I forsake such general descriptions and grapple with particulars, coming to the closest possible quarters with the facts, *it is difficult for me to detect in the activity any purely spiritual element at all. Whenever my introspective glance succeeds in turning round quickly enough to catch one of these manifestations of spontaneity in the act, all it can ever feel distinctly is some bodily process, for the most part taking place within the head.*"[13] (original italics)

Later in the same book James adds that, contrary to what we normally assume, the agent is not experienced from moment to moment in the stream of experience but is known only in subsequent reflection.

Instead, then, of the stream of thought being one of *conscious*-ness, "thinking its own existence along with whatever else it thinks . . .," it might better be called a stream of *Scious*ness pure and simple, thinking objects of some of which it makes what it calls a "Me", and only aware of its "pure" Self in an abstract, hypothetic or conceptual way.[14]

Unlike Hume who concluded from his inability to discover a Self through introspection that such an agent did not exist, James leaves open the possibility that it is there but knowable only as an abstraction. From this autobiographical writings, we know that he eventually took a decisive stand in favor of free will ("My first act of freedom shall be to declare a belief in free will") – an act which served as a major turning point in his recovery from a prolonged depression.

Watts takes a position similar to Hume's when he argues that, if the agent exists, we should be able to detect it in any conscious activity, e.g., in the act of reading this very book. His conclusion, of course, is that it can't be done.

> While you are watching this present experience, are you aware of *someone* watching it? Can you find, in addition to the experience itself, an experiencer? Can you, at the same time, read *this* sentence and think about yourself reading it? You will find that, to think about yourself reading it, you must for a brief second stop reading. The first experience is reading. The second experience is the thought, "I am reading." Can you find any thinker, who is thinking the thought, "I am reading?" In other words, when present experience is the thought, "I am reading," can you think about yourself thinking this thought?
>
> Once again, you must stop thinking just, "I am reading." You pass to a third experience, which is the thought, "I am thinking that I am reading"... But what has happened? Never at any time were you able to separate yourself from your present thought, or your present experience. . . . You are never able to separate the thinker from the thought, the knower from the known. All you ever found was a new thought, a new experience.[15]

Every time we go looking for the thinker of our thoughts, Watts is telling us, we come up with another thought. Just when we think we have caught the agent/I, our experience turns out to be just another thought about agency.

As Hume might have put it, we can never experience the thinker without a thought, and never can experience anything but the thought.*

William Barrett takes issue with Hume, Watts, and James when he asserts that we are always conscious of our Selves.

> I am not only aware of the sensory datum – the brown of the table on which I write and the white of the wall opposite – but I am aware of my own consciousness perceiving it. And I am also aware of the I – an ego, a self that is at the center of this consciousness. And I am aware also that I am the same conscious self as yesterday, however different the sensations I am now bombarded with.[16]

Thus we have a variety of positions on the relationship between agency and consciousness: James' position that the agent/I lies beyond the limits of introspection but can be inferred rationally from other things we know about ourselves; the Hume-Watts position that, if the agent were real, we should be able to observe it introspectively but we can't; and Barrett's position (the conventional position) that we are, in fact, aware of it. To help you decide the issue for yourself (or, at the very least, to rule out one of the latter two positions), I propose that you perform a simple experiment: If you look systematically at the way images, thoughts, feelings, and choices enter your mind, can you find a Self, spirit, or soul that seems to be making them happen? Can you find, hidden among the evanescent, tangled contents of consciousness, an entity that serves as their creator – the creator you have always assumed yourself to be?

THE EXPERIMENT

There is no reason why we should have to take anyone else's word for the reality of something as important as the Self. Nor need we rely on the results of anyone else's personal investigation. If there is anything to learn from

---

* Wittgenstein took a similar position when he said: "If I wrote a book called *The World as I Found It*, I should have to include a report on my body, and should have to say which parts were subordinate to my will, and which were not, etc., this being a method of isolating the subject, or rather of showing that in an important sense there is no subject; for it alone could *not* be mentioned in that book." From *Tractatus Logico-Philosophicus*, quoted by Jonathan Glover, *I: The Philosophy and Psychology of Personal Identity*, London: The Penguin Press, 1988, p. 64.

scrutinizing consciousness carefully, the best way to learn it is by scrutinizing our own. The only thing required is a little patience and a willingness to take a fresh look at the way our minds work.

The object of this brief investigation is to examine more carefully than ever before the way in which thoughts, feelings, and images arise in our minds. To get anything out of the experiment, we are going to have to suspend, or at the very least, loosen, our prior assumptions about the way consciousness works. The best way to do that is to start by admitting that we have probably never paid much attention to how thoughts enter our minds.

I would suggest that you start by closing your eyes and taking several slow, deep breaths. This should have the effect of slowing down the stream of thoughts flowing through your mind. When that stream has slowed to a trickle, get ready for an image to appear, any image at all. Don't force it. If you wait patiently for a few seconds, an image will appear. [TRY THAT NOW]

If I can assume that by now you have experienced at least one image, I would like to ask this: At the moment you first became aware of an image, were you aware of any entity in your mind that seemed to have manufactured it or to have somehow brought it into existence? Or did the image simply present itself? If you have trouble answering that question, try the experiment again. Try this time to catch the image – any image – at the very moment it enters consciousness. Focus your attention on how the image is formed. [CLOSE YOUR EYES, BREATHE DEEPLY, AND WAIT FOR AN IMAGE]

When I perform this exercise along with you, I experience my image arising spontaneously (the content is irrelevant). One moment there is nothing there; the next moment I "see" the image. While its particular form might be related to immediately preceding thoughts, or events, it appears to come on its own. I can find no little person, center of energy, or entity of any kind fashioning that image out of memories, wishes or other conscious materials.

We are unlikely to learn much about the workings of consciousness from exploring images, however, since we already assume that most of them come "out of the blue." It may strike us as extreme but hardly bizarre that when Mozart was asked about the source of his musical ideas, he replied: "Whence and how do they come? I do not know and I have nothing to do with it."[17] If our experiment is to reveal anything new, it is more apt to be with the way thoughts arise. With that in mind, let us try the same exercise now substituting thoughts for images. As soon as a thought comes to mind, recall what you can about the way in which it actually entered consciousness. Given the stream of worries normally racing through our minds, it may be difficult to isolate a single thought. If you have more than one thought at a time, concentrate on the first of them. See if you can find an entity apart from the thought that seems to be creating it. Look for some sign of an agent actually engaged in the process of manufacturing that thought. [CLOSE YOUR EYES, BREATHE DEEPLY, AND WAIT FOR A THOUGHT].

Even if you did not find such an agent, you may be tempted to report that, "True, I did not find an agent, but it was still I who did the thinking. Since no one else came up with it, it is clearly *my* thought." But the *I* implied in those statements is the positional I-as-person. When you say that, "I did the thinking," you are simply indicating that the thought occurred *here* (i.e., in your body), rather than somewhere else (i.e., in someone else's body). This is true enough. But my question is aimed at that other *I*. I am asking whether you experienced, apart from the thought itself, an interior entity that served as the author or creator of that thought. Based on my own experience with this exercise, I am willing to bet that you did not.

Let us try something more deliberate and see if it makes any difference. I am going to ask you a question and I want you to watch what happens in your mind as you proceed to answer it. It will help once again to clear away some of your "internal dialogue" by breathing deeply and closing your eyes. [TRY THAT BEFORE READING FURTHER]

Here is the question: How old do you think I am? [MAKE A GUESS BEFORE GOING ON]

Looking back now at the manner in which your guess entered consciousness, were you aware of both the guess and an agent creating it, or did the guess seem to present itself? If you think you detected some kind of agent at work, can you recall how it managed to get the guess into consciousness? Was the agent there in consciousness first, before the guess appeared? If so, what was it like? What was that agent doing when it was not engaged in guessing? Did it have any kind of recognizable attributes apart from its activities? Or did it have to be doing something (like guessing) before you could detect its presence. And if that is the case, is it not possible that you have confused the agent with what it *does*?

For most people this confusion stems from assuming that every activity must have a doer. To test that assumption, see if you can discover a guess*er* separate from the guess*ing*. Don't be satisfied with the guessing itself; keep looking until you have found, or realize that you can't find, an entity that exists independently of the guessing, i.e., an agent that can be observed in the act of manufacturing a guess.

If your guess was an intuitive one, it will already be obvious to you that it arose "by itself." If, on the other hand, that guess emerged only after a long process of deliberation in which several guesses were weighed in the light of things I said about myself earlier, it might be harder to see just how spontaneous the whole process really was. To do so, you must look carefully at how each thought arose. Don't assume that, because your speculations form a logically related series, there must be a supervisor there managing the sequence. The point of the experiment is to see whether you can actually find such an entity. According to Hume and Watts, if there is a manager there, it should be available to introspection, just like the thoughts themselves.

After trying this exercise several times, most students seem willing to grant that thoughts, even decisions, do indeed come bubbling up on their own. It is common for them to insist, however, that *acting* on those decisions still requires an agent. Someone, the argument goes, has to be there to put the decision into practice. Converting a decision about going to the store into the physical act of going requires the presence of an inner director with the power to make the body move.

This is what our conventional wisdom tells us. To answer the question for yourself, check your experience the next time you act on a decision, e.g., the next time you get up from your chair to get a drink. Observe your mind carefully. Can you find any evidence of an agent that initiated the getting up? Presumably you will be able to recall the decision to get up, perhaps even some of the thoughts leading up to that decision, but can you find the entity that caused your body to move? Was there a *you* that moved your body, or did your body simply move itself? Is it possible, in other words, that the physical act of getting up out of the chair was just as spontaneous as the decision which preceded it?

When I say that all thoughts, perceptions, feelings, decisions, and behavior are spontaneous, I am using the term in a specific sense to indicate that there is no autonomous entity initiating them. Who, then, you might ask, is performing this present experiment? Who is viewing this experience and drawing conclusions about the presence or absence of an agent? Is there not, after all, a witness to these "spontaneous" events? And is not this witness the very *I* we have been seeking?

The formal practice of "witnessing" or observing the flow of one's mind is encouraged in some spiritual traditions as a way of helping the adept to disengage from the contents of consciousness. To anyone who stays with the practice long enough, however, witnessing proves to be simply another

activity arising on its own – just like the thoughts and feelings being wit-
nessed. When we go looking for the agent "doing" the witnessing, we find
nothing beyond the act of witnessing. We can watch as witnessing presents
itself to consciousness, but can never catch the "witness" independently of
what it is witnessing.

Sustained meditation, in fact, confirms the absence of a witness – or,
for that matter, any agent at all. We see this most clearly in the Buddhist
practice of Vipassana or Insight meditation. Western psychologist Jack Engler
describes the process as following:

> My sense of being an independent observer disappears. The
> normal sense that I am a fixed, continuous point of observa-
> tion from which I regard now this object, now that, is dis-
> pelled. Like the tachistoscopic flicker-fusion phenomenon
> which produces the illusion of an "object" when discrete and
> discontinuous images are flashed too quickly for normal
> perception to distinguish them, my sense of being a separate
> observer or experiencer behind my observation or experi-
> ence is revealed to be the result of a perceptual illusion, of
> my not being normally able to perceive a more microscopic
> level of events. When my attention is sufficiently refined
> through training and kept bare of secondary reactions and
> elaboration of stimuli, all that is actually apparent to me
> from moment to moment is a mental or physical event and
> an awareness of that event. In each moment, there is simply a
> process of knowing (nama) and its object (rupa). Each arises
> separately and simultaneously in each moment of awareness.
> No enduring or substantial entity or observer or experiencer
> or agent – no self – can be found behind or apart from these
> moment-to-moment events to which they could be attributed
> (an-atta = no-self).[18]

Our brief experiment is no substitute for years of Vipassana meditation. And yet, in a very rudimentary way, it reveals the same truth, namely
that consciousness is filled with events but devoid of agents. In a sentence
that could have been taken from Hume but is meant instead to describe a
spiritual practice twenty-five hundred years old, Engler concludes that "the
only observable reality at this level [of meditation] is the flow of mental and

physical events themselves. There is no awareness of an observer. There are just individual moments of observation."[19]

Hume, James, Watts, and the Buddhists agree that if there are agents creating our experience, those agents are not available to introspection. The only way to prove their existence, therefore, is to infer them from other things we know about ourselves. And this, of course, is exactly what some philosophers have attempted to do. Descartes, we have already seen, argued that the soul could be inferred from the simple fact of thinking. Over a thousand years earlier, Augustine claimed that "If I am deceived, I am." Kant agreed with Hume that it was impossible to confirm the existence of the Self empirically, but went on to claim that it could be done through "practical reason" or what we might call intuition. Practical reason tells us, or at least it told Kant, that the soul has to exist because it is necessary for the efficient operation of the human organism.

Like those natural rights philosophers before and after him, Kant argued that practical reason represents an infallible guide to those truths that cannot be determined empirically (Anyone in his right mind can see that . . .). As more than one person has pointed out, however, this kind of philosophizing invites arbitrariness, as in Hegel's insisting on the *necessity* of sequences in history, and then changing his mind repeatedly as to which sequences were necessary.[20]

This sort of arbitrariness seems especially evident in Kant's further attempt to prove that the soul is immortal. Despite his insistence that we can never know anything about the soul, he argued that it must be immortal since, otherwise, we should not have enough time to become holy. Walter Kaufmann summarizes the argument:

> Practical reason demands that the achievement of holiness should be possible. Since it is not possible in this life, "it therefore can be encountered only in a progressus ad infinitum," and this "is possible only if we presuppose an infinitely enduring existence and personality of the same rational being (which one calls the immortality of the soul)."[21]

Unless we take holiness as an absolute good, which we have no obligation to do, Kant's argument that souls must be immortal because an eternal life is necessary for achieving holiness makes no sense at all. This illustrates how easily "practical" reason can be bent to serve the demands of a priori values.

I personally see nothing at all necessary about a soul, mortal or immortal, either for becoming holy, holding the pieces of my personality together, or keeping the social order from collapsing. Not only do I find the idea of a soul unnecessary, I find it inconsistent with a naturalistic view of human history.* How can it be that, in a universe where every other living and non-living thing participates in a chain of cause and effect, we humans managed to extricate ourselves from that chain? How did we ever get to be agents that cause thoughts and actions without, at the same time, being at the effect of previous events? Gods are usually thought to have the power of causal autonomy – but do we seriously regard ourselves as divine? Is each of us really an island cut off from the rest of nature – a separate entity operating according to a different set of rules from everything else?

Think of it historically. Why should the emergence of an upright-walking hominid suddenly yield an organism exempt from the rules by which the universe had governed itself for the preceding five billion years? And at what point in time did that miraculous emancipation actually take place? Did Lucy, the three and a half million year old Ethiopian female with a head no larger than a softball, have free will? Or did free will have to wait another million years for the arrival of those huge-molared, nut-eating Australopithecines? This is not a likely hypothesis since the participants in that particular experiment soon died out, perishing perhaps in competition with Homo Habilis or Homo Erectus. Even if we argue that free will required a rational, language-based consciousness (an event which scholars place no further back than ten thousand years ago), we are still caught in the trap of trying to find causes for a phenomenon which, by definition, is uncaused. We are left with the conundrum: if free will emerged historically, how did it manage to wriggle free from the causal chain we know to be a part of that history?

That puzzle cannot be solved unless we assume that the power to cause without being caused was introduced arbitrarily into the world by some divine force whose influence stopped short of specifying how that freedom was to be used. This assumption forces us to grant a world external to our own and a super-consciousness capable of abrogating the basic laws of the universe. If we ask how this cosmic entity acquired its own freedom from the laws of nature, we must pose another super-super-consciousness – and then still another, ad infinitum.

---

* Naturalism holds that there exists a single world of phenomena of which man is an integral part. All events, however strange, can be explained without positing the existence of a supernatural realm populated by spiritual entities.

There are many who are wary of the infinite regress implied in the concept of a divine creator but who fail to see that the concept of free will suffers from the same logical flaw. Nor do they seem aware that free will implies a similar assumption of divinity. Consider this: if one's will is truly free, one's choices cannot be explained in terms of past or present events. Those choices are caused not by other events (e.g., genetic inheritance and conditioning), but by an inner agent acting independently of past or present circumstances. The power to cause without being caused – that is, the power to create ex nihilo – is something we ordinarily reserve for God. In declaring that we too have that power, we have, in effect, laid claim to divine status, thereby elevating ourselves above anything else in nature. We have turned ourselves into minor gods.

I find it more congenial to think of the emergence of human consciousness as a part of nature, as natural as the birth and death of the most distant star. With the development of a cerebral cortex and the ability to think, plan, and control our own lives, we have not escaped from nature's web. Thinking, planning, and controlling are all tied to the rest of the universe through circumstance. As complex and difficult to predict as we know them to be, those activities have their origin in other events of this world. Like everything else in nature, they arise out of what has gone before and, in turn, impart their own shape to what comes afterwards.

For my own part, when attempting to get to the truth of agency, I feel safer generalizing from the data of introspection, however subjective, than trusting to the vagaries of intuition (especially someone else's, but my own as well). The data of my own consciousness reveal no agent of any kind. When this finding is confirmed by others using a similar technique, my confidence is increased. The burden of proof remains on those who insist that there is someone there. Until they can show me where to look or convince me that agency follows logically from other assumptions I can accept, I must take the position that the agent/I is an illusion.

REFERENCES

1. Beardsley, M. (ed.), *The European Philosophers from Descartes to Nietzsche*, New York: Modern Library, 1960, pp. 82-83.
2. Beardsley, M. (ed.), *The European Philosophers from Descartes to Nietzsche*, p. 85.
3. Searle, J., *Minds, Brains and Science*, Cambridge: Harvard University Press, 1984, p. 95.
4. Skinner, B.F., "The Origins of Cognitive Thought," *American Psychologist*, 1989, vol. 44., No. 1, p. 14.

5. Minsky, M., *The Society of Mind*, New York: Simon and Schuster, 1985, p. 306.

6. James W., *The Principles of Psychology*, Cambridge: Harvard University Press, 1983, p. 288. First published in 1890.

7. Watts, A., *The Essence of Alan Watts*, Millbrae: Celestial Arts, 1974, pp. 15-19.

8. Watts, A., *The Essence of Alan Watts*, p. 19.

9. Nietzsche, F., *On the Genealogy of Morals*, New York: Vintage, 1969, p. 45.

10. Turkle, S., *Psychoanalytic Politics*, London: Burnett Books, 1979, p. 146.

11. Nietzsche, F., *On The Genealogy of Morals*, p. 45.

12. Hume, D., *A Treaties of Human Nature*, p. 300.

13. James, W., *The Principles of Psychology*, p. 287.

14. James, W., *The Principles of Psychology*, pp. 290-291.

15. Watts, A., *The Wisdom of Insecurity*, New York: Vintage, 1951, pp. 83-84.

16. Barrett, W., *Death of the Soul*, Garden City: Anchor Press, 1987, p. 42.

17. Quoted in Dennett, D., *Elbow Room*, Cambridge: MIT Press, 1984, p. 13.

18. Engler, J., "Therapeutic Aims in Psychotherapy and Meditation," in *Transformations of Consciousness* by Ken Wilber, Jack Engler and Daniel P. Brown, Boston: Shambhala, 1986, p. 41.

19. Engler, J., "Therapeutic Aims in Psychotherapy and Meditation," p. 42.

20. Kaufmann, W., *Goethe, Kant, and Hegel*, Vol. 1 of *Discovering the Mind*, New York: McGraw-Hill, 1980, p. 244.

21. Kaufmann, W., *Goethe, Kant, and Hegel*, pp. 119-120.

4

Linguistic and Social Origins of Agency

If free agency is only an illusion, how did the Western world fall victim to its spell? It is hard to imagine a whole civilization taken in by a simple but critical cognitive error – and then persisting in that error throughout its four thousand year history. In light of the impressive accomplishments of that civilization, moreover, it may strike many as inappropriate to worry over a possible error in basic premises. Still others, quick to agree that free will is only an illusion, will be equally adamant in insisting that the West would never have achieved its greatness without it. Voltaire, for one, attributed the finest products of Western art and science to vanity and personal ambition, both of which he conceded owe much of their motivating power to our belief in the soul.[1]

Whether or not Western art and science would have flourished as well without a commitment to free will is a moot point. Whatever our speculation, we can justify questioning the place of agency in Western culture on the a priori grounds that truth is preferable to illusion. There is also the practical possibility that human life, in particular the emotional life of the individual, would be more satisfying without a belief in agency. Documenting that latter claim is one of the primary concerns of this book. In the meantime, our task in this present chapter is to account for the origins of the illusion itself.

An inquiry into the origins of free agency must deal with two facts: first, that the germ of agency can be found in all cultures, and second, that the concept of *free* agency is primarily a Western phenomenon. By the germ of agency I mean some rudimentary notion of an essence, soul, or spirit that exists apart from the individual's experience and behavior. By free agency I mean an essence, soul, or spirit that exercises a causal influence on that experience and behavior without itself being caused. The fact that all cultures contain at least the germ of agency suggests that in searching for an explanation of the basic illusion, we must look for factors indigenous to human life itself. The specifically Western character of free will, on the other hand, requires an examination of the particular social and economic conditions in which it arose.

Some writers have argued that the basic illusion of agency represents a distortion in perception. Engler, whom I quoted earlier, takes the Buddhist position that our sense of being a substantial self emerges from the illusion of continuity, in the same way that "objects" appear when separate images (like the frames of a film) are flashed in succession too quickly for the human eye to distinguish. Our thoughts, feelings, and physical movements succeed each other too quickly for us to see ourselves as the momentary constellations of body and mind that we really are. What we see instead is a unitary, enduring entity, not unlike the illusion, Watts reminds us, of a continuous circle of fire created by whirling a burning stick.[2] We are fooled by our inability to make microscopic discriminations into seeing something that does not exist. According to the Buddhists, this illusion of object constancy represents the ultimate source of all our problems.

The trouble with this explanation is that it fails to address the more specific belief that inside this object called "me" there is another entity which serves as manager, soul, spirit, or agent. Engler and Watts are both talking about the tachistoscopic illusion underlying our perception of objects in general – persons, trees, cars, houses, mountains – all of which are actually in flux but which give the appearance of remaining the same over time. From their Eastern perspective, they are challenging something much more basic than our belief in agency. They are asking us to see beneath the perceptual continuity of all *things*, including ourselves as persons. While this question is fascinating in its own right, I am content for now to assume that the things we perceive are real, and concentrate instead on explaining our belief in those mysterious agents thought to reside inside of things.

THE ROLE OF LANGUAGE

The illusion that things are animated by agents is a linguistic rather than a perceptual problem. Our thinking and the language in which we express that thinking rest on an ability to symbolize what we perceive. Names are among our most common symbols. Whether we are referring to people or objects in nature, the names we use allow us to communicate about the phenomenal world without having to point. This ability to symbolize the entities we see, hear, and touch lies at the very heart of civilized life. It also lies, unfortunately, at the heart of our mistaken image of ourselves.

Naming objects makes it easier to infuse them with agency by creating the illusion of a separation between the object itself and the qualities that it possesses or the things it does. Thanks to language, houses *have* roofs and cars *need* new tires. Once we differentiate verbally between an object and its component parts, we forget that the parts help to define the object, that roofs are part of what we mean by house and tires a part of what we mean by car. With animate things the separation is even more obvious. We say that trees *send out* roots and *grow* new leaves, quickly forgetting that roots and leaves are part of what we mean by the term tree in the first place. Once an object has been conceptually differentiated from its parts, we begin thinking of it as an entity in its own right – an entity that stands in a possessive or even causal relationship vis-à-vis its own parts. It is but a short step from the "tree" that sends out roots and grows leaves to a vague, undefinable "tree spirit" that dwells within the observable object and animates all aspects of its existence. The illusion of agency has its origins in the linguistic separation of an object from its attributes and activities.

The temptation to infuse objects with agency is most compelling with sentient beings, those that feel, choose, and move around. I easily fall into thinking of "Fred" (the neighbor's cat) as something *apart* from "his" black, furry, shoebox-sized body and the sleeping, jumping, and eating I see him "doing." When I say to you that "Fred" is eating his supper or that "Fred" has a nick in his ear, it is difficult for me to avoid assuming that "Fred" is something separate from both the eating (in which he is engaged) and the nicked ear (which he possesses). My ability to use linguistic symbols seduces me (as Nietzsche put it) into distinguishing between doer and deed, between the object and what the object "does." What the object "does," of course, is very much a part of what the object "is." Giving the object and its parts separate names tends to obscure the fact that the whole and the parts represent two ways of looking at the same set of phenomena.

The temptation to infuse objects with agency presents itself whenever we try to say something about the phenomenal world. Any noun with an empirical reference (sea, sky, forest) represents a candidate for agency. While we prefer to think of animism as a relic of Stone Age culture, there are few among us who have not experienced the temptation to infuse our own world of animals, trees, sun, and wind with spirits, and then project onto those spirits our distinctly human thoughts and feelings. Our degree of success in resisting that temptation is determined primarily by our cultural training. The greater our exposure to rational-empirical thinking, the less likely we are to take spirits of any kind seriously. It is testimony to the strength of the animistic temptation that, even in Western culture where science is so highly regarded, we continue to populate our own human world with spiritual agents. While few of us continue to think of trees and rocks as harboring souls, the majority of us remain convinced that all humans and many animals are so endowed. That insistence on projecting spirits into objects, however sophisticated its theological justification, can be raced ultimately to the distorting effects of language.

THE RISE OF FREE WILL

Our belief in souls and spirits has its roots in a variety of conditions. I am suggesting here that language is one of those conditions. Giving names to objects invites us to differentiate those objects from their constituent parts, thereby creating the illusion of entities which are not only separate from their parts but, in the case of living things, capable of acting upon those parts. In imputing *free* agency to homo sapiens, we take the further step of investing those ghostly abstractions with causal power. Free agency is born when an object is differentiated from its parts and then elevated to the status of uncaused cause vis-à-vis the very qualities and activities of which it is composed.

While the germ of agency can be found in all languages, the idea of free will is specific to Western and Near Eastern culture. Agents did not gain their miraculous freedom to operate as uncaused causes until Zeus slew Typhon, Yahweh vanquished Leviathan, and the heroic age broke upon a world in which both men and their deities were enslaved to nature symbolized as the Great Goddess. Into the massive, hieratic, city-states of lower Mesopotamia poured legions of aggressive warrior tribesmen from herding societies to the north and south. Prior to their victorious assault (2000-1500 B.C.), there had prevailed

> an essentially organic, vegetal, non-heroic view of the nature
> and necessities of life that was completely repugnant to those
> lion hearts for whom no patient toil of earth but the battle

spear and its plunder were the source of both wealth and joy.[3]

With them the invaders brought or soon fashioned myths in which warrior heroes took on and defeated monsters symbolic of the passive, cyclical mentality that had emerged with the rise of agriculture several thousand years before. Against those tyrannous symbols (Leviathan, Typhon, etc.), Joseph Campbell tells us that

> the warrior principle of the great deed of the individual who matters flung its bolt, and for a period the old order of belief – as well as of civilization – fell apart. The empire of Minoan Crete disintegrated, just as in India the civilization of the Dravidian twin cities, Harappa and Mohenjodaro. However, in India the old mythology of the serpent power presently recovered strength, until, by the middle of the first millennium B.C., it had absorbed the entire pantheon and spirit of the Vedic gods – Indra, Mitra, Vayu, and the rest – transforming all into mere agents of the processes of its own, still circling round of eternal return. In the West, on the other hand, the principle of indeterminacy represented by the freely willing, historically effective hero not only gained but held the field, and has retained it to the present. Moreover, this victory of the principle of free will, together with its moral corollary of individual responsibility, establishes the first distinguishing characteristic of specifically Occidental myth.[4]

As a sign of this radical shift in thinking, Campbell points to the difference between the traditional Mesopotamian concept of the Deluge as a terminal event in a recurring, mathematically determined cycle of events fixed by nature, and the Sumerian-Hebrew idea of the Flood as a punishment sent by Yahweh for sins against his commandments.[5] With this momentous leap from an impersonal cosmic order to divine retribution, the illusion of free will entered human history and along with it sin, virtue, guilt, pride and all the other correlates of moral responsibility.

The Mesopotamian view of the world as endlessly and impersonally cyclical reflected the repetitive, seasonal nature of life in a static agriculturally-based society, while serving the interests of the priests whose role it was to anticipate and interpret those cycles for the king. Free agency had its origins in a radically different socio-economic setting. The invaders' view of the world as an expression of will – both divine and human – arose out of a life-situation in which the individual herdsman was repeatedly forced to make his own decisions far from either priests or court. His high plains environment demanded the ability to exercise independent judgment to a degree unknown to the agrarians below who were rewarded for subordinating their thoughts and impulses to the larger community.

From a life characterized by autonomy, we can surmise that it was but a short leap to the belief that causality lay in the mind of the individual rather than in the irresistible forces of nature. With the internalizing of causal power came guilt, pride, the beginnings of moral responsibility and, in time, the rise of a distinctly Western individualism. We, the heirs of the herdsmen's daring, can only marvel at a gesture no less bold than Prometheus' theft of fire from the gods. What the herdsmen stole was nature's power to create. In doing so they won for themselves a divine power hitherto enjoyed only by the Great Goddess herself.

Our life-situation shapes our habits of thought; it trains us to think in specific ways not only about daily affairs but about life, death, and all the other issues which religion and philosophy traditionally address. The belief that our behavior is caused not by the irresistible forces of nature but by an internal force presumably grew out of the need for autonomous judgment imposed by the exigencies of life as a wandering herdsman. Throughout Western civilization that belief has been supported most strongly by those in entrepreneurial positions – and least by those (e.g., peasants and factory workers) whose work favors cooperation over independent judgment.

The rapid proliferation of myths extolling the virtues of the individual hero arose out of the violent clash between herdsman and agrarian world views. In the context of that clash, the herdsmen's claim to causal autonomy burst forth as a protest against a culture that threatened to smother individual initiative in the embrace of priestly fatalism. In the Mesopotamian world of caste and privilege, one had no choice but to accept social conditions

> as unalterable destiny in the same way that we shall probably always have to accept such natural and inevitable limitations as birth and death. Together with this outlook there went an ethical principle – the ethics of fatalism, the main tenet of which was submission to higher and inscrutable powers. The

first break in this fatalistic outlook occurred in the emergence of the ethics of conscience in which man set his self over against the destiny inherent in the course of social events. He reserved his personal freedom, on the one hand, in the sense of retaining the ability through his own actions to set new causal sequences going in the world ... and, on the other hand, through the belief in the indeterminateness of his own decisions.[6]

From the perspective of our own commitment to free will, the shattering of a cosmology in which the individual counted for little looms as a great and unqualified victory. That same commitment, however, makes it difficult to see at what price the victory was gained. What we lost, Campbell reminds us, was our "essential identity with the organic, divine being of a living universe."

The universe is no longer itself divine, radiant of a mystery beyond thought, of which all the living gods and demons, no less than the plants, animals, and cities of mankind, are functioning parts. Divinity has been removed from earth to a supernatural sphere, from which the gods, who alone are radiant, control terrestrial events.[7]

By wresting causal primacy from nature and reapportioning it to God and themselves, the warrior invaders demystified the world and, in the process, disconnected themselves from it. Never again would they, nor we, their heirs, belong wholly to the eternal, seamless order of things. If the price of individual freedom was alienation from nature, they seemed willing to pay, even though the freedom they won was no more real than their former servitude. They simply substituted one illusion for another, the illusion of free agency for the illusion that the order of man could be deduced from the order of the stars. In their eagerness to escape from the tyranny of a depersonalizing cosmology, they overlooked solutions that would have granted the individual greater autonomy while retaining his place as a functioning part of the universe. As a result, they inadvertently created a tyranny of their own, that of the autonomous, ever-responsible, ever-nagging agent/I.

Whatever its failings, the concept of a free and causally autonomous soul quickly found widespread acceptance in the West. Within a few hundred years of its appearance, the myth of the "free-willing, historically effective individual" spread from the city-states of Sumeria to the Levant, Greece, and Europe until the whole West lay under its spell. The East, meanwhile, took a separate path. After experimenting briefly with free agency, India led the way back to a collectivistic, vegetal world view in which the individual resumed a subordinate position in the eternal, cyclical order of things.

FREE WILL IN THE MODERN WORLD

Today, some four thousand years after the herdsmen's victory over the Mesopotamians, free agency remains a core belief in the cultures of Europe, America and the Near East. While the herdsman's way of life is now practiced by only a tiny minority, other roles have emerged over the centuries to provide comparable training in autonomous thinking. Not strangely, it is the entrepreneurs, individual farmers, salesmen, merchants, and independent professionals who have most strongly supported the ideology of agency in the West.

Many of these roles, however, have recently been absorbed by the growth of large organizations. In the process, the capacity for orienting and motivating oneself (what Riesman called inner-directedness) has lost much of its value.[8] Success in a bureaucratic world demands teamwork, that is, the ability to synchronize one's thinking with that of others and to subordinate one's idiosyncratic style to the operating procedures of the larger unit. While corporate managers, government officials, and hospital physicians must still be capable of thinking autonomously, most of their problem solving occurs in conjunction with others. Success in a bureaucratized world increasingly requires that one be able to think collectively, that is, in harmony with the thoughts of one's colleagues.

What will be the effect of this training in cooperative thinking on our basic Western beliefs – on our belief in free agency in particular? Thus far, despite some signs of erosion in traditional individualistic values, our faith in free will would appear to be as strong as ever, particularly in the American upper middle class. Is it possible that our beliefs have not yet caught up with our changing occupational structure?

> The critical role of culture in structuring social action cannot be understood apart from the fact that the ideas which make it up are extremely abstract and hence unlikely to be affected significantly by changes in the immediate task environment. . . . Despite their seemingly absolute character,

[however,] they are never completely divorced from their origins. While they may appear to follow a course of their own, they are still subject to the vagaries of human experience. To the extent that they represent inductions from situationally specific task experiences, they are amenable to change. The fact that they change slowly is what gives them their autonomous appearance.[9]

To the degree that free will has its roots in autonomous thinking, the bureaucratization of the workplace common to all mature industrial societies may signal an eventual change in belief. That change may be slow in coming, however, because of support for agency among all Western religions, as well as the fact that, throughout the West, the concept of agency is fully institutionalized in the law, the economy, government, the family, and education. By itself, further rationalization of the occupational structure appears unlikely to dislodge free agency from its pivotal position in European and American thought. Dispelling that illusion may have to wait for a related development which began as long ago as the Renaissance but which, some six centuries later, remains unfinished. I refer to the replacement of what Carl Becker called "the conception of existence as divinely composed and purposeful drama..." with a view of existence as the spontaneous but orderly play of energy.[10] If we are to move beyond the limits of agency, we may have to wait, in other words, for the ascendance of naturalism over spiritualism.

If recent developments in artificial intelligence and the neurosciences are any indication, we may not have to wait too long. With every success in computer emulation of human thinking, perception, and physical movement, we inch closer to the realization that we do not need souls to behave like humans. From the laboratories of the neurobiologists, evidence is mounting to suggest that for every sensation of pain, pleasure, depression, craving, and anger that we feel in what we call our minds, there is a correlative physio-chemical state in the brain. The dualistic premise of two distinct realms, one mental and one physical, is rapidly becoming untenable. To more and more scientists and philosophers, mind and brain appear to be one and the same thing. Consistent with that view is the discovery that many of our psychological states (including depression, schizophrenia, and the craving for alcohol) are tied directly to the actions of neurotransmitters (dopamine, serotonin, norepinephrine) in the brain – a discovery that leaves little room for the exercise of spiritual agents.

51

> We humans feel as we do not because we are guided by the invisible edicts of the gods, . . . but because of the peculiar sensitivities, densities, locations, and metabolisms of our receptors and transmitters. Those, in turn, are products of natural selection. Thus the behavior we identify as uniquely human is as fundamentally Darwinian as our characteristically hairless bodies and the distinctive type of hemoglobin that flows in our veins.[11]

While structural changes in the workplace favoring "other-directedness" may loosen our attachment to agency, research demonstrating the material nature of mind threatens to undermine our faith in free will completely. Free will is a spiritual concept. The power to cause without being caused requires the assumption of a non-physical domain from which agents can operate upon the physical world while remaining immune to material influence. If mind and brain turn out to be two sides of the same coin, that assumption, while not categorically disprovable, becomes superfluous.

By contrast, the concept of human beings as constellations of body and experience arising spontaneously out of genetic and environmental circumstance is a thoroughly naturalistic one. There are no ghosts in such a concept - just flesh and bones, mind-brain states, genes, and environment. To many, that may suggest that we are machines, or, more to the point, no better than machines. It is quite possible that we *are* machines (albeit organic ones), but such a description is unlikely to help us to understand ourselves until we become more knowledgeable about what machines are capable of doing.

> For centuries, words like "mechanical" made us think of simple devices like pulleys, levers, locomotives, and typewriters. . . . But we ought to recognize that we're still in an early era of machines, with virtually no idea of what they may become. What if some visitor from Mars had come a billion years ago to judge the fate of earthly life from watching clumps of cells that hadn't even learned to crawl? In the same way, we cannot grasp the range of what machines may do in the future from seeing what's on view right now.[12]

Whatever we may be, we are of this physio-chemical world. Whether or not that qualifies us as machines depends, as Minsky says, on what we mean by machines. As the computer revolution matures, our concept of the mechanical is bound to mature along with it. The day may not be far off when the term machine has a different ring to it, one that we shall find no more objectionable when applied to ourselves than the term animal. As Sherry Turkle argues in *The Second Self*, the computer is already challenging our traditional way of viewing ourselves.

One thing is certain: the riddle of mind, long a topic for the philosophers, has taken on new urgency. Under pressure from the computer, the question of mind in relation to machine is becoming a central cultural preoccupation. It is becoming for us what sex was to the Victorians – threat and obsession, taboo and fascination.[13]

REFERENCES

1. Cassirer, E., *The Philosophy of the Enlightenment*, Princeton: Princeton University Press, 1951, pp. 106-107.
2. Watts, A., *The Wisdom of Insecurity*, New York: Vintage, 1951, p. 85.
3. Campbell, J., *Occidental Mythology*, New York: Penguin Books, 1964, p. 21.
4. Campbell, J., *Occidental Mythology*, p. 24.
5. Campbell, J., *Myths To Live By*, New York: Bantam Books, 1972, p. 76.
6. Mannheim, K., *Ideology and Utopia*, New York: Harcourt, Brace & Co., 1936, pp. 170-171.
7. Campbell, J., *Myths To Live By*, p. 76.
8. Riesmann, D., *The Lonely Crowd*, New Haven: Yale University Press, 1950.
9. Breer, P., and Locke, E., *Task Experience as a Source of Attitudes*, Homewood: Dorsey Press, 1965, pp. 20-21.
10. Becker, C., *The Heavenly City of the Eighteenth-Century Philosophers*, New Haven: Yale University Press, 1932, p. 15.
11. Franklin, J., *Molecules of the Mind*, New York: Dell Publishing Co., 1987, p. 262.
12. Minsky, M., *The Society of Mind*, p. 30.
13. Turkle, S., *The Second Self*, New York: Simon and Schuster, 1984, p. 313.

A Question
of
Survival

5

The Self-governing Organism

If the agent/I is only a conceptual fiction, we are left, as was Hume, with some critical questions. For one thing, if there is no inner agent overseeing our daily activities, what prevents our flying off spastically in a thousand directions at once? Without a psychic supervisor, how do we manage the complex synchronization of thoughts, perceptions, emotions, and physical movements required in everyday affairs? How do we even maintain a continuous sense of identity?

All of these questions so perplexed Hume that he began to doubt his discovery. In the Appendix of the *Treatise*, he returned to the problem of "no-self" and confessed that he could not make sense of it.

> But upon a more strict review of the section concerning *personal identity*, I find myself involv'd in such a labyrinth, that, I confess, I neither know how to correct my former opinions, nor how to render them consistent. . . . If perceptions are distinct existences, they form a whole only by being connected together. But no connexions among distinct existences are ever discoverable by human understanding.[1]

If each of our perceptions is distinct from all others, Hume asks, and no connections among those perceptions can be observed in our minds, what is it that "unites our successive perceptions in our thought or consciousness?" He takes it for granted that our perceptions somehow get "united" or bound together and given an "identity," but, if there is no self apart from the perceptions themselves, how does it all happen?

Because Hume could not explain to his own satisfaction how the psyche functions without a self, his novel and puzzling insight went for naught, at least in his own lifetime. Stymied as he was by the question of "psychic management," he never got around to raising a second, equally knotty issue. If there is no agent in charge of the individual's behavior, how can society hold its members responsible for what they do? Without the assumption of moral responsibility, what is to prevent the social order from collapsing into a Hobbesian dog-eat-dog world of cutthroat sociopaths?

In most discussions of free will, social control is, in fact, the central issue, whether it is referred to directly or not. Those philosophers who start with the assumption that social survival depends on a belief in free agency must either commit themselves wholeheartedly to that belief or take the position that it is necessary to act "as if" the belief were true. To anyone who has gone looking for such an agent and come away empty-handed, neither alternative is likely to be palatable.

Our problem lies in assuming that social control is impossible without guilt, pride, conscience and all the other trappings of a belief in agency. At the individual level, the cognate problem lies in assuming that a stable personal existence is impossible without an agent to serve as supervisor. Both problems dissolve when we give up our obsession with control and learn to recognize nature's ability to organize itself. In this chapter we shall examine the control issue from the point of view of the individual. In chapter six shall look at it again from a social systems perspective.

Managing Without a Manager

Although Hume continued to write into his sixties, he never returned to this disturbing insight of his youth. What had disturbed him the most was his inability to explain how a consciousness devoid of self managed to unite "a bundle or collection of different perceptions, which succeed each other with an inconceivable rapidity and are in a perpetual flux and movement."[2] No matter how carefully he looked for an agent engaged in the process of uniting these perceptions, all he ever found was the perceptions themselves.

There are two questions implicit in this search for psychic unity: "How can we be sure that these successive perceptions belong to a single person?" (the problem of personal identity), and "How do these perceptions get organized into a smoothly functioning whole?" (the problem of personal management).

A. J. Ayer speaks for a number of contemporary philosophers in answering the first question with the argument that "personal identity depends upon the identity of the body, and that a person's ownership of states of consciousness consists in their standing in a special causal relation to the body by which he is identified."[3]

The second question is more relevant to the issue of free agency. If there is no interior self to organize our constantly changing thoughts and feelings, what keeps them from stumbling over each other? What keeps us from changing our minds unpredictably, doing one thing while saying another, acting contrary to our best interests, or becoming immobilized by indecision? As Hume himself asked, how can a bundle of perceptions in constant flux coordinate itself? The simple rejoinder, of course, is that it doesn't have to because there *is* an agent there performing the task. William Barrett takes that position when he states,

> Certainly, the Humean conception of the ego as a momentary heap of impressions or perceptions here collapses. A self that is only a heap of impressions could not count up to five. It would not have the continuity of beliefs required to do so; nor could it have the center of consciousness, the ego, that can direct attention to the future and then gather it together with the past (a passive heap of impressions cannot project toward the future).[4]

Without an agent/I to oversee consciousness, Barrett insists, we would be unable to count, plan, remember – or, others might add, make decisions, evaluate behavior, and assess the consequences of our actions.

The answer to the "management question" is much simpler than we might suppose. Consider, first, how an ordinary decision like that of getting out of bed in the morning gets made without benefit of an agent. At first blush the absence of an interior supervisor would seem to invite perpetual indolence. If there is no *I* inside of me responsible for my thoughts and behavior, what is to prevent me from staying right there between the sheets all day long? As anyone who has ever tried doing it knows, the answer lies in what will happen if I do. Getting up is controlled by its consequences, that is, by what we have learned from similar experiences in the past and by our anticipation of what might happen in the future. If we get up, it is because we have been reinforced positively in the past by the pleasures of breakfast, by friendly greetings at the office, and by getting paid for working. Remaining in bed, by contrast, is more likely to have brought an empty stomach, glares from office mates, and threats of dismissal. Getting up is shaped by our perception of the consequences of staying in bed. That shaping process does not require the presence of an interior agent. The decision to get up arises spontaneously out of previous experience.

The same logic applies to any situation requiring self-control, whether that be control of our drinking, temper, spending, appetite, or desire to gossip. Self-controls are built into the normally socialized individual through conditioning and arise as spontaneously as the very feelings and behavior to which they are directed. If they fail to arise (as in addictive behavior), it is not because of any delinquency on the agent/I's part, but because of previous circumstances.

According to years of biological, psychological and sociological research, the roots of addictive behavior lie in heredity, individual conditioning, and exposure to a subculture in which addictive behavior is normative. Those of us for whom self-control has never been a problem can thank an advantageous combination of genes, personal experience, and cultural exposure. It makes no more sense to attribute our self-control to a causally autonomous will than it does to give thanks to our lucky stars. In the normally socialized person, internal warnings are triggered automatically by previous learning and, when the threat is extreme enough, are followed by a decision to act on those warnings. The whole process is spontaneous in that no agent can be found, nor need be assumed, behind either the warning or the decision to obey it.

While interpersonal situations are usually more complex than those involving a single individual, the basic principle remains the same. Imagine that a man has been invited to a dinner party to meet some friends of a friend. While he is seated at the table, the following thoughts and perceptions begin racing through his mind:

> "I find the middle-aged woman across from me quite attrac-
> tive; I wonder if she realizes that I do; I would like to find out
> more about her, but I don't want to appear nosey; The food
> is a bit plainer than I had hoped; Are the others listening to
> my conversation with the middle-aged woman?; Do they find
> me intellectually interesting?; My anxiety is increasing; Do I
> dare let them know how conservative I am politically?; I can
> feel that first glass of wine; I'm still anxious; I'd like another

one right now, but no one else seems to have taken a second glass yet; I wish I didn't need a drink to feel relaxed; The middle-aged woman has been talking to the man on her left for the last three minutes; I wonder if she got bored with me; I should probably be telling a funny story, but I can't think of any except the one __ "

In a matter of minutes, he has experienced a variety of visual and auditory sensations, sexual arousal, a desire for respect, judgments about others, curiosity about how others perceive him, anxiety, a craving for alcohol, jealousy, fear, and an assessment of group norms with respect to politics, drinking behavior, and story-telling. And the dinner party has only begun. Unless he manages to bring some order to these "successive perceptions," he is unlikely to survive the evening.

If, for example, his craving for another drink and his awareness that others are drinking more slowly remain disconnected perceptions, he will probably go ahead and have a second glass of wine, and maybe a third, and thus risk being perceived as someone with a drinking problem. Only by integrating these two experiences will he be able to escape embarrassment. If this act of integration appears to be a simple matter, consider all the phenomena involved: a feeling of anxiety, a desire to conceal that anxiety, the knowledge that a few drinks will make it easier to do so; the observation that other people are drinking more slowly, the thought that they would probably frown upon his having a second drink so quickly, the awareness that they are listening to his conversation and observing his behavior, and a feeling of personal inadequacy at needing a drink to relax.

Now, how do all those perceptions get sorted out so as to make some kind of behavior possible, whether this involves having a second drink now or choosing to wait? Traditionally, we have assumed that his ego, soul, or self surveys the situation, makes a judgment, and then relays that decision to the sensory-motor system which initiates the act of either asking for another glass of wine or refusing when someone offers to pour him one. This is part of the executive function Freud had in mind when he described the ego's role in terms of reality testing and "secondary process" (as opposed to the instinctual primary processes of the id).

There can be little doubt that the executive process is critical for organizing the many thoughts, sensations, and feelings streaming through our friend's mind at the dinner table. It is far from clear, however, that the observing, judging, and decision-making which make up that process require an autonomous agent. Since no one seems to be able to find such an agent, the alternative is to assume that the executive process is part of the body/mind system itself. More accurately, it is part of a field of interaction involving both organism and environment. By looking at that field cybernetically, we can begin to view reality-testing and decision-making as aspects of a self-correcting system in which no agent is needed. It is the system which "does" the thinking and choosing. Gregory Bateson provides us with an example.

> Consider a man felling a tree with an axe. Each stroke of the axe is modified or corrected according to the shape of the cut face of the tree left by the previous stroke. This self-corrective (i.e., mental) process is brought about by a total system, trees-eyes-brain-muscles-axe-stroke tree.... But this is *not* how the average Occidental sees the event sequence of tree felling. He says, "*I* cut down the tree" and he even believes that there is a delimited agent, the "self," which performed a delimited "purposive" action upon a delimited object.[5]

This is a very different way of thinking about ourselves. The agent/I to whom we traditionally ascribe intentions and choices is excluded from the model Bateson is describing. Even volitional behavior is seen as a system product, something that emerges out of the interaction of body/mind with environment. Bateson continues:

> The total self-corrective unit which processes information, or, as I say, "thinks" and "acts" and "decides" is a *system* whose boundaries do not at all coincide with the boundaries either of the body or what is popularly called the "self" or "consciousness"... (original italics)

That self, he says,

> is only a small part of a much larger trial-and-error system which does the thinking, acting, and deciding. This system includes all the informational pathways which are relevant at any given moment to any given decision. The "self" is a false

reification of an improperly delimited part of this much larger field of interlocking processes.[6]

Bateson is not alone in arguing that the "subject" in any interaction between organism and environment is actually a system of forces rather than an autonomous entity. Philosopher Thomas Nagel draws the same conclusion in his analysis of how split-brain patients manage to achieve unity of consciousness despite a "plurality" of separate minds.

> The fundamental problem in trying to understand these cases in mentalistic terms is that we take ourselves as paradigms of psychological unity, and are then unable to project ourselves into their mental lives, either once or twice. But in thus using ourselves as the touchstone of whether another organism can be said to house an individual subject of experience or not, we are subtly ignoring the possibility that our own unity may be nothing absolute, but merely another case of integration, more or less effective, in the control system of a complex organism. This system speaks in the first person singular through our mouths, and that makes it understandable that we should think of its unity as in some sense numerically absolute, rather than relative and a function of the integration of its contents.

> But this is quite genuinely an illusion. The illusion consists in projecting inward to the center of the mind the very subject whose unity we are trying to explain: the individual person with all his complexities. The ultimate account of the unity of what we call a single mind consists of an enumeration of the types of functional integration that typify it. We know that these can be eroded in different ways, and to different degrees. The belief that even in their complete version they can be explained by the presence of a numerically single subject is an illusion. Either this subject contains the mental life, in which case it is complex and its unity must be accounted for in terms of the unified operation of its components and functions, or else it is an extensionless point, in which case it explains nothing.[7]

For most of us, it is wrenching to give up the idea that it is we as agents who are deciding things. It is even harder to accept that this inner agent with whom we so deeply identify is "a false reification of an improperly delimited part of [a]... field of interlocking processes." But such a conclusion is consistent with the failure of Hume, James, Watts, and the Buddhists to find any such agent standing apart from experience. It is not only consistent with that discovery; it begins to explain how our perceptions and behavior (and those of our friend at the dinner party) organize themselves into a coherent whole without benefit of an internal manager.

The process by which our friend's perceptions and behavior get sorted out is self-corrective in that, within the total system of players, each person's actions are modified or corrected by the reactions of others. A series of remarks on our friend's part, for example, may be modified by a subtle expression of disapproval on the part of the woman seated across from him. Her own flirtatiousness, in turn, may be modified both by our friend's overeagerness and hints of interest from the man next to her. Each person brings to the situation a unique set of behavioral propensities based on genetic inheritance and personal history. Those propensities consist, in part, of sensitivities to changes in the environment. When a specific threshold is reached, the individual responds – with a laugh, a sigh, anger, disapproval, disgust, etc. Each response has the capacity to shape the behavior of other members in the system through its impact on their own response thresholds.

The individual's behavior is organized, not by an interior agent, but by a combination of propensities (genetic and environmental in origin) which he or she brings to the situation, and the propensities of others to respond to that behavior in certain ways. The system works automatically in that no agents are required for integrating any one person's perceptions or guiding the interaction between two or more people. Although the process is wholly automatic and self-correcting, it is just as subtle and complex as the agent-driven process we usually imagine to be going on when people interact.

This non-agent model of interaction is consistent with the behaviorists' rejection of agency as a concept necessary for explaining human behavior. While he stops short of referring to the "inner man" as an illusion, B.F. Skinner clearly sees him as an impediment to science:

> Unable to understand how or why the person we see behaves
> as he does, we attribute his behavior to a person we can-
> not see, whose behavior we cannot explain either but about

whom we are not inclined to ask questions. We probably adopt this strategy not so much because of any lack of interest or power but because of a long-standing conviction that for much of human behavior there are no relevant antecedents. The function of the inner man is to provide an explanation which will not be explained in turn. Explanation stops with him. He is not a mediator between past history and current behavior; he is a center from which behavior emanates. He initiates, originates, and creates, and in doing so remains, as he was for the Greeks, divine. We say that he is autonomous – and, so far as a science of behavior is concerned, that means miraculous.[8]

Skinner would have us follow the path taken by physics and biology by "turning directly to the relation between behavior and the environment and neglecting supposed mediating states of mind."[9] Mediating states of mind include all of those beliefs, values, intentions, thoughts, fears, and desires which we conventionally rely on for explanations of why people act the way they do. Highest on any list of such states, of course, is that grandest mediator of them all, the agent/I. In any mentalistic housecleaning, the concept of an autonomous inner agent represents the most obvious candidate for disposal. For Skinner, however, the inner man is just one of many illusions to be dispelled. If we are to build a true science of behavior, he argues, we must rid ourselves of *all* mentalistic constructions and turn directly to the relationship between behavior and environment.

Getting rid of the illusory agent/I has obvious advantages; jettisoning all mental explanations, however, may be carrying a good idea to unwarranted extremes. Along with "autonomous man," Skinner wants to throw out the mind altogether, which he sees as nothing more than an "explanatory fiction." From his perspective, ideas (beliefs, intentions, desires) are simply "imagined precursors of behavior." The only thing that counts is behavior – and the determinants of behavior are to be found exclusively in the organism's genes, history of reinforcement, and current environment.

But what about a belief that affects the meaning of the environment, a belief (like the belief in agency) that affects the contingencies of reinforcement in a given situation through its impact on the value of potential reinforcers? If I believe, for example, that I am the creator of my actions, I am likely to interpret any approval I get as a comment on my worthiness as a creator. If I do not believe in agency, I am more likely to interpret that same approval as a comment on behavior which has arisen here out of circumstance. The power of approval to influence my behavior depends on the meaning I assign to it, a meaning which is rooted in my basic beliefs about agency. Barring beliefs (or other mediating states of mind) from our explanations of behavior on the grounds that they are "mentalistic" handicaps our efforts to understand and predict differences in behavior. Just because mental states are shaped by their own history of conditioning does not make their use in scientific investigation spurious. Without using beliefs and other mediating states as explanations, we are forced to look for the causes of behavior in the organism's genes and history of reinforcement, however distant or elusive that history might be.

Instead of giving up mentalistic explanations entirely, we can use them in conjunction with behavioral and cybernetic concepts to form a rudimentary model capable of answering Hume's question of how separate perceptions become united without a unifying agent. The unifying of a single person's perceptions takes place within the context of a larger system of self-correcting exchanges between the organism and its environment in which responses, both mental and physical, are shaped by their consequences. The individual unity which Hume found so hard to explain arises spontaneously out of repeated transactions between the organism and its environment. However complex the organism's behavior, the process by which it becomes integrated is a spontaneous one, unfolding on its own through a complex set of feedback mechanisms and response thresholds. Its success depends not on the effectiveness of an internal soul-manager but on the presence of a relatively stable environment.

For many readers it will appear that, in all this talk about self-correcting systems, we have lost sight of the individual. Is there any room left for "soul-searching," for that volitional process by which individuals confront and then seek to change themselves? A non-agency systems approach to behavior, Barrett contends, can tell us nothing about

> an actual subject who is possessed by self-concern and who makes decisions about himself and his life. . . . We are here at the farthest remove from the empiricist view of David Hume, that the self is merely a passive bundle of sense impressions; an aggregate of sense impressions does not make decisions about itself. And the same point might be made against our present-day behaviorists, who would seek to treat the human

self as nothing but a bundle of behavior patterns: A bundle
of behavior patterns does not confront itself decisively in
self-questioning and seek its change.[10]

To speak of a bundle (Hume's own word) of behavior patterns does
not do justice to the highly structured, integrated quality of human action.
Barrett may be right in claiming that a bundle of behavior "does not confront
itself in self-questioning," but there is no reason why an integrated system of
thoughts, feelings, and behavior should not be able to do exactly that. Our
conventional way of approaching self-induced change forces us to assume
that, for a system to question and then seek to change itself, it must first get
outside of itself. But, as Watts has made clear, there *is* no getting outside of
the self. Every attempt to view the self from a vantage point outside the self
turns out to be just another expression of self.

Barrett assumes that the desire to change who we are emanates from a
center of will and energy located somewhere inside the person to be changed.
Our own investigation has failed to reveal any such autonomous center of
will. We are forced to the conclusion, therefore, that will and energy are
aspects of the person itself; like all other experiences, they arise on their own
out of interaction between genes and environment. Once they arise, they have
the capacity to cause changes in other aspects of the body/mind complex. In
viewing that process, however, we should keep in mind that it is the will*ing* or
intend*ing* that precipitates the change, not the illusory will*er* or intend*er*.

For example, a woman's decision to enter therapy may arise out of a
long-standing frustration with relationships, a frustration which, unknown
to her, has its roots in her unwillingness to accept others for who they are.
No agent is needed to account either for that intention to seek help or for the
energy to act upon it. In therapy, feedback from the therapist and other group
members may alter her awareness of how others perceive her. Some of these
insights may intersect with her desire to change ("I didn't realize the effect
my criticism was having on people. I don't want to go on alienating people
this way."). Any changes emerging from the therapeutic experience, e.g., an
intention on the client's part to be less critical in the future, can be attributed
to the interaction among a variety of perceptual, motivational, and behavioral
processes. Those changes are a systems product, not an act of free agency.

The process is analogous to what takes place in a corporation when it
seeks to change itself. To understand how that happens, there is no need to
posit the existence of a separate corporate soul or Self which confronts the

organization and persuades it to change. What it takes to produce change is an awareness of the problem, a solution, and a plan for implementing that solution – all of which are indigenous to the corporation and its environment. The same is true for the human qualities that are needed to produce that change – motivation, intelligence, imagination, and skill. No matter how daring or self-confrontive the final result is, it will represent the product, not of an autonomous agent (either internal or external), but of the organization-environment system as a whole.

SELF-GOVERNING IN NATURE

We can gain further insight into the way complex systems govern themselves from considering what we know about our own bodies. If Hume had stopped to reflect on how complex the human body is and how well it operates without any visible manager, he might have grasped how the mind functions without a separate self. Consider all the intricate processes going on night and day in a healthy human body: we breathe, digest our food, exchange carbon dioxide for oxygen, grow hair, get taller, replace cells, ovulate, and manufacture antibodies to fight disease – all without benefit of conscious supervision. Our capacity for self-government probably reveals itself even more clearly in the way our bodies deal with sharp fluctuations in external and internal conditions. These "homeostatic" processes, found in all living organisms, were first elucidated in 1932 by physiologist W.B. Cannon.

Through evolution, Cannon reminds us, we have developed methods for "maintaining constancy and keeping steady in the presence of conditions which might reasonably he expected to prove profoundly disturbing."[11] Of the many examples of homeostasis given, the simplest is the process by which the human body maintains a relatively constant temperature. When vigorous muscular activity generates an excess of internal heat, arterioles dilate, thereby allowing the blood to carry the heat through the capillaries out to the skin where it is released by radiation and conduction. If it is hot outside, body heat passes out instead through the evaporation of sweat formed on the skin's surface. The opposite happens when body temperature threatens to fall. Perspiration is reduced, capillaries contract to prevent exposure of warm blood to cold air at the surface, heart beat accelerates, muscles contract repeatedly (shivering), and adrenalin is discharged into the blood stream causing an increase in combustion and heat throughout the organism. Together the interlocking processes form a cybernetic heat control system in which nerve centers in the brain serve as thermostat.[12]

Whether it be maintaining body temperature, stabilizing blood sugar and fat, making internal adjustments in oxygen supply, or maintaining water and salt content, the body responds automatically to changes which threaten its equilibrium by neutralizing or repairing the disturbance. While this ability to maintain a steady state is common to all organisms, "the higher in the scale of living beings, the more numerous, the more perfect and the more complicated do these regulatory agencies become."[13]

Despite their automatic, unconscious nature, these physiological processes are no less complex than conscious, volitional ones – and their synchronization no less prodigious a feat. And yet we accept the fact that our body's ability to maintain a steady state takes place without *our* having to intervene. It is only when the system is disturbed that we are even aware that there are self-correcting processes taking place inside of us. Even without technical knowledge, we tend to view our bodies as self-governing systems in which separate functions get integrated automatically. We do not insist, as we do with mental phenomena, that, if the system is being regulated, there must be someone apart from the process who is "doing" it.

There are complex physical systems other than the human body which, without thinking about it directly, we also assume to be self-governing. The solar system is certainly one of them. Consider for a moment how intricate that system is. Planets, some with their own circling moons, revolve while whirling around the sun at fantastic speeds. The sun pursues its own course within the Milky Way, which is itself in the process of pulling away from other galaxies as the universe expands. Everything is in motion, yet, thanks to gravity, the movements are orderly. Velikovsky's *Worlds in Collision* notwithstanding, planets do not often collide. Nor do they leave their orbits, reverse directions, or change speeds. Millennium after millennium the system continues to function without a cosmic supervisor (unless one assigns that role to God). What makes it work smoothly is a network of interlocking controls, no one of which requires an autonomous manager to set it in motion. Every object exerts a controlling influence on its surrounding objects, and is in turn controlled by them. Like the human body, the physical universe governs itself.

Consider further how this applies to our own earth and the change of seasons. Many species of mammals and fish spend the winter hibernating, lying low, or hiding in the mud. During that time most plants appear to die off altogether, storing their energy in roots or seed pods given up to the wind. Insects tend to give up the ghost at the first chill, leaving a new generation hidden in branches and rocks. With the coming of spring, hibernating mammals and fish wake up just as edible plants and insects emerge. Early wildflower seeds germinate at a rate that produces blossoms just as insects appear to pollinate them. The insects, in turn, are programmed to hatch at the same time that nectar becomes available. All in all, it is an incredibly complex system which, if it is to work, must be synchronized in exquisite detail.

Fortunately it is. But there is no one managing the drama, making sure that each creature emerges in the right place at the right time. The system which has evolved over the course of four billion years of life is clearly self-synchronizing. A change in the angle of the sun's rays provides a central mechanism around which both plants and animals have adapted themselves. Other self-correcting mechanisms have emerged to regulate the size and location of each population. The number of woodchucks likely to survive into summer, for example, is controlled by the availability of plant food and the number of predators. An excess of woodchucks is quickly "corrected" by a dwindling supply of grasses and/or a growing number of hungry foxes. We say that Mother Nature sees to it that a certain balance is preserved, but the simpler truth is that the system takes care of itself.

It makes sense to think of the whole universe as a self-organizing system. Activity in any part of the system is influenced by events taking place in other parts. We do not need the assumption of agency to explain the structure we observe when we examine either the system as a whole or any sub-system within it. All events are mutually controlling and controlled by other events; all processes are held in place by other processes. The world is one vast self-regulating system.

In the context of what we know about the human body, the planets, and indeed the whole universe, the idea of a self-organizing mind should not appear strange at all. It does, however, most likely because we have been trained to think of organization as something done *to* the mind, rather than an activity *of* the mind itself. According to conventional thinking, the mind is organized only because id, ego, and superego are there to initiate and coordinate the experiences which pass through it. Desire can flood consciousness, but only if id opens the libidinal gates. Guilt can quickly dampen that desire, but only if superego sounds the alarm. Conflict between guilt and desire can be resolved, but only if ego chooses to resolve it.

In view of the self-correcting nature of the universe itself, it seems more reasonable, albeit less poetic, to conceptualize id, ego, and superego as processes rather than agents. Fewer assumptions are needed if we see them as intimately related parts of a self-regulating cybernetic system in which each process modifies and is, in turn, modified by the others. Viewing the psyche as a self-governing system allows us to dispose of those ghostly entities which, in one guise or another, have haunted human consciousness since the beginning of modern civilization. Once we are convinced that our minds will not collapse without them, we can do what Hume never got around to doing. We can ask ourselves what giving up those ghosts implies for pride, guilt, ambition, love, power, and all the other staples of what we take to be the human condition.

Some may question whether dispelling the illusion of agency implies anything at all for the way we live. Such doubts are reasonable in the light of Western philosophy's long-standing indifference to the practical application of ideas. If you are having doubts of your own, I would like to assure you right now that giving up the ghost of agency will turn your life upside down, or, more likely, right side up. Once you realize that you *are* your experience and not some agent responsible for making that experience happen, every aspect of your life involving the assumption of personal responsibility will change. That includes the goals you set for yourself, your ambition, the way you respond to failure, the pride you take in your work, the guilt you feel when you let others down, your need to defend yourself against criticism, your readiness to put yourself down, your grasping for power, your admiration of others who already have power, your need for love and respect, your need to talk about yourself, your bragging, your sensitivity to insult and rejection, and your willingness to be emotionally honest.

Personal responsibility is the key. Dispelling the illusion of agency means replacing the notion that we cause our own behavior with the more realistic idea that all behavior arises spontaneously out of genetic and environmental circumstance. If it is the circumstances of our birth and training rather than the agent/soul within us that causes our behavior, we cannot be held morally responsible for who we are. This awareness is what changes our lives. It does not follow, however, that we because we are not agents, we are not responsible for our actions. The purpose of the next chapter is to explore a naturalistic kind of responsibility which does not require a belief in free agency. Once we are assured that giving up the illusion of agency will not undermine the social order, we can turn our attention to what it implies for our personal lives.

REFERENCES

1. Hume, D., *A Treatise of Human Nature*, Middlesex: Penguin Books, 1984, pp. 671-678.
2. Hume, D., *A Treatise of Human Nature*, p. 300.
3. Ayer, A., *The Concept of a Person*, New York: St. Martin's Press, 1963, p. 118.
4. Barrett, W., *Death of the Soul*, Garden City: Anchor Books, 1987, p. 64.
5. Bateson, G., *Steps To an Ecology of Mind*, New York: Ballantine Books, 1972, p. 317.
6. Bateson, G., *Steps To an Ecology of Mind*, p. 331.
7. Nagel, T., "Brain Bisection and The Unity of Consciousness," in Perry, J. (ed.) *Personal Identity*, Berkeley: University of California Press, 1975, pp. 242-243.
8. Skinner, B.F., *Beyond Freedom and Dignity*, New York: Bantam Books, 1971, pp. 11-12.
9. Skinner, B.F., *Beyond Freedom and Dignity*, New York: Bantam Books, 1971, pp. 11-12.
10. Barrett, W., *Death of the Soul*, p. 126.
11. Cannon, W.B., *The Wisdom of The Body*, New York: Norton, 1932, p. 22.
12. Cannon, W.B., *The Wisdom of the Body*, pp. 177-201.
13. Fredericq, L., quoted in Cannon, W.B., *The Wisdom of the Body*, p. 21.

6

MORAL RESPONSIBILITY AND SOCIAL CONTROL

Our Occidental sense of what it means to be human rests heavily on our belief that we are morally responsible for what we do. To a great extent, our resistance to the idea of non-agency stems from our fear that, if the agent within us turns out to be an illusion, so will our image of ourselves as moral beings. Without that image, we shall lose our special place in the universe, in particular the status which comes from our unique ability to transcend the chain of cause and effect.

There may be more at stake here than being special. Our freedom to walk safely among each other demands that all of us behave reasonably. It may not be our own moral responsibility to which we cling so much as the responsible behavior of others. The two, of course, are intimately related. As Daniel Dennett puts it,

> Perhaps we think that if the price we must pay for holding others responsible is holding ourselves responsible, this is a bargain well worth striking.[1]

The cost of accepting responsibility lies in foregoing the satisfaction of some of our less worthy impulses, but this is a sacrifice we are more than willing to make because, aside from conferring dignity on ourselves, it gives us control over each other.

Whether for reasons of dignity or social control, we continue to hold firmly to the assumption that we are morally responsible for our behavior. But can we go on doing so if free agency turns out to be an illusion? If everything we do can be traced to either antecedent circumstance or the vagaries of chance, does it make sense to maintain that we are morally responsible for our conduct? Philosopher Thomas Nagel draws his own conclusion reluctantly:

> If one cannot be responsible for consequences of one's acts due to factors beyond one's control, or for antecedents of one's acts that are rare properties of temperament not subject to one's will, or for the circumstances that pose one's moral choices, then how can one be responsible even for the stripped-down acts of the will itself, if *they* are the product of antecedent circumstances outside of the will's control?
>
> The area of genuine agency, and therefore of legitimate moral judgment, seems to shrink under this scrutiny to an extensionless point. Everything seems to result from the combined influence of factors, antecedent and posterior to action, that are not within the agent's control. Since he cannot be responsible for them, he cannot be responsible for their results . . .[2]

Before going any further, it might be wise to remind ourselves that non-agency does not mean that the agent inside of us lacks the power to cause behavior; it means more simply that there is no such agent. There is no entity inside of us which is either free or not free, no entity to play the role of either prime mover of subsequent events or hapless victim of previous events. It makes no more sense to interpret that lack of agency as a sign that there is nothing we as agents *can* do (and get depressed as a result) than to interpret it to mean that there is nothing we as agents *have* to do (and feel relieved). Both interpretations are misleading in that they suggest the lingering presence of either an *I* pacing the corridors of the mind, frustrated by its inability to bend the world to its own image, or an *I* smugly observing the ebb and flow of a life in which it has no further responsibilities.

If there is no inner agent either causing our experience or serving as mediator between antecedent circumstances and experience, it seems safe to conclude that our behavior, thoughts, and feelings are caused by the circumstances themselves. That is, if they are caused by anything at all. It might be argued that, on certain levels, those events are to some degree random, not unlike the subatomic particles whose behavior cannot be measured without changing either their position or momentum. In approaching the issue of moral responsibility, it makes no difference whether we insist that all events are caused or whether we accept the possibility that, at certain levels of aggregation, the universe is indeterministic. In either case, there is no agent that can be held responsible for making events happen. And that is the crux of the matter.

If all our behavior is a function of either genetic and environmental factors or random fluctuation, does it follow that we are not morally responsible for our behavior? If what we mean by moral responsibility is agent-driven responsibility, the answer must be yes. And that is, in fact, what we ordinarily mean. In common parlance, an action is not considered moral unless the person faced with the choice of taking that action is free to choose otherwise. We consider others virtuous or sinful only on the condition that they are the causes of their own behavior. When we learn that their behavior is traceable to clear-cut antecedents, as in the case of the sports hero who turns out to be using drugs, or the murderer who is revealed as mentally retarded, we quickly withdraw our respect or opprobrium. Unless we assume that our behavior is caused by an inner agent which is free to choose otherwise, we cannot consider ourselves morally responsible. Without that assumption of free agency, our behavioral choices are neither moral nor immoral. They are simply normative or abnormative, i.e., they either conform to or deviate from agreed upon rules. Whether voluntary or involuntary, they represent products of circumstance and chance. In neither instance is there any entity free to do the choosing, hence no occasion to speak of moral responsibility, or, for that matter, of morality itself.

Many philosophers have worked hard to avoid this very conclusion, primarily because they cannot imagine society's functioning without a belief in free agency. Many of those same thinkers have, nevertheless, embraced a deterministic view of the universe. As a brief sampling of recent theorists will demonstrate, reconciling moral responsibility and determinism is a feat requiring considerable imagination and intellectual agility. William James' term for the attempt was "soft determinism." Today we refer to it more simply as compatibilism.

At the heart of compatibilism is a distinction between behavior that is determined and behavior that is constrained. All acts are determined but only a few are constrained (e.g., performed at gunpoint or as part of a compulsive syndrome). Starting with that distinction, philosophers such as Hobbes and

Hume have concluded that, so long as a person's behavior is not constrained, it is free. John Searle summarizes the argument:

> Of course it [voluntary behavior] is also completely determined, since every aspect of his behaviour is determined by the physical forces operating on the particles that compose his body, as they operate on all of the bodies in the universe. So, free behaviour exists, but it is just a small corner of the determined world – it is that corner of determined human behaviour where certain kinds of force and compulsion are absent.[3]

What follows from this reasoning (which Searle himself disavows) is that, unless our behavior is compelled, we are morally responsible for it even though it is completely determined by antecedent forces. Uncoerced behavior which violates community norms remains "inexcusable" no matter how clear its causes are. From this perspective, there is nothing incompatible between viewing behavior as determined while continuing to express moral judgments about it. In support of that position, one philosopher cites the hypothetical case of a professor who gives a student a poor grade for no apparent reason and then refuses to listen to the student's protest or give him a recommendation to graduate school.

> Do we, when we reflect on the determinism in human behavior, find our indignation melted – in the way it is melted if we hear that his (the professor's) attitude was based on some serious misunderstanding, or even that he has been under severe emotional strain on account of personal difficulties?[4]

The author seems to be saying that, if we can point to a specific cause of the professor's unfair behavior, our indignation will be melted. If all we have to go on, however, is an abstract belief that all human behavior is determined, we shall probably remain indignant. What does that suggest? Does it really mean that determinism is compatible with indignation, or merely that an abstract belief in determinism is insufficient to make any difference in how we feel toward people who break the rules? I think clearly the latter. In my wanderings through academia, I have met many professors who claim to be determinists, but who quickly hedge their claim when I personalize the issue with a reference to their own lives. Moral judging and a belief in determinism seem to be compatible only if you take your determinism lightly. For those who take it seriously, indignation, scorn, spite resentment, bitterness and vindictiveness rarely arise and tend to be short-lived when they do. Those feelings are all tied to the assumption that, lurking somewhere inside the offending person, there is an entity that made the offensive behavior happen. As we begin questioning that assumption, our moralistic fervor abates; once we are absolutely convinced that there is no one there to condemn, it vanishes altogether.

Yale philosopher Brand Blanshard took a different tack. He argued that determinism works at different levels of causality; at the mechanical or asso-ciative level, our choices are clearly brought about by antecedent conditions, while at the level of morals, art, and logic, those choices are determined by the "necessities of the case."

> The determination is still there, but, since it is a determina-tion by the *moral necessities of the case*, it is just what the moral man wants and thus is the equivalent of freedom. For the moral man, like the logician and the artist, is really seeking self-surrender. Through him as through the others an imper-sonal ideal is working, and to the extent that this ideal takes possession of him and molds him according to its pattern, he feels free and is free.

> *This good necessitates certain things*, not as means to ends merely, for that is not usually a necessary link, but as integral parts of itself. It requires that he should put love above hate, that he should regard his neighbor's good as of like value with his own, that he should repair injuries, and express gratitude, and respect promises, and revere truth.[5] (italics added)

Blanshard attempts to reconcile determinism, freedom, and moral re-sponsibility by arguing that our moral choices, like our creative efforts, are fully determined, but because they are determined by the "necessities of the case" rather than by antecedent circumstances, we feel free in making them and thus willingly take responsibility for them. The argument hangs on the precarious assumption that morals, logic, and art mold us "according to their own pattern." If that were true, we should be able to present a hundred people with a moral dilemma or musical theme to elaborate on - and have them come up with the same result, an outcome too unlikely to consider seriously. In any event, if, at this higher level of causality, moral and aesthetic problems generate their own solutions, it still makes little sense to hold ourselves responsible for the solutions *they* come up with.

Daniel Dennett has submitted the latest and probably the most interesting in a long line of compatibilist solutions. Dennett's solution is not to give up the notion of agency, but to replace the traditional "magical and mysterious" version of that concept with a more natural one rooted in the developmental process. This new entity Dennett calls the "self-made self."[6] By using our capacity to represent our "current beliefs, desires, intentions, and policies in a detached way, as objects for evaluation," we gradually develop our powers of "meta-level reasoning" and in doing so learn to control ourselves at increasingly higher levels of sophistication. Among other things, this power to control includes deciding what basic strategies we should use in gaining satisfaction, how much risk to take in pursuing those strategies, and, basic to all others, what kind of selves we want to be. After years of self-evaluation and self-improvement, a self-made self emerges which enjoys considerable "elbow room," and is capable of true moral responsibility.

Dennett anticipates our doubts when he asks:

> How could any deterministic process of "character trans-formation" beginning with a being that was *not* responsible for any of its "decisions" ever yield a being who was not only responsible for its decisions, but responsible for having the sort of character that would make those decisions?[7]

The question rings true; the answer does not. The answer Dennett provides hinges on the assumption that advancing to meta-levels of self-control allows us to wriggle free from the constraints of genetic and environmental circumstance. To this writer, such an assumption smacks of wishful thinking. While the kind of breadth and maturity to which he is referring give the appearance of autonomy (partly because behavior at that level is harder to predict), they remain forms of learned behavior. As we go about developing the kind of thinking skills that enhance and enlighten our choices, we interact with and are affected by our environment no less intimately than when we are learning to talk. The self-made self that Dennett has in mind remains a product of the interaction between genes and environment. That self is simply another name for what we have called the person; there is no reason to think of it is as an autonomous agent.

MORAL VS. POSITIONAL RESPONSIBILITY

Hovering over all of these attempts to reconcile morality with cause and effect is the fear that loosening the bonds of responsibility will spell the end of civilized life. If the attempts cited all have a strained quality, it stems from the shared conviction that, in any thinking about human nature, we *must* make room for moral responsibility, however incommodious the fit. Such attempts overlook the fact that the rest of the natural world is held together by a different kind of responsibility, one which requires no belief in spirits, in fact, no belief in anything at all. That natural responsibility I would like to call "positional responsibility" to distinguish it from moral or causal responsibility.

We assign moral responsibility to someone when we assume that his or her behavior is caused by an inner agent acting free of physical or psychological constraint. As Merriam-Webster's puts it, we are morally responsible when we are "liable to be called to account as the primary cause, motive, or agent" of an act. The definition implies that we are free to choose otherwise, i.e., are not forced or caused by either previous events or present circumstances to behave in a certain way. In short, we are morally responsible whenever we serve as the cause of our own behavior.

While moral responsibility assumes the presence of a causal agent, positional responsibility does not. By the term positional, I mean the same thing I did in chapter two where I defined the positional *I* as the speaker's body and all those experiences taking place at or in that body. To say that *I* am positionally responsible for a given act means that, because the act arose here in this body/mind rather than somewhere else, I am liable for whatever the consequences may be of its arising. I am positionally responsible for my behavior, not because I am an agent who willed it to happen, but because I am the body/mind in which it arose. It doesn't matter that my behavior has arisen out of a combination of genetic and environmental circumstances – or even that it represents a random event. Like all events in the natural world, that behavior has consequences; it serves as a stimulus to which other objects in the environment respond. Because I am the body/mind in which the behavior arose, I am positionally liable for those consequences.

Moral responsibility implies positional responsibility, but the reverse is not true. It is impossible to be the cause of one's actions without also serving as the body/mind in which they arise. It is quite possible, however, to be positionally responsible without serving as the soul-agent responsible for making that behavior happen. Theoretically, we are positionally accountable for everything that arises within us, even when our behavior is controlled by factors outside our awareness (e.g., by our genes, unconscious wishes, or unnoticed events in the environment). Being positionally responsible implies that we are liable for the consequences of our actions – including punishment for acts that violate community norms. When our responsibility is purely positional rather than moral, however, deliberate punishment makes sense only if it has some kind of deterrent or rehabilitative value. In the case of crimes committed under duress, punishment of the offender in whom the criminal behavior arose has no value at all and is thus inappropriate.

You may want to protest at this point, claiming that if we do not cause our own behavior, we should not be punished or even blamed for *any* of the things we do. To the extent that blame and punishment imply moral responsibility, your point is well taken. But the two terms do not always carry that implication. When we have to cancel an outdoor event because of rain, for example, we blame the cancellation on bad weather. Similarly, we place the blame for lung cancer on smoking. When used this way, blaming is simply a way of explaining events. We cancelled the outing *because* of the weather; individuals get lung cancer *because* they smoke.

When we place blame in this fashion, we are not morally judging; we are identifying one event as the proximate cause of another. If the subsequent event is a negative one, we say that the first event is to blame for the second. This kind of non-moralistic or positional blame applies to people as well. Positionally blaming someone for violating agreed upon rules is equivalent to identifying the proximate cause of the offensive behavior. Since the precipitating conditions themselves tend to be obscure, we usually have to settle for identifying where that behavior arose: *He* is the man I saw breaking into the store. *He* is the person where the offending behavior arose. *He* is the body/mind complex to which we should go if we decide to administer punishment, exact restitution, or attempt rehabilitation.

Punishment can have the same non-moralistic kind of meaning, although that particular usage is less common than is the case with blame. We usually confine the term punishment to intentionally arranged aversive contingencies, but the term can be broadened to include naturally occurring aversive consequences as well.[8] If one animal, for example, tries to take another's food, it runs the risk of being attacked (punished). If we touch a bee, we may get stung. If we eat too much, we may get a stomach ache. If we step on someone else's toes in the subway, we may be yelled at. These are all punitive events in that they have negative consequences for the behaving organism. There is no moral responsibility involved in this broader meaning of punishment, no moral blaming. The responsibility is there but it has nothing to do with morality; it is purely positional. If we are liable for punishment, either natural or social, it is because behavior with punishing consequences has arisen here and not somewhere else.

Being punished for acts we have not intended or wished for is an everyday occurrence for all of us. If the process seems unfair, we can console ourselves with the reminder that it is universal. As Skinner has observed, if it were not for this natural form of punishment, we would have fewer opportunities for learning. Organized punishment, on the other hand, strikes us as something dramatically different. Our vast system of police, courts, prisons, and execution chambers seems to demand real culprits, i.e., bona fide agents that can be morally condemned for their crimes. Our whole concept of justice rests squarely on the assumption that a criminal is morally responsible for his crime. Giving up that assumption would appear to throw into question the legitimacy of intentionally punishing anyone for anything. On what grounds can we deliberately fine, imprison, or otherwise punish offenders if their offending behavior is explainable in terms of bad genes or a bad environment, or can be attributed to chance? Isn't it just a matter of bad luck that circumstances cause crimes to arise when and where they do? With a slight change in circumstances, might not any given crime have arisen somewhere else – or nowhere at all?

It seems contrary to our notion of justice to let luck play any role at all in determining guilt and in meting out punishment. As Thomas Nagel reminds us, however, luck already plays an important role in our legal system.[9] Consider Nagel's example: After drinking too much at a party, you lose control of your car and swerve onto the sidewalk where you hit three people. The way the law is constituted now, your punishment will depend on whether or not any of them die. If there are no pedestrians at all on the sidewalk when you lose control, your punishment will be mild; nonexistent, in fact, if no one sees you. Despite the fact that your behavior remains the same regardless of outcome, the possibilities for punishment range all the way from a brief spell of anxiety to life imprisonment. Whether or not you are punished depends on more than your intentions or even your behavior; it depends on the state of the environment at the time your behavior takes place. Your punishment is, to some degree, a matter of luck.

The point of the example is that, in judging offenders, we often (although certainly not always) set aside questions of intention and base our decision to punish on the consequences of the action. We already have a tradition of jurisprudence which, although based firmly on the assumption of agency, grants ample room for this sort of luck. It would not be that much of a departure from our present system, then, to punish offenders while simultaneously acknowledging that their behavior has been determined by circumstance or chance rather than agency. That punishment can be justified, not on moral or retributive grounds, but on the basis of its usefulness as a deterrent to certain kinds of behavior (e.g., drinking before driving), or as restitution, or as a way of incapacitating someone whose behavior threatens the community.

Giving up moral responsibility does not mean that we have to give up the distinction between coerced and uncoerced behavior. Even when the offender is only positionally responsible, it remains true that crimes committed under duress need not qualify as punishable acts. In the case of moral or causal responsibility, punishment is justified whenever the agent/I is considered free to choose otherwise. In addition to serving as a deterrent, punishment constitutes a form of moral retribution, i.e., a way of retaliating against the agent thought to have initiated the offending action. When responsibility is defined in purely positional terms, there is no agent left to be retaliated against. The only justification for punishment is its deterrent, restitutive, or rehabilitative value. If none of these applies, as is the case with crimes committed under duress, it follows that no punishment is called for. Crimes committed by individuals who are unable to distinguish between right and wrong are exempt for the same reason as those who act under duress. The same is true for criminals suffering from an impairment which prevents their evaluating the consequences of their actions. While the person involved in each case may serve as the proximate cause of the offense, it is not by virtue of any characteristics amenable to change by punishment.

SOCIAL SURVIVAL

Latent in most compatibilist solutions to the determinism-responsibility dilemma is the conviction that society cannot survive without widespread acceptance of the idea of moral responsibility. It is consistent with that premise to speculate that thirty to forty thousand years ago our own species won out in competition with other hominids precisely because of our rivals' failure to implant in their young that belief in free agency which makes individuals morally accountable for their behavior. That speculation rests on the long-held assumption that all societies require both an internal and an external line of defense against deviance. According to that conventional wisdom, internal sanctions such as pride and guilt represent society's first and primary line of defense. It is only when our ability to reward and punish ourselves fails that the external system of police, courts, civil and criminal penalties has to be invoked. The assumption is that both lines of defense are critical. Without the inhibiting power of individual pride and guilt, the police and courts could never hope to contain the vast pool of anti-social impulses that constantly threatens to inundate the social order. On the other hand, without the threat of fines and imprisonment, inadequately socialized individuals would be free to commit crimes with impunity.

While internal sanctions depend to a great extent on a belief in agency, many of the external sanctions do not. It is impossible to feel proud of ourselves or guilty for what we have done unless we can assume that, to some extent, we are the causes of our behavior. While some of the external sanctions, particularly the informal ones such as approval and disapproval, ridicule, admiration, gratitude, and humiliation also require that assumption, the more formal ones – like fines, revocation of licenses, suspension of privileges, ostracism, and imprisonment – do not. Relinquishing our belief in agency would shift the burden of enforcing the norms to those external sanctions that do not require a belief in agency. The question is this: Is that system of external sanctions powerful enough by itself to hold deviance in check?

Giving up the illusion of agency would certainly change our attitude toward criminals. Consider the difference it would make in our approach to murder. "YOUNG NURSE RAPED AND STABBED TO DEATH IN HER COMMONWEALTH AVE. APARTMENT", screams the headline. Our blood begins to boil immediately and is unlikely to subside until the killer is found, tried, convicted, sent to prison, and, ideally, put to death. While we are moved by the loss itself and the grief it implies for the victim's family and friends, what raises our passion to fever pitch is the thought that the murderer chose to kill when he could have chosen otherwise. Our wrath is focused on the unmoved mover inside of him that *made* the murder happen.

Without the assumption of an interior agent freely choosing to kill, our desire for revenge would never reach the bloodthirsty heights we have come to accept as a normal response to murder. Consider the fact that animals, all of which seem to have escaped the burden of agency, rarely kill other members of their own species, however heinous the offense. When protecting their territories, mammals, birds, and fish all show a capacity for intense, sustained aggression, but that aggression is quickly dissipated once the intruder is driven away. Despite flashing teeth, intimidating growls, and hot pursuit, there is nothing in most animals' response to threat resembling our own response to serious crime. For us, it is not enough to drive the intruder away, to strip him of his ability to hurt anyone else. We want him to suffer, at least as much as if not more than he has made his victim suffer.

While some have argued that the retributive impulse is indigenous to human nature and that our belief in free will *allows* that natural impulse to be satisfied, it seems more likely to me that our belief in free will *arouses* the need for revenge.[10] The fact that no other species of animal consistently engages in retributive behavior supports that speculation. It is supported as well by the common experience of seeing our own desire for revenge abate when we learn more about the circumstances that led the criminal to commit his crime. It is when we can find no extenuating circumstances that our blaming becomes most blatantly moralistic and our wrath most inflamed. Without a belief in agency, both our feelings and behavior can be expected to lose much of their retributive quality.

To see the difference that agency makes, consider how you might feel if, instead of reading about the murder of a young nurse on Commonwealth Ave., you had just read about a tornado taking ten lives and threatening to take more. Would your blood boil? Would you demand revenge against those agents, either meteorological or divine, that made it happen? Not likely, because most of us see tornadoes as arising out of circumstance. Even though we don't know exactly what those circumstances are, we assume that they have something to do with the spinning of the earth, gravity, moisture, and temperature – all natural phenomena, themselves the products of other circumstances.

The way we react to tornadoes can teach us something about how we might treat murderers in a world without agency. What most of us would do if we were in immediate danger of a tornado would be to stay indoors and make our houses as safe as possible, perhaps retreating to the basement or even moving temporarily to a public shelter. If the technological know-how were available (as it probably will be some day), we would wait for the meteorological specialists to neutralize the tornado, perhaps by isolating it over an unpopulated area or deflecting it out to sea. In the meantime, scientists would continue working on the problem of how to prevent winds of tornado-like proportions from arising in the first place.

There is no rage in any of this. All attempts are directed toward modifying the behavior of the tornado or, initially, toward getting away from it. While the analogy is far from perfect, is there any reason why we cannot do the same *kind* of thing with murder? We can start by making our homes safer with better alarms, locks and lighting. Once the offender has been caught, we can isolate him (i.e., put him in prison) until such time as we consider him no longer a threat. In the meantime, we can continue exploring the social and psychological causes of murder with an eye to preventing or at least reducing its occurrence in the future.

Despite their many differences, murder and tornadoes are both natural phenomena that can be explained and controlled without resorting to assumptions about agency. They may be similar in other respects as well. For most of history, tornadoes were thought to be caused by spirits of one sort or another – malevolent ghosts, not unlike the ghost of agency that we still insist on blaming for murder. In the context of our species gradual ascent from animism, the ghost of an autonomous, free-willing agent capable of inciting us to murder may represent the last of the spirits to go.

Giving up our belief in ghosts relieves all of us from moral judgment. The murderer is no exception. He remains positionally but no longer morally responsible for his crime. Because his crime has emerged out of anteced-ent conditions, we feel no need to seek revenge; for the community's sake, however, it remains critical to identify and neutralize him. Shorn of all moral fervor, that task becomes more rational and, other things being equal, less repressive. Because it no longer has to carry the extra baggage of retribution, punishment can be judged in terms of its deterrent or incapacitative value. An atmosphere free of moralizing permits experimenting with alternative, nonpunitive responses, such as restitution and rehabilitation. In the long run, a non-moralistic approach to crime calls for a shift of resources away from the task of punishing to the task of identifying the social and psychological circumstances out of which crime evolves, and initiating measures for chang-ing those conditions.

Once we give up agency, however, we can no longer count on the anticipa-tion of guilt and pride to forestall crime. It becomes important, therefore, to make the learning of social norms and the application of external sanctions to violations of those norms all the more effective. This leaves a big question: Until such time as we understand the origins of crime better, can we make external sanctions effective enough to maintain our security? Among those who have answered no, Freud was perhaps the most outspoken.

> It is in keeping with the course of human development that
> external coercion gradually becomes internalized; for a

special mental agency, man's super-ego, takes it over and includes it among its commandments. Every child presents this process of transformation to us; only by that means does it become a moral and social being. Such a strengthening of the super-ego is a most precious cultural asset in the psychological field. Those in whom it has taken place are turned from being opponents of civilization into being its vehicles.[11]

The turning point in this development is the differentiation of the superego from the ego, a step that Freud sees occurring in two stages: "First comes renunciation of instinct owing to fear of aggression by the *external* authority... After that comes the erection of an *internal* authority, and renunciation of instinct owing to fear of it – owing to fear of conscience."[12] In the first stage, the instincts are held in place by anticipatory anxiety, i.e., by the fear of being found out and punished by others. A true superego does not emerge until the second stage in which the individual becomes capable for the first time of *self*-punishment through guilt. It is characteristic of the fully developed superego, moreover, that guilt follows the mere *intention* to break the rules, whether or not that intention is ever acted upon.

The first stage requires no belief in agency, just the learning of an association between certain kinds of behavior and their aversive consequences. This is the stage of the child who acts out of a "fear of loss of love," or the primitive who, "if he has met with a misfortune, ... does not throw the blame on himself but on his fetish, which has obviously not done its duty, and . . . gives it a thrashing instead of punishing himself."[13] The fully developed superego, on the other hand, accomplishes the ends of renunciation and conformity not through anxiety but through guilt.

Guilt is more than the fear of getting caught, a feeling which vanishes quickly when one realizes that one is unobserved. Nor can it be equated with shame, which requires public knowledge of one's anti-social behavior or feelings. Guilt arises even when we are alone, even when we are only considering an action or desire. What distinguishes guilt from other emotions is its tie to self-blame; guilt is the emotional corollary of blaming ourselves for what we have done or what we would like to do. As such, it requires a belief that we cause our own behavior, i.e., a belief in free agency. Given the role Freud assigned to guilt as the ultimate safeguard of civilized life, it is clear that, despite his avowed determinism ("... all psychic events without exception are determined"), he must have harbored such a belief himself.

The differentiation of the superego from the child's ego requires that a belief in agency has already been implanted. In resolving its Oedipal conflict through identification with the parent of the same sex, the child internalizes both the parent's rules *and* the blaming/praising posture (the moral judging) that goes with those rules. That judging posture requires an agent as its object. Before the parents can instill a conscience in the child's mind, they must implant the illusion of an ego that is free to choose otherwise and is thus punishable for its choices. From its inception, then the superego is given the task of watching over a ghost.

But the superego has all the earmarks of an agent, and thus an illusion, itself. We are really talking about the division of a single illusion into two equally illusory parts, one unmoved mover giving birth to another. The status of the superego as an agent in its own right is confirmed by the fact that, when we break a rule and our superego fails to blame our ego, our superego is blamed by others for letting our ego off the hook. We end up being seen as morally irresponsible, not only for our original transgression, but for not blaming ourselves for that act, for not feeling guilty. Superego is as free to judge as ego is free to act.

Yet it is just as true of superego as of ego that introspection reveals no agent there. There is no entity making normative reminders surface, no agent that can be seen meting out punishment or rewards to another agent. Just as ego (executive) processes operate without anyone making them happen, remembering rules and anticipating punishment for violating those rules arise without any agent's bringing them into existence. Desiring, remembering, anticipating, and deciding form a self-corrective system in which equilibrium is maintained through interaction among the processes themselves. The organism has the capacity to control itself. That control arises spontaneously out of antecedent conditions just like all other behavior. Self-control is simply a "sub-routine" in a larger program which is determined by a combination of genetic inheritance and personal history. There is no need to assume an autonomous agent doing the controlling.

If the superego is just as illusory as the ego, where does that leave us with respect to Freud's contention that civilization hangs on our ability to punish and reward ourselves? It obviously leaves us without the two primary weapons in what sociologists refer to as our first line of defense against deviance. It leaves us without either guilt or pride. Both represent the interplay between two putatively free entities, one choosing our actions for us (ego), the other responding judgmentally to those choices (superego). All internal punishing and rewarding rest on the assumption that those agents are real and that they are morally responsible for what they do. Without that assumption, we may continue to experience anxiety before and after breaking a rule, or satisfaction after behaving appropriately, but we will feel no guilt or pride. Anxiety and satisfaction may be better than no defense at all, but, if we are to believe Freud, they are probably not powerful enough to restrain the destructive impulses with which, he says, all humans are born, and which pose a constant threat to civilization.

If civilization really is held aloft by the superego and its handmaidens, guilt and pride, it would appear that we cannot afford to give up our belief in agency, whether that belief is true or not. Philosopher Hans Vaihinger was the first in a long line of thinkers who have argued that agency (free will) is, indeed, a fiction, but no less necessary because of that.

> We encounter at the very threshold of these fictions one of the most important concepts ever formed by man, the idea of *freedom*; human actions are regarded as free, and therefore as "responsible" and contrasted with the "necessary" course of natural events. We need not here recapitulate the familiar antinomies found in this contradictory concept; it not only contradicts observation which shows that everything obeys unalterable laws, but is also self-contradictory, for an absolutely free, chance act, resulting from nothing, is ethically just as valueless as an absolutely necessary one. In spite of all these contradictions, however, we not only make use of this concept in ordinary life in judging moral actions, but it is also the foundation of criminal law. . . Our judgment of our fellowmen is likewise so completely bound up with this ideational construct that we can no longer do without it. . . But this does not prevent our realizing that it is itself a logical monstrosity, a contradiction; in a word, only a fiction and not an hypothesis.[14]

Life is full of fictions, according to Vaihinger, fictions such as three dimensional space, matter, atoms, infinity, paradigms, utopias, the "average person", etc. We employ these fictions heuristically as a matter of course in physics, logic, mathematics, religion, economics, and philosophy. We must not, however, insist upon their status as ultimate truths; what is essential is that they have practical value, even if they are false. The point is to act *as if* they were true and suspend what we know about their fictitious status.

The implication in all of this is that we are not ready for the truth. While it may be safe for an elite handful of thinkers like Vaihinger and Minsky to know what is going on, it would be dangerous to let the average person in on the secret. Society can survive, both writers are claiming, only if the vast majority of citizens allow themselves to be deluded into thinking that they cause their own behavior and are thus morally responsible for what they do. The truth, as Vaihinger bluntly puts it, is that free will "is itself a logical monstrosity, a contradiction; in a word, only a fiction . . ." Minsky, writing some seventy-five years later, leaves no doubt as to how we should deal with that truth: "Such thoughts must be suppressed."[15]

The recommendation that we deal with a truth by suppressing it usually indicates fear – in Vaihinger and Minsky's case, fear of social chaos. Despite the ease with which we accept their warnings, it is not clear what their basic premise is. Are they arguing that the illusion of causal autonomy is necessary for preserving *any* kind of social order, or are they making the more limited claim that it is necessary for upholding society as we know it in the Western world? In light of the stability of cultures (both Eastern and Paleolithic) which rely primarily on shame (community disapproval) rather than guilt (self-punishment), it is clear that a belief in free agency is not essential for human survival.*

How important a role that belief plays in maintaining our own Western culture is more problematical. Despite the obvious restraining influence of guilt and pride, it can be argued that free agency represents one of the primary sources of the very anti-social sentiments against which civilization must defend itself. Teaching our children that they cause their own behavior and

---

* "True shame cultures rely on external sanctions for good behavior, not, as true guilt cultures do, on an internalized conviction of sin. Shame is a reaction to other people's criticism. A man is shamed either by being openly ridiculed and rejected or by fantasying to himself that he has been made ridiculous. In either case it is a potent sanction. But it requires an audience or at least a man's fantasy of an audience. Guilt does not. In a nation where honor means living up to one's own picture of oneself, a man may suffer from guilt though no man knows of his misdeed and a man's feeling of guilt may actually be relieved by confessing a sin. . . . We [Westerners] do not harness the acute personal chagrin which accompanies shame to our fundamental system of morality. The Japanese do. . . . Shame has the same place of authority in Japanese ethics that a 'clear conscience,' 'being right with God,' and the avoidance of sin have in Western ethics." Ruth Benedict, *The Chrysanthemum and the Sword*, Boston: Houghton Mifflin Co., 1946, pp. 223-224.

thus must take responsibility for it, leaves them open to far more than guilt. For those who do not succeed in love and work, a belief in agency invites self-loathing, bitterness, isolation, and spite. Those are all feelings that can alienate one from the world; they are also feelings that easily lead to violating social norms. Not strangely, they are the very feelings that arise in response to retributive punishment and that often induce offenders to commit further crimes. Given these considerations, one is on tenuous ground arguing that a belief in free agency, despite its fictional status, is essential for avoiding the collapse of Western civilization. At the very least, we must consider the possibility of surviving without that fiction an open question.

Freud was aware of Vaihinger's insistence on the practical necessity of conceptual fictions and was not impressed with it:

> This line of argument is not far removed from the "*Credo quia absurdum.*" But I think the demand made by the "As if" argument is one that only a philosopher could put forward. A man whose thinking is not influenced by the artifices of philosophy will never be able to accept it; in such a man's view, the admission that something is absurd or contrary to reason leaves no more to be said. It cannot be expected of him that precisely in treating his most important interests he shall forgo the guarantees he requires for all his ordinary activities.[16]

While Freud was thinking about religion when he wrote that response, it is reasonable to assume that he had similar feelings about other illusions. The idea that the survival of civilization depends on our ability to pretend is contrary to the rational spirit which runs throughout his writing. For Freud, civilization rests squarely on our capacity to punish ourselves. That capacity requires the assumption of two centers of activity, each free to choose its own course of action, each causally responsible for the choices it makes. Unlike Vaihinger, Freud is not asking us to act *as if* our freedom and responsibility were real; he is convinced that they are.

Like Freud, I find it hard to believe that our species depends for its survival on our ability to invent illusions and then to forget that we have done so. Unlike Freud, I am convinced that the superego and ego are just such illusions. Whether one takes them to be real or illusory, there is good reason to question the claim that they are important to our social survival. Freud's view of guilt as the cornerstone of civilization seems to have blinded him to the possibility that free agency (manifested as ego-superego) has an anti-social side as well. The other side of guilt, as Fritz Perls reminds us, is resentment.[17] One of the ways we express resentment is through aggression.

Freud argued that much of our innate aggressiveness gets expressed safely through the "superego's whipping of the ego." The presence of an introjected parent (superego), eager to turn on its new owner (ego), enables us to deflect our aggressiveness inward, thereby sparing society the trouble of dealing with it externally.

> What happens in him to render his desire for aggression innocuous? Something very remarkable, which we should never have guessed and which is nevertheless quite obvious. His aggressiveness is introjected, internalized; it is, in point of fact, sent back to where it came from – that is, it is directed towards his own ego. There it is taken over by a portion of the ego, which sets itself over against the rest of the ego as super-ego, and which now, in the form of "conscience," is ready to put into action against the ego the same harsh aggressiveness that the ego would have liked to satisfy upon other, extraneous individuals. The tension between the harsh super-ego and the ego that is subjected to it, is called by us the sense of guilt; it expresses itself as a need for punishment. Civilization, therefore, obtains mastery over the individual's dangerous desire for aggression by weakening and disarming it and by setting up an agency within him to watch over it, like a garrison in a conquered city.[18]

But is it not equally possible that the superego's hostility toward ego (in the form of guilt), rather than restraining our behavior, makes us more hostile toward others? While it is true that judging ourselves adversely often makes us depressed, there are many occasions when self-judging arouses a desire to hurt others. When the superego's "whipping" of the ego reaches a certain threshold, displacing that anger onto others, as in mass murder, may be the only way to handle the pain of self-hate. Even in its milder forms, the transmutation of self-hate into aggression raises serious doubts about the role of free agency as protector of civilization.

The real impact of agency on aggressiveness, however, shows up most clearly in our reaction to being judged by *others*. When someone else puts us down, degrades, humiliates, ridicules, or scorns us, we very often respond with fury. It is the assumption of agency that makes negative judgment so painful. The message that hurts so much is that *we* are bad, that we as agents have failed to win the respect or approval we wanted. Adding to our fury is the assumption that the other is *causing* the judgment, that in his or her role as ego/superego, the other could have chosen to withhold judgment but failed to do so. Our need to strike back is fueled by the illusion of both our own and the other's causal freedom. Without that dual illusion, it is unlikely that negative judgment could arouse such violent emotions.

One way to concretize the relationship between agency and aggressiveness is to consider a real-life situation. Imagine a scene in which a driver, anxious to avoid late afternoon city traffic, pulls out of lane abruptly and in doing so scrapes the fender of the car next to him. Both cars come to an immediate halt. From your front row seat a few cars away, you sense the possibility of violence. As the two leap out of their cars and head for each other, ask yourself this question: Will their belief in free agency serve to inhibit their anger – or to inflame it? Keep in mind that the very belief in causal autonomy which makes conscience and guilt possible is the same belief that ignites moral blaming, pride, indignation, fear of humiliation, and self-righteousness. Can we say with confidence that the two men's view of themselves and each other as causal agents makes them better citizens? Or does it have the opposite effect?

In light of the intimate connection between agency and aggressiveness, I think we must reconsider the premise that a belief in moral responsibility is critical for civilized life. At the very least, the issue appears to be more complex than we have been led to believe. On the one hand, it seems true enough that a belief in agency and moral responsibility gives society more control over its members than it would have otherwise. Through guilt and pride, that belief creates an internal "police force" which may often prevent criminal impulses from erupting into behavior. Giving up that belief may rob society of its first line of defense against deviance and force it to rely exclusively on public sanctions.

On the other hand, that same belief may, in some people, foster the very emotions which make criminal behavior more probable. Without the sense that we make things happen, we would be less likely to feel frustrated, angry, and bitter, and less compelled to seek compensation for our inadequacies in anti-social acts. The belief in agency, then, may have the effect of strengthening

society's defense against crime while at the same time arousing the very sentiments which threaten that defense. Taking away the belief would presumably
leave society more vulnerable to attack while simultaneously reducing the
likelihood that such an attack would be forthcoming.

Of course, if agency really is an illusion, all this talk about the implications
of that belief for social control is beside the point unless we are willing to
follow Vaihinger's advice and go on acting as if the belief were true anyway.
My own investigation into agency tells me that the belief is an illusion and
that Freud was exaggerating when he implied that civilization would collapse
without it. I find it difficult to believe that the rise of conscience was the
turning point in history that Freud believed it to be. Can we really say that
conscience turned men from being "opponents of civilization into being its
vehicles"? Would it not be equally accurate to say that it turned men into
the anxious, depressed, easily-angered, self-conscious, inadequate, guilty,
remorseful, and self-doubting creatures so many of us seem to be today?
Freud might have agreed that both consequences were true but gone on to
justify one as the price we pay for the other.

> . . . the price we pay for our advance in civilization is a loss of
> happiness through the heightening of the sense of guilt.[19]

Did Freud ever consider that the price might be too high, or, better yet,
that it needn't be paid, at least in the currency of self-punishment? No one is
likely to question that restraint is necessary if we are to live together peace-
fully. But in assessing that need for restraint, we may have exaggerated the
importance of moral responsibility. It may be possible to cultivate responsible
behavior without perpetuating the illusion that we are free to choose our
behavior independently of previous events. To borrow one of Freud's own
phrases, we may have "overrated the necessity" of free agency for mankind.

When Freud used that phrase, he was referring to religion rather than
free agency. Many of his comments on the illusoriness of religion, however,
seem to work as well for agency. For example, substitute agency for religion
in the following statement:

> While giving up religion would involve a certain amount of
> renunciation, more would perhaps be gained than lost, and
> a great danger would be avoided. Everyone is frightened of
> it, however, as though it would expose civilization to a still

greater danger. When St. Boniface cut down the tree that was venerated as sacred by the Saxons, the bystanders expected some fearful event to follow upon the sacrilege. But nothing happened, and the Saxons accepted baptism.[20]

Is free agency another sacred tree that has managed to escape the axe by the threat of consequences too dire to contemplate? Are we continuing to pay too high a price for our civilization on the assumption that the price is necessary when, in fact, it is based on an illusion? Most of us, philosophers, psychologists, and lay people alike, expect some fearful event to follow upon any disavowal of free agency. I think rather that, like the Saxons, we shall find when it happens that life does not collapse under the weight of the sacrilege. If anything, the burdens of living should become lighter. The next eight chapters of this book are devoted to examining those aspects of life most likely to be affected by a change in our beliefs about agency.

REFERENCES

1. Dennett, Daniel, *Elbow Room*, Cambridge: The MIT Press, 1984, p. 154.
2. Nagel, Thomas, *Mortal Questions*, Cambridge: Cambridge University Press, 1979, p. 35.
3. Searle, J., *Minds, Brains, and Science*, Cambridge: Harvard University Press, 1984, pp. 88-89.
4. Brandt, R., "Determinism and The Justifiability of Moral Blame," in S. Hook (ed.), *Determinism and Freedom*, New York: Collier Books, 1958, p. 153.
5. Blanshard, B., "The Case for Determinism," *Determinism and Freedom*, p. 29.
6. Dennett, D., *Elbow Room*, ch. 4.
7. Dennett, D., *Elbow Room*, p. 84.
8. Skinner, B.F., *Beyond Freedom and Dignity*, p. 56.
9. Nagel, T., *Mortal Questions*, ch.3.
10. Clark, T., "Why We Want Free Will," unpublished MS, 1988.
11. Freud, S., *The Future of An Illusion*, New York: W.W. Norton, 1961, p. 11.
12. Freud, S., *Civilization and Its Discontents*, New York: W.W. Norton, 1961, p. 75.
13. Freud, S., *Civilization and Its Discontents*, p. 74.
14. Vaihinger, H., *The Philosophy of As If*, London: Routledge and Kegan Paul, 1935, p.43, first published in 1911.
15. Minsky, M., *The Society of Mind*, p. 307.
16. Freud, S., *The Future of an Illusion*, p. 29.
17. Perls, F., *The Gestalt Approach*, Palo Alto: Science and Behavior Books, 1973.
18. Freud, S., *Civilization and Its Discontents*, pp. 70-71.
19. Freud, S., *Civilization and Its Discontents*, p. 81.
20. Freud, S., *The Future of an Illusion*, p. 40.

PSYCHOLOGICAL IMPLICATIONS OF GIVING UP FREE WILL

BLAMING OTHERS, BLAMING OURSELVES

Esteem and disgrace are, of all others, the most powerful incentives to the mind, when once it is brought to relish them. If you can once get into children a love of credit, and an apprehension of shame and disgrace, you have put into them the true principle, which will constantly work and incline them to the right.[1]

Instilling in our children a love of credit and fear of blame sensitizes them to our opinions, thus rendering them more amenable to our control. It may not always incline them to the "right" as Locke suggests, but it will certainly incline them to what we want. The way we ordinarily go about instilling that love of credit and fear of blame is to convince our children that there exists within them an agent that is responsible for how they behave, and that this agent constitutes their real self. Children fully socialized to that belief can then be expected to interpret praise and blame as judgments of the agent/I and not simply as comments on behavior which happens to be arising "there." From the child's point of view, the two messages are bound to be very different. Being approved or disapproved of for something we have made happen feels quite different from being approved or disapproved of for something that has arisen here on its own. One represents a judgment of us as the creators of our actions, while the other constitutes an evaluation of us as the stream of actions taking place here. The two judgments not only evoke different feelings; they have a different effect on how we behave toward our judges.

The contrast will become clearer as we examine what moral and positional evaluation imply, first, for blame, guilt, and defensiveness, and, in the next chapter, for credit, pride, and virtue.

BEING BLAMED

Because most of us believe in agency, we tend to interpret blame received from others as moral blame, i.e., as a judgment aimed at our causal or agent selves. Moral blame has the power to intimidate and depress us, especially when we concede its validity. More often than not, however, we refuse to make that concession and respond to blame by defending ourselves, often counterattacking with blame of our own regardless of the validity of the judgment against us. We automatically defend whatever we consider to be *us* or *ours*, and there is nothing we consider more *us* or *ours* than the agents within us that think our thoughts and make our behavioral choices. Because moral blame represents an attack on our deepest, most personal selves, it often causes more pain than being attacked physically. Given the nature of civilized society, it is also more common.

Defending ourselves against moral judgment constitutes one of the most visible signs of our belief in agency. We react defensively to blame because we are convinced that there is an entity inside of us to defend. If we cannot afford to stand by calmly while someone reproaches us for our behavior, it is because we see ourselves as authors of that behavior. The assumption of authorship changes the meaning of our behavior, and thus the meaning of any judgment made upon it. It is ours, our creation, that which we have chosen to make happen when we could have chosen otherwise.

The strategies we use to defend ourselves depend to a great extent on the way we judge ourselves as causal agents. Being judged negatively by others is most difficult to defend against when we already doubt our worthiness as soul-agents. Each day presents an endless gauntlet of insults, barbs, affronts, accusations, snubs, insinuations, and outright rejections, our only defense being to keep bobbing and weaving until our tormentors tire of attacking. An unflattering opinion of ourselves as author-agents makes us vulnerable to the most innocent of criticisms and, by redirecting our anger inward, renders us too depressed to fight back.

Others among us, less burdened by self-doubt, seek to protect the agent/I by an assortment of evasive moves including denial, pretense, lying, and rationalization. The key to success lies in having an answer for everything, a "yes, but" for every possible thrust made by every possible adversary. When confronted with having made an offensive remark, we respond, "Yes, but I didn't mean it that way," when that it is exactly how we meant it. When we are late for work, we respond, "Yes I'm late, but the bus never came," when we couldn't possible have known since we were in bed at the time. Success at evading judgment comes at a stiff price: such people are rarely liked and can never afford to relax their guard. Worse yet, they may end up believing their own lies.

At other times, our best defense against moral judgment may be a counterattack. Rather than retreating or contenting ourselves with deflecting the enemy's slings and arrows, we ride out to initiate attacks of our own. The secret to successful retaliation lies in undermining our adversary's view of himself as a worthy causal agent. The simplest and most direct way to do that is to blame him for having blamed us unfairly. To the extent that we are successful in doing so, we shift the burden of responsibility (and all the pain that goes with it) back to its source. The interplay becomes a game, the object of which is to establish the innocence of our own agent while destroying the integrity of our adversary's.

I consider defensiveness (my own included) one of the uglier forms of human behavior. No matter how loving or generous we might be under most circumstances, the possibility of censure can reduce us to levels of pettiness ordinarily reserved for spoiled children. Those rare individuals who manage to take adverse judgment in stride are especially attractive because they are so easy to get along with. When, on the contrary, we are confronted with someone whose defenses are up, we generally become wary of saying anything that might prove threatening, a constraint which limits our freedom to argue openly, ask questions, make suggestions, or respond with humor. At its worst, trying to interact with a highly defensive person resembles greeting someone through barbed wire or trying to chat with someone with a rattlesnake coiled in his lap. The risks are obvious, and, in most cases, not worth taking.

When we interpret blame as positional (aimed at our behavior) rather than moral (aimed at our agent), we both feel and respond differently. Being identified as the person in whom an offensive act has arisen, as opposed to the agent who has made that act happen, is less likely to make us defensive. As persons instead of agents, we have less to defend; while our value as body/minds remains open to judgment, our worthiness as creators of experience and behavior is no longer at stake. Once relieved of the fear of being proved unworthy agents, we are unlikely to develop feelings of rage or harbor thoughts of seeking revenge against our accuser. If our behavior needs explaining, we need only point to our genes, our previous conditioning, and certain features of our present environment. Because the behavior has arisen here, however, we will still suffer the consequences. If those consequences are punitive, it behooves us to defend ourselves against false accusation. The choice may even arise to defend ourselves against a legitimate charge. Whatever the decision, our belief that we are positionally but not morally responsible makes it easier for us to be objective in weighing the evidence presented.

Although blame is most often directed at violations of socially agreed upon norms of conduct, it can just as easily take the form of aesthetic or intellectual criticism. Not surprisingly, the way we interpret that criticism has a direct effect on our feelings. For example, I expect a lot of criticism from readers of this present book and will react according to the meaning I attach to that criticism. I certainly intend to defend the content of the book against misunderstandings. I also leave open the possibility that certain comments could lead me to change my future line of reasoning or manner of expression. I cannot think of any comment, however, that would arouse in me a desire to strike back. Even if critics were to couch their comments in terms of agency ("You completely misunderstand the meaning of morality"), I know how to translate those comments into non-agency terms ("A true understanding of morality is not arising here"), and then decide whether I agree with what is being said. I will still feel uncomfortable reading hostile reviews, or seeing scowls on readers' faces in the bookstore. It will still bother me to hear someone say that the ideas were not presented clearly or consistently. But such criticism will be easier to accept if I view it as a comment on what has arisen here out of the circumstances of my birth and training than if I take it as a sign that I as agent have failed to create something of merit. For that change in perception to occur, all that is needed is the reminder that, while the book has arisen at a particular place and time on this planet, it remains the product of a thousand circumstances.

BLAMING OTHERS

As any subway ride or coffee shop lunch will verify, blaming qualifies as one of our most popular pastimes. The frequency with which we put other people down, especially when they are not around to object, is so great that we might even be tempted to call the impulse instinctive. Before doing so, however, we would do well to remind ourselves of how blaming is affected by our basic cultural beliefs about responsibility. At the very least, our belief that behavior is caused by agents rather than circumstance makes our disapproval of others more passionate. What intensifies our fear and anger is the assumption of an interior entity that could have chosen to behave differently. In blaming others, our belief that an agent inside the other person could have caused something less offensive to happen makes acceptance of the actual behavior far more difficult. The more freedom we assume that agent to have had in its choosing, the angrier we are likely to feel over the choice actually made.

When we view offensive behavior as a product of circumstance rather than an expression of free will, we become less angry and more accepting. Linking that behavior to circumstance provides us with an explanation, and, as Schopenhauer argued in *The World As Will And Representation*, understanding *why* others behave the way they do alters our feelings toward them.

> Of ten things that annoy us, nine would not be able to do so if we understood them thoroughly in their causes, and therefore knew their necessity and true nature . . . [2]

When we become indignant at someone, it is almost automatic to say, "How could you have done that?" The question is transparently rhetorical, and almost always leads to counter-blaming. Imagine, however, how you might react if the other person took the question seriously, and made a genuine attempt to give you an explanation of his behavior. What if that person could cite all the genetic, psychological, and sociological factors involved, and then weave them into a coherent and convincing account of what triggered the offending behavior? Would you still feel indignant?

Once you understood, for example, that your husband's accusing you of infidelity was fed by jealousy, itself the product of self-doubt built up from many previous rejections, would you continue to feel as angry as you did when he first accused you? You might continue to blame him for his behavior, but, knowing the "necessity" of that behavior, you would be less likely to condemn him morally. Your blame would be directed at your husband-as-accuser rather than your husband-as-causal-agent. In blaming him positionally, you would be identifying him as the body/mind where the jealousy arose rather than the agent which made the jealousy happen. That blaming, of course, might still imply that if the relationship is to survive, something needs to be done about his jealousy.

Positional blaming arouses less anger than moral blaming. The anger may be there, but it tends to be milder and briefer. To pursue the example just used, your initial reaction to being falsely accused of infidelity might very well take the form of an angry denial. That initial explosion could be instinctive, i.e., independent of any beliefs you might have about the causes of human behavior. In my own experience, such beliefs do not enter the picture until the reflexive, visceral response has spent itself. Once engaged, however, those beliefs have an almost immediate effect on our emotions. It only takes a moment to place an offensive act, e.g., being falsely accused, in a deterministic perspective. What arises first is the diffuse awareness that the accusation was caused by previous events. With more time for speculation, it is possible to entertain ideas about the specific causes of your husband's behavior – his relationships with his mother, his later involvements with other women, his self-image etc. As Schopenhauer implied, the more concrete our understanding, the easier it is for us to respond without anger. In my own experience, however, the bulk of the work is done at the outset when we place the act in a broad, deterministic perspective. Speculation about specific causes and later confirmation of those speculations may serve to deepen our understanding, but they are not critical for responding in a non-punitive, accepting way. In the long run, the most critical factor in learning to view personal attacks from a non-agency perspective may not be our speculations about the exact causes of other people's behavior, but rather the reinforcing effect of a reduction in our own anger. Every time our reinterpretation of events in non-agency terms leads to a lessening of anger, our new perspective is strengthened.

In many situations, positional blaming is more effective than moral blaming in getting people to change their behavior. What arises for me immediately following that thought is a string of memories involving attempts to get neighbors to turn down their stereos. Years of struggling to socialize new generations of Bostonians have convinced me that moral wrath does not work. With all but the most guilt-prone (who never seem to make any noise anyway), judgments about thoughtlessness and selfishness usually boomerang by making the offender defensive and unwilling to listen to the facts of the case. What works best, and it is that which follows from a belief in non-agency, is positional blaming with a sprinkle of warmth: "I can hear your stereo upstairs over my living room (addresses the behavior not the agent). I would appreciate it if you would turn it down." If that doesn't work, and there will be occasions when it doesn't, it is always possible to move things up a notch or two. "If the sound continues, I will (1) call the police, (2) call the landlord, (3) circulate a petition to have you evicted." The important thing is to stay focused on the offending behavior and avoid judgment of the agent/I ("How could you be so thoughtless as to play your stereo that loud?"). Although moral rage certainly works in some cases, it usually causes more harm than good. Most of the time, we maximize our effectiveness by taking a firm but unemotional stand. What makes that calmness possible is our perception of the offending behavior as a product of circumstance rather than an expression of will.

When we view other people's behavior as determined, some of life's sharpest barbs lose their sting. I am thinking as I say that of the hostess in a restaurant where I once worked as bookkeeper. Her persistent unfriendliness caused me considerable discomfort until I began to see the behavior not as *her* doing, but as something happening *there* in response to a whole network of circumstances of which I could only get an occasion hint. That simple change in perception enabled me to continue being friendly long after such friendliness would ordinarily have been extinguished by her coldness. Perhaps, if I had given up my belief in agency altogether, I might have hung on long enough to win her trust and even her friendship. As it was, I occasionally lapsed into censuring her for her aloofness, which prompted her to cling to it all the more tightly.

Accepting someone's offensive behavior doesn't mean that we must go on putting up with it forever. No matter how spontaneous an act is, the person in whom it arose has to live with its consequences. One of the consequences of persistently hostile behavior is that it eventually drives people away. We can accept the causal necessity of someone's hostility, or aloofness, or lack of humor, and at the same time choose to withdraw from that person's company. In withdrawing we may feel disappointment, sadness, frustration, or pity, but, without the assumption of agency, we are unlikely to feel disgust, rage, or a desire for revenge. Without a belief that the offender is causing his or her own behavior, our passion tends to give way to a more objective concern either with putting an end to the offensive behavior or getting away from it.

As worthy as it might seem, learning to forgive an offender for what he or she has done bypasses the basic truth that there is no one apart from the behavior who can be forgiven for making it happen. To hold forgiveness aloft as an ideal simply confuses the issue. What non-agency calls for is not forgiveness but acceptance; this is a cognitive rather than a spiritual process. Giving up hatred, bitterness, and the pleasures of retribution happens automatically with dispelling the illusion of agency. There is no need to pursue acceptance as a moral virtue. Straining to cultivate it may, in fact, delay its arising. If it is to arise, it will have to arise by itself. The condition most likely to trigger that arising is a shift in our thoughts about who we are.

BLAMING OURSELVES

Much of our hostility is tied up with blaming and being blamed by others. That same desire to hurt or strike back shows up again, less noisily but just as acutely, in the way we blame ourselves. Among the many varieties of self-blame, the quieter, less visible forms tend to be the most painful of all. When we exclaim for all to hear, "I could kick myself for being so stupid," our anger is usually mild and short-lived. Guilt, remorse, and regret are another matter. They can persist for years and make life so painful that we occasionally provoke others into punishing us in order to avoid the greater anguish of having to punish ourselves. At their worst, they have the power to make life too painful to endure. We acknowledge their power over us when we speak of being "stricken by conscience," or suffering "pangs of guilt," or being "guilt-ridden." Despite the lofty place he assigned guilt in the evolution of culture, Freud did not hesitate to characterize the superego's treatment of ego as cruel.*

As I write that, I am thinking of two people whose lives intersected briefly with my own years ago. One was a cocaine addict who, right up to the time she committed suicide, blamed herself for the automobile accident in which her six year old daughter was killed, a tragedy which she felt she could have averted if she hadn't been using drugs at the time. Years of therapy were unsuccessful in alleviating her remorse. Throughout her torment, she clung to the belief that, if she had only been stronger, she could have altered the course of events. The pain of acknowledging her inadequacy ultimately proved to be more than she could stand.

The other was a bright man in his late thirties who was obsessed with the thought that he had wasted his youth. By his own anguished account, he chose to explore the drug scene after college instead of going on to get his Ph.D. and wound up in mid-life waiting on table to support his wife and two children. He saw his life as a train which, by means of his own unfortunate choices, he had diverted from a promising path onto a sidetrack that was going

---

* Emotions which are not only tolerated but expected of all healthy individuals in an agency-dominated culture become symptomatic of pathology in a culture where a belief in agency is defined as psychotic. The absence of those same emotions, conversely, becomes a sign not of impairment but of good health. In Freud's culture, for example, the inability to feel guilt was taken as prima facie evidence of mental disturbance. If agency is only a fiction, however, all guilt is based on a distortion in thinking – a delusion. Far from constituting a sign of mental health, the capacity to feel guilt must be seen, from the perspective of non-agency, as a sign of pathology.

nowhere. Much of his energy was dissipated in regretting his decision to try drugs, and fantasizing about what kind of life he could be living now if he had made wiser choices earlier in life.

How different would the lives of the cocaine addict and the waiter have been if they had viewed themselves as constellations of experience rather than causal agents? At the very least, the addict would not have experienced any guilt. Guilt and remorse constitute forms of self-punishment and require identification with an agent which was free to do other than what it did. The waiter's case is not as clear. Regret is more complicated in that it can be interpreted both as a form of self-blaming (which requires the assumption of an inner entity deserving of blame), and as an expression of disappointment in the way events have turned out (which does not require such an assumption). When the waiter said that he regretted his choice to experiment with drugs, I got the impression that he was registering more than disappointment in the way his life had turned out. He seemed to be blaming himself for having caused the unwise choices (his "regret," in other words, was equivalent to guilt). If I had succeeded (which I did not) in convincing him that his choices were fully determined by circumstance, he might have continued lamenting their arising, but he would probably have stopped blaming himself for making them happen.

Even without a belief in agency we can lament past choices. We can grieve for children or careers lost as a result of those choices. But we cannot logically punish ourselves for what arose unless we see ourselves as having caused those choices. In fact, the ability to punish ourselves requires that we identify simultaneously with two agents, the one which did the original choosing (ego), and another (superego) which now stands in judgment of the first. The addict's remorse and the waiter's regret have their roots in the belief that ego and superego are real entities with the freedom to choose and judge without restraint. Without that belief and the dual identification which accompanies it, their lives would certainly have been different, not just in the torment they might have been spared, but in all the specific thoughts and actions to which self-punishment gives rise.

Once we give up our belief in agency, our self-blaming becomes purely positional. When I blame myself positionally, I am acknowledging that behavior not to my liking has arisen here. I am identifying myself as the body/mind where something offensive to me has arisen. The behavior at issue might have been a hurtful remark, a poor stage performance, an unwise investment decision, or a thoughtless career choice made years ago. To take a hypothetical example, assume that it was the latter – a choice to follow my parents' advice and become a dentist instead of the composer I really wanted to be. Imagine that, because of that choice, I am stuck now, five thousand fillings later, with a job that has no meaning beyond the livelihood it provides me and my family. Having given up the illusion of agency, I am not even tempted to condemn myself for that choice, knowing that it was determined by the circumstances of genetic inheritance and early socialization. Although I may not be sure of all the factors involved, I know that my parents' concern for my financial security and my own eagerness to win their approval played important roles in shaping my decision. I am positionally "at fault" in that the eagerness to please my parents arose *here*. This admission, however, does not imply an *I* inside of me which, at the time of the decision, stood apart from the process and miraculously called my eagerness to please into existence. It came on its own out of my genes and the way I was treated early in life. Since that need for approval arose here, however, I am the one (the body/mind) that will have to bear the consequences of its arising. One of those consequences is that I am now filling cavities instead of writing string quartets. Seeing events that way, I am sad, disappointed, and, to some degree, frustrated with my present circumstances. But, unlike the middle age waiter who wanted to teach English literature, I do not spend my days flagellating myself with regret about my early decision. I accept what happened as a result of antecedent conditions. I recognize that, given all the factors involved, this is what had to arise. (I also plan to retire early.)

Unlike moral self-blaming, positional self-blaming arouses no guilt or remorse. It represents an evaluation of the choices which have arisen here without implying the existence of any entity presumed to have caused those choices. Even without guilt and remorse, however, that evaluation has the power to change my behavior. In my fantasy life as eager-to-please dentist, for example, it might stir within me some concern that choices based on a desire to win approval could arise again and lead to equally unsatisfactory consequences. In interacting with my spouse, my colleagues, or other people close to me, that concern might prevent my giving in to pressure in order to win favor. Acknowledging the role of my eagerness to please in past decisions might even prompt me to enter therapy in an attempt to free myself from its constraints. Whatever I do, without guilt or regret to contend with, I am in a better position to use my self-blaming constructively.

Conventionally, apologizing for something we have said or done implies an admission of guilt or wrong-doing. Does it follow that, in giving up a belief in moral responsibility, we relieve ourselves of any obligation to say that we are sorry? Merriam-Webster defines apology as "an admission of error or discourtesy accompanied by an expression of regret." The two halves of the definition would seem to suggest two different answers to the question. Admitting to "error or discourtesy" does not require a belief in agency; expressing regret (with implied admission of guilt) does. Apologizing for our errors, despite their having arisen on their own, makes sense in light of the fact that we remain positionally responsible for everything which arises *here*. Being positionally responsible means having to take the consequences of our actions. We might be prompted to apologize for a statement, for example, simply because of the effect of that statement on someone we care about. Such an apology comes out of empathy, however, rather than out of guilt or obligation. We are sorry, not that we as agents have caused something untoward to happen, but that someone we care about is suffering as a result of what has arisen here spontaneously. There is no guilt in such an apology; it is an expression of concern and resolve, concern for what the other is feeling, and resolve to avoid such statements in the future.

SIN

One of the great appeals of Christianity is its promise of true justice in the hereafter. The Bible tells us that on Judgment Day those who have obeyed God's laws will be compensated for their pains, while those who have sinned against Him will get their comeuppance. Before the books are closed, all wrongs will be righted, all evil punished, all virtue rewarded. It is a perfectly just system in which luck, causal necessity, and statistical probability play no role whatsoever. What matters is will. God judges us according to our desires and intentions, a yardstick which assumes, of course, that we are always free to choose our thoughts and feelings. For perfect justice to reign in the hereafter, it is essential that we have free will here on earth.

If we do not have that miraculous power, does it make any sense to talk about sin at all? The obvious answer would seem to be no. Sin, guilt, and remorse – in fact, all behavior and feelings involving moral responsibility – rest on the assumption that we cause what we do and are always free to cause something else instead. If we were to give up our belief in free agency, we could no longer regard our violations of God's commandments as sinful. Without the assumption of agency, we would be forced to view all transgressions of religious law as either determined or random. And sin, if it is to have any spiritual significance at all, can be neither determined nor random; it must be willed – freely and deliberately.

At least so it would seem. Many Christians, however, believe that we are all sinners even at birth, a state of affairs caused not by anything we have done personally, but by something that Adam did back in the Garden of Eden. The concept of original sin changes the relationship between sin and free will and ends up making sin a matter of inheritance rather than a matter of choice. Despite the fact that it makes no sense logically, original sin has survived because of its pivotal role in a theodicy which attempts to reconcile God's goodness with the realities of human suffering by attributing that suffering to our own sinfulness rather than to His lack of mercy or power. Augustine of Hippo was the first to formalize the doctrine:

> And since this great nature has certainly been created by the true and supreme God, Who administers all things He has made with absolute power and justice, it could never have fallen into these miseries. . . had not an exceeding great sin been found in the first man from whom the rest have sprung.[3]

Such thinking, Augustine reveals in his *Confessions*, allowed him to avoid "the hell of that error, where no man confesses unto You [God], the error which holds rather that You suffer evil than that man does it."[4]

Blaming ourselves for our misery saves us from having to blame God for it. It allows us to go on believing in an infinitely good, just, and powerful God, despite the suffering so apparent in His creation. Self-blaming, Freud suggested, serves the additional function of preserving the illusion of our own specialness.

> The people [Jews] met with hard times; the hopes on the favour of God were slow in being fulfilled; it became not easy to adhere to the illusion, cherished above all else, that they were God's chosen people. If they wished to keep happiness, then the consciousness of guilt because they themselves were such sinners offered a welcome excuse for God's severity. They deserved nothing better than to be punished by him, because they did not observe the laws; the need for satisfying this feeling of guilt, which, coming from a much deeper source, was insatiable, made them render their religious precepts ever and ever more strict, more exacting, but also

more petty. In a new transport of moral asceticism the Jews imposed on themselves constantly increasing instinctual renunciation, and thereby reached – at least in doctrine and precepts – ethical heights that had remained inaccessible to the other peoples of antiquity.[5]

At times the human capacity for self-judgment seems inexhaustible. The Western mind seems particularly inventive in discovering things to feel guilty about, and then concocting ways to absolve ourselves of the guilt we ourselves have created. Fortunately, perhaps, the worst is behind us. While guilt still plays a central role in modern life, from the voice of the individual conscience to religious dogmas designed to reconcile God and evil, it no longer wields the power it had in previous centuries. A life totally without either guilt or sin, however, is bound to seem unreal, a child's fantasy that has no place in a world of adults. And yet the world as we know it already rests precariously on a fantasy of its own - the fantasy that each of us harbors a secret agent endowed with eternal life and the magical power to cause events without itself being caused. Behind that fantasy lies a very different reality in which all events, including our most sordid thoughts, our cruelest feelings, and most heinous crimes arise on their own unaided by an agent of any kind. In that world there are no sins or sinners – just a stream of events, some desirable, some undesirable, all arising spontaneously out of circumstance.

More than any other writer, it is B.F. Skinner who has sought to de-homunculize our thinking about behavior. It seems only fitting, then, to give him the last word on sin.

> To say that a man is sinful because he sins is to give an operational definition of sin. To say that he sins because he is sinful is to trace his behavior to a supposed inner trait. But whether of not a person engages in the kind of behavior called sinful depends upon circumstances which are not mentioned in either question. The sin assigned as an inner possession (the sin a person "knows") is to be found in a history of reinforcement. . . . As we have seen, man is not a moral animal in the sense of possessing a special trait or virtue; he has built a kind of social environment which induces him to behave in moral ways.[6]

REFERENCES

1. Locke, J., *Some Thoughts Concerning Education*, 56, quoted in Adler, M., and Van Doren, C., *Great Treasury of Western Thought*, New York: R.R. Bowker, 1977, p. 543.
2. Schopenhauer, A., *The World As Will and Representation*, vol. II, tr. by E.F.J. Payne, New York: Dover Publications, 1966, p. 213.
3. Augustine, *City of God*, XXII, 24, quoted in Adler, M. and Van Doren, C., *Great Treasury of Western Thought*, p. 973.
4. Augustine, *Confessions*, VII, 3, quoted in Adler, M., and Van Doren, C., *Great Treasury of Western Thought*, p. 374.
5. Freud, S., *Moses and Monotheism*, III, II, 9, quoted in Adler, M., and Van Doren, C., *Great Treasury of Western Thought*, p. 1289.
6. Skinner, B.F., *Beyond Freedom and Dignity*, New York: Ballantine Books, 1971, p. 188.

8

BEYOND PRIDE AND VIRTUE

Giving up the ghost of agency exposes guilt, remorse, and sin as demons whose power to torment us rests on an error in our thinking. In light of the pain those demons continue to inflict upon us, it seems reasonable to ask why we continue to tolerate the error. In part, the answer lies in what we stand to lose by changing our thinking. We are attached to a view of ourselves as causal agents who are not at the effect of other causes. We enjoy seeing ourselves as islands of freedom in a sea of determinism. From this perspective, every time we act out of will we perform a small miracle. We are gods who move the world of experience and behavior without ourselves being moved. Once a god, it is hard to settle for less, hard to leave that island and join the other creatures of the sea, hard to accept that we are bound by the same laws of motion, heredity, and conditioning as the rest of nature. Giving up the illusion of agency implies rejoining the natural world, or, more accurately, recognizing that, despite our dreams of divine status, we have never been parted from it.

If we give up our identity as soul-agents, we also stand to lose the satisfactions of pride and approval, which, some would argue, more than compensate for the pain of guilt and disapproval. The fear of losing credit for our accomplishments is certainly one of the reasons we have resisted attacks on free will. Just how realistic is that fear? What exactly is lost when we give up our belief in agency? Can we still take delight in hearing someone praise our ideas or good deeds when we know that they are the product of circumstance? Can we still admire other persons when we no longer view them as creators of their experience and behavior?

111

RECEIVING CREDIT

According to the theory of agency, we are free to choose our own behavior, except for those occasions when we are constrained either by force or by the physical laws of the universe. That causal autonomy gives to our choices a quality found nowhere else in the universe: it makes them moral. Because we are free to choose otherwise, we are both positionally *and* morally responsible for the choices we make. One of the perquisites of that status is the right to interpret any positive response to our actions as a comment on our worthiness as prime movers.

While sincere praise of any kind has reinforcement value for the normal individual, that which we interpret as judgment on ourselves as agents has a special power to move us. The anticipation of such praise can lift us to heights of effort not otherwise possible and sustain us through extended periods of deprivation. Planted early in life, the illusion of agency changes the meaning of praise and blame. The reinforcing value of affection, rejection, approval, and disapproval is magnified by the belief that we are the authors of our own behavior. Once that belief is implanted, a mother's smile conveys far more than "I love you" or "I am enjoying your behavior." It carries the judgment that "I think you are a fine and worthy child for the way you are choosing to act." To someone convinced of his or her freedom to choose otherwise, that judgment is music to the ears. It tells us not only that our behavior is good, but, more importantly, that we are good agents for having made that behavior happen.

To anyone still convinced of agency, the concept of positional credit is bound to seem disappointing. Something important is lost when we give up the view of ourselves as causally autonomous entities. Without agency, the comment, "You did a fine job" means simply that a fine job arose "here." We are the body/minds where the fine job arose, not the causes of its arising. The causes lie elsewhere – in our genes, the way we were treated growing up, and certain facets of the present situation. Without agency, the appropriate way to interpret, "You did a fine job," is to see it as we would a favorable judgment on the color of our eyes. We are not being rewarded for something we have made happen, but for something which has arisen here on its own. We can enjoy the compliment and have our behavior reinforced by it without drawing any conclusions about our worthiness as causal agents.

Although we may never have conceptualized them as such, we are already familiar with both moral and positional credit. In its purest form, the latter is usually directed to features of our anatomy, like our height, the color of our hair, and the shape of our nose, all of which we assume to be genetic in origin. There are, however, other aspects of our physical being (e.g., our figure) which lend themselves to both forms of credit. When someone praises our figure, we are apt to feel praised both for what we as agents have accomplished through dieting and exercising, and for the raw material our genes have put at our disposal. Intelligence can also work both ways. When someone says, "You are very bright," we tend to interpret the credit partly as a reflection on our agent-driven efforts and partly as a comment on our genetic heritage. "You are very wise" or "You certainly know a lot about history" are more clearly judgments of us as agents. "You seem to be good at numbers like your father" may be both moral (causal) and positional (determined), but primarily the latter.

The point is this: positional credit is nothing new. We can get a sense of what credit would feel like in a world without agency by focusing on those judgments we already interpret as directed to us as body/minds rather than to us as agents. We know what it is like to hear someone say they like the color of our eyes. With the giving up of agency, all credit comes to feel that way. In the beginning of the giving up process, it may feel as if *we* were being ignored, that none of the credit coming this way is really directed at *us* – a sign, of course, that the ghost of agency is still at large. To anyone still hanging onto agency, something pleasurable gets lost when credit aimed at the agent/I ("I really like the idea you came up with") is transformed into credit aimed at the behavior itself ("I really like the idea that arose there"). With time and further erasing of the agency illusion, however, that feeling of loss can be expected to fade and ultimately disappear. Credit continues to leave a warm feeling, but our response to it is less emotional and more matter of fact.

Writing a book raises many issues involving credit. For example, if this present book arose on its own out of circumstance, should I have my name listed as author? Does the book even have an author? In the positional sense of the word it does, and I qualify as that author in so far as the book arose *here* in this body/mind complex called Paul Breer. And because it arose here rather than somewhere else, I feel entitled to any rewards associated with "positional authorship" of the book. Those rewards include royalties and, more importantly for me, the opportunity to meet readers who want to discuss the ideas of the book further. You may argue at this point that I could just as easily attract people if I said that the book was written at the Institute for Naturalistic Philosophy (which is where the discussions are held), making no mention of my own name. The response which comes to mind is that, if

I move to another city, I want interested readers to be able to find me. Being known as the author of the book may also result in invitations to give talks to other groups or to contribute essays to other people's books. At the very least, being identified as the person in whom this book arose implies new opportunities for friendship and the sharing of ideas.

While these arguments all seem valid enough, I suspect that my wish to have my name on the cover also reflects a lingering belief that I deserve some old-fashioned causal credit for making the book happen. While eight years of assimilating non-agency have dried up much of my oceanic need for recognition, many pools (perhaps even seas) of agent-inspired desire remain. Even though life seems infinitely easier than it did eight years ago when this process began, it is clear to me that a complete surrendering of agency has not yet arisen here.

GIVING CREDIT

As any parent knows, moral credit represents a very powerful means of controlling other people's behavior, more powerful, it would seem, than its counterpart moral blame. Our families, schools, and work organizations all rely heavily on moral credit for motivating and controlling their members. When a first grade boy produces a creditable painting, for example, the teacher is apt to respond with, "What a good little painter you are," thereby reinforcing the behavior by flattering the illusory agent/I. If the child shows significant talent, subsequent teachers may attempt to arouse further effort by cultivating fantasies of his "becoming a great painter." And sometimes it works. Appealing to the child's desire for moral credit may get him to work harder at his art, thereby making him a better artist than he otherwise would have been.

But there are dangers as well in all this "agent-stroking." For one thing, the child may confuse the joys of flattery with the joys of painting and embark on a career that holds little intrinsic meaning for him. And even if his choice of painting proves to be a sound one, his concern for moral credit could distract him from his work or frighten him into conforming to what everyone else is doing. At the very least, his concern with agent-evaluation will have the effect of making him more dependent on other people than he would have been otherwise. Paradoxically, by convincing him that he is a free agent, society makes him more eager for moral approval and, thus, ends up limiting his creative freedom.

Moral credit draws much of its reinforcing power from our doubts about our efficacy as causal agents. The implanting of the agency illusion early in life leaves us in the precarious position of needing to prove and continually confirm our innate worthiness. As uncaused causes, it is we who must give shape to our own lives, we who must turn the raw materials of biology and chemistry into ideas and action. We claim the divine power to create experience out of nothingness but, without God's omnipotence, we remain prone to errors in judgment and failure of nerve. As creators ex nihilo, we can never be certain that we have discharged our responsibilities adequately and so we look to each other for validation. What we need to hear over and over is that we are good and worthy agents. Not that we have pretty blue eyes, or that we look young for our age, but that we are loving mothers, shrewd businessmen, or respected contributors to the community. It is our doubts about our effectiveness as causal agents that give this validation its power to move us. Without a belief in agency, we would have no reason to be concerned about our adequacy as creators of experience and behavior. Moral approval plays a critical role in our motivation only because of our mistaken notion of who we are.

Giving positional credit is a very different matter. When the first grade teacher says to the little boy, "That's a lovely painting" (rather than "What a marvelous little painter you are"), she is giving positional credit. She is directing her enthusiasm to the painting itself rather than to the agent-soul that created it. In a culture like our own, however, where children are steeped in agency long before they enter school, most children will interpret the teacher's comment as an evaluation of their ability as causal agents. To get around that interpretation, the teacher would have to be more explicit by saying, "That's a lovely painting *that arose there.*" She might go on to explain what makes it a good painting and in the process teach the child something about form, composition, and color. Her comments would all be directed to the painting or the behavior (technique) which produced that painting, much the way painting instructors teach in schools of art. What the teacher omits in giving positional credit is any reference to the artist as agent. The undeluded teacher assumes that all paintings are products of inherited ability and training, and that the painter is simply the body/mind where those various factors have intersected.

While less reinforcing than moral credit, positional credit can nevertheless have a powerful effect on another person's behavior. Telling a colleague, "That's a great idea that arose there," can spur her on to developing the idea further. I know from personal experience how encouraging it can be to have a friend say that the ideas arising here are exciting. Positive evaluation coming from someone whose opinion we respect confirms the worthiness of our ideas (and ourselves as *persons*), even though it says nothing about our worthiness as causal agents. The more often our ideas are confirmed by approval, the more often new ones are likely to arise in the future.

Giving positional credit feels different from giving moral credit. When I say, "I think it's great that you lost thirty pounds," I am saying three different things, none of which has anything to do with agency: first, that you look good, secondly, that your happiness makes me happy, and thirdly, that I am slightly in awe of the genetic and environmental forces which have conspired to produce this outcome. Because I am not commending you as causal agent for having accomplished this feat, my remarks are apt to seem less laudatory than those to which you may be accustomed. I might be just as elated as anyone else, but that elation will be marked less by admiration for your indomitable Will than by happiness over your good fortune. The more I care for you, the more pleasure I will probably feel. If I try to reinforce your behavior with the thought of getting you to lose another ten pounds, I will avoid any comments directed to you as agent ("It's incredible what you can do when you put your mind to it"), directing them instead to you as person ("The perseverance arising there is remarkable"). If moral credit is what you want, all of this will probably leave you feeling unappreciated and, therefore, less motivated to go on dieting. If, on the other hand, you have already given up your belief in agency, it may be just what you need to hear.

TAKING CREDIT

Pride is what we feel when we give ourselves moral (i.e., causal) credit for our thoughts or actions. Western culture is ambivalent about pride, regarding it sometimes as a sin, other times as a virtue. While all the major religious traditions condemn pride as an obstacle to spiritual growth, secular society not only accepts it, but goes so far as to fault those who lack it. Religious leaders warn us that "pride goeth before the fall" at the same time that therapists and friends encourage us to take more pride in what we do. Our reaction to others' taking pride seems to depend on *how much* credit they try to take. We respect people who know what they want and who go after it with the expectation of achieving success. We even tolerate a certain amount of boasting in the process, as long as the boaster can back up his or her claim. Justified or not, however, self-congratulation eventually reaches the point where it suggests the very condition it would seem to deny, namely a lack of self-assurance.

At that point we are repelled and interpret the taking of credit as a sign of insecurity.

Taking moral credit for our actions is woven into practically every aspect of our lives. We find it perfectly normal for an employee to harangue her colleagues at lunch with boasts such as, "You should have seen me at the meeting this morning. When the department head walked in and announced her new regulations, I stood up and really told her off." Nor do we find it particularly objectionable when a friend comes right out and asks to be credited for her behavior: "Didn't I tell you that you would regret leaving your old job? Well, I was right, wasn't I?" Of course, not all our boasting is that obvious. Often a smile is all others see as we go about our day privately congratulating ourselves for incredibly witty thoughts, breath-taking insights, and Christ-like acts of humility. While we might prefer to hear ourselves praised by others, it is always easy to do unto ourselves what we would have others do unto us. In the privacy of our minds, there is no one to object if we choose to exaggerate our accomplishments, minimize our shortcomings, or rewrite personal scenes substituting lines and gestures more suited to the image we have of ourselves.

At other times our bragging is overt, but so subtle that no one, including ourselves, recognizes what we are doing. Years ago, when I was in training to do Gestalt Therapy, I recall being asked at a weekly supervision meeting to choose one of my clients to discuss in class. There were several I could have chosen; one was doing very well, while the others, for reasons I could not understand, did not seem to be improving at all. I chose my "success" story and was quite shocked when the supervisor interrupted my presentation to say, "So you want to brag." I dismissed the comment as peevish and continued talking. It was not until I got home that night that I realized how right he was. I had spent the whole session demonstrating to the class what a good therapist I was and consequently hadn't learned anything at all. It was obviously more important for me to chalk up additional moral credit than to find out what I might have been doing wrong with my less successful clients.

It is a symptom of our inability to accept ourselves that we are always looking for opportunities to convince others (and, in the process, ourselves) of our excellence. We rarely feel so confident that we can afford to let our accomplishments go unrecognized, or so magnanimous that we allow them to be attributed to someone else. This hunger for credit impoverishes our lives in many ways, chief among them being our ability to establish close relationships. Our need to be heard makes it difficult to listen openly to others and to enter into their lives without bringing our own emotional baggage with us. If most of our conversations are superficial, it is because we can't wait to talk about *our* accomplishments, *our* hurts, all that *we* have been through. We want sympathy for our troubles and we also want credit for our skill in dealing with all the indignities life has heaped upon us. When both parties are driven by the same need, intimacy has no chance at all. Interaction quickly degenerates into a competition in which contestants pretend to listen to each other while rehearsing their own stories.

Taking pride in our accomplishments is not so much a sign of defective character as it is a sign of defective thinking. We are entitled to speak of accomplishments as *ours* only in that they have arisen *here*. It makes no difference whether we are talking about the successes themselves or the choices and actions which serve as their proximate causes. Those precipitating acts also arise spontaneously and, as with the deeds that follow, belong to us only in the sense that they have arisen here and not somewhere else. Means and ends are both part of a spontaneous chain of cause and effect in which free will plays no part at all. All events are determined by other events, not by autonomous agents.

That is true not simply for our inspirations, but, Thomas Edison notwithstanding, our perspiration as well. Sustained, hard work is built up out of a thousand moment-to-moment choices, each of which, if we look carefully enough, can be seen to arise on its own. An artist's choice to continue painting for another fifteen minutes, for example, is as spontaneous as the choice of subject matter itself. The fact that some artists are willing to work that extra fifteen minutes while others are not is determined by the circumstances of heredity, socialization, and present environment. Taking pride in that effort is no more justified than taking pride in the ideas which have inspired it.

Giving myself positional credit for an idea (or for the effort spent in working that idea out) is equivalent to recognizing that something of value has arisen here. It implies nothing about agency and, thus, need not trigger feelings of pride or lead to bragging. It says that I value what has arisen; I think the idea is interesting, significant, or whatever. Instead of triggering feelings of pride, that assessment arouses feelings of joy. I am glad that something which I consider good has arisen here. If there were someone (e.g., a cosmic agent) to thank for what has arisen, I would undoubtedly want to register my appreciation. In lieu of such an entity, I content myself with feeling fortunate that the idea and all the effort involved in working it out have arisen here in this body/mind.

My appraisal of what is arising in this body/mind affects my behavior as well as my feelings. A positive self-evaluation of the ideas in this book, for example, will increase the probability of similar ideas arising in the future. What is critical for shaping those future thoughts is my judgment of what is arising, not any pride I might feel as initiator of those thoughts. Evaluation of myself as body/mind (positional credit) and evaluation of myself as agent (moral credit) are not always easily distinguished. If I have any doubts about who or what is being evaluated, I can always use the language test mentioned earlier. To do so, I take the behavior at issue (e.g., getting a good idea) and try expressing it in two different ways: "I just got a good idea," versus, "A good idea just arose here." If the latter way of expressing it leaves me feeling overlooked or left out, chances are that I have been giving myself moral credit.

VIRTUE

If we are only positionally responsible for what arises within us, can we ever be said to possess that "moral excellence" called virtue? The answer would appear to be no. For one thing, who is there to possess it? If the agent/I is a ghost, all that remains is the person, i.e., the body/mind of which the "virtuous" behavior is already a part. As persons we *are* the kindness, the patience, and the generosity arising here; we are also the body in which these socially approved traits are arising. In neither capacity, as the behavior arising or as the place in which it is arising, can we consider ourselves the creators of our behavior.

Once we identify the causes of someone's behavior, we can no longer call that behavior a virtue, regardless of how much we might admire it. If doctors were to trace a friend's exceptional patience to a malfunctioning thyroid, for example, we would be compelled to withdraw all moral credit. Unless we can take credit for causing our own behavior, it makes little sense to apply the term virtuous to anything we do. If all behavior is either random or a product of genetic and environmental circumstance, it would be sensible, in fact, to drop the concept of virtue altogether, along with sin, pride, guilt, and all other concepts associated with moral responsibility.

In the meantime, the concept of virtue continues to rest on the assumption that we as causal agents can change our behavior through an application of will. It follows from that same assumption that we should be able to make ourselves more virtuous. Because our will is free, it is presumably within our grasp at any time to make ourselves kinder, more patient, and more courageous – or less stingy, less envious, less cowardly. Given that freedom, it follows that, if we don't at least try to improve ourselves, we leave ourselves open to moral censure. Not surprisingly, the effort to cultivate virtue and reap the social approval that goes with it often lead to strained efforts at self-improvement. Because that struggle is socially approved, we find it easy to fool both others and ourselves that our motives are pure, that we are inspired solely by a love for virtue in and of itself.

> The would-be saint walks straight into the meshes of this web because he would become a saint. His "I" finds the deepest security in a satisfaction which is the more intense for being so cleverly hidden – the satisfaction of being contrite for his sins, and contrite for taking pride in his contrition. In such an involved vicious circle the masks behind masks are infinite. Or, to put it in another way, he who would stand outside himself to kick himself, must then kick the self that stands outside. And so on forever.

> So long as there is the motive to become something, so long as the mind believes in the possibility of escape from what it is at this moment, there can be no freedom. Virtue will be pursued for exactly the same reason as vice, and good and evil will alternate as the opposite poles of a single circle. The "saint" who appears to have conquered his self-love by spiritual violence has only concealed it. His apparent success convinces others that he has found the "true way," and they follow his example long enough for the course to swing to its opposite pole, when license becomes the inevitable reaction to puritanism.[1]

When we strain after saintliness, we wreak havoc with our psyches by denying our true feelings and pretending to be something we are not. If saintliness (or at least socially valued behavior) has any chance at all, it is more apt to arise from accepting who we already are as persons than from twisting ourselves around to fit some conception of who we should be. Straining to be kind, loving, and charitable when we really don't feel that way creates a pool of frustration that ultimately leads to intolerance, resentment, and a holier-than-thou attitude. Accepting others who are different from us can be difficult enough under ordinary conditions; when we do not accept ourselves, it becomes virtually impossible. If we deny ourselves for the sake of an ideal, how can we possibly accept others who fall short of that same ideal? We can't. We displace onto them all the resentment which comes out of our struggling to be something we are not. Often that resentment shows up as an attempt to make others conform to our own ideals. The greater the resentment, the more heavy-handed the bid to exert control. We judge, we preach, we shake our fists in outrage, and all the while it is our inability to accept what is arising *here* that is firing our indignation.

Real tolerance comes from accepting what is arising here. We cannot let others be themselves unless we first accept ourselves for the persons we are. This means not running away from or otherwise defending ourselves against the frailties and shortcomings that arise from our own genetic and environmental background. Accepting our thoughts and feelings doesn't necessarily mean acting on them. It means being fully aware of them and not condemning ourselves for having them, all of which follows automatically from giving up the illusion of agency. Once we accept all the thoughts and feelings arising within us, it is but a short step to accepting what arises in others.

Many of our efforts to leave the world a better place are inspired by either a desire for moral credit or a nagging sense of duty to our fellow human beings, which is to say a desire to avoid moral blame. Both motives are saturated with agency. And, as Lao-tze was fond of saying, that is why those efforts usually cause more harm than good. When we strain to be socially responsible in order to win approval or assuage our guilt, we are doomed to make a mess of things. Our heart is not in our work and we end up resenting the very people we are trying to help. The more desperate our need for self-justification, the more energy we waste in competing for praise and the more rigid we become in asserting our own ideas. We are better off waiting until we are moved to act not by duty but by genuine concern. This need not mean abandoning the world to all its pain and ugliness. It means abandoning the well-intentioned but intrusive notion that, in order to justify our existence as moral agents, we should be doing something to improve the world.

Much of the behavior that Western religion defines as virtuous and exhorts us to emulate will arise spontaneously when we give up our belief in agency. I refer to humility, patience, forgiveness (acceptance), turning the other cheek (non-defensiveness), not craving or clinging to objects or people, not seeking our own glory, and not protesting adversity. If "virtues" of this kind seem out of reach to most of us, it is primarily because we insist on seeing ourselves as the causes of our own behavior. Our belief in free agency gets in the way by fostering the illusion that we are centers of will capable of forcing the world and ourselves to conform to our wishes. That premise is perfectly designed to breed arrogance, egocentricity, defensiveness, pride – qualities just the opposite of those we are taught to value most highly. Once instilled, our belief in agency makes it unlikely that acceptance, humility and other valued kinds of behavior will arise on their own. We are left, then, with the necessity of *making* them arise through good works and self-denial, a strategy which practically guarantees that they never will.

As Watts reminds us, striving for moral perfection arises from the same desire for power and approval as the "vices" which that striving is designed to overcome. Once we give up our belief in agency, it becomes clear that no great spiritual effort is needed to rid ourselves of our shortcomings. Many of them stop arising spontaneously, according to the workings of our genes and environment, once we realize that all behavior is determined by circumstance. The primary obstacle to getting rid of them is our belief that it is within our power as causal agents to do so. Paradoxically, the single most important things we can do to realize our cultural ideals is to give up our belief in moral responsibility. Until we do so, life will remain a treadmill where, no matter how fast we run, we can never get to where we want to go because we are convinced that it is up to us to get there.

REFERENCES

1.   Watts, A., *The Wisdom of Insecurity*, New York: Vintage Books, 1951, pp. 129-130.

9

RELEASING THE WHEEL

Henry David Thoreau was living in rural mid-nineteenth century Concord when he declared that, "The mass of men lead lives of quiet desperation." If he were still with us in this late twentieth century world of freeways and nuclear arms, he would have little reason to alter his pronouncement. We remain as desperate as ever, even more noisily so, as we go about the task of bending the world to our personal will. If the last four thousand years are any indication, chances are that we shall go on feeling desperate as long as we continue to hold ourselves morally responsible for achieving the success, health, peace, contentment, and love we desire.

A life without desperation remains as elusive and mysterious to us as the other side of the moon. The side of life we know most intimately resists our desires; it confronts us with adversity and challenges us to impose our will. We know it best as an adversary that can be conquered only with determination and vigilance. In our preoccupation with winning the battle, we seldom catch even a glimpse of life's other side. When we do, it is usually through art or, as Isak Dinesen reminds us, in our dreams:

> People who dream when they sleep at night know of a special
> kind of happiness which the world of the day have holds not,
> a placid ecstasy, and ease of heart, that are like honey on the
> tongue. They also know that the real glory of dreams lies in
> their atmosphere of unlimited freedom. It is not the freedom
> of the dictator, who enforces his own will on the world, but

the freedom of the artist, who has no will, who is free of will. The pleasure of the true dreamer does not lie in the substance of the dream, but in this: that there things happen without any interference from his side, and altogether outside his control.[1]

Remaining true to that "freedom from will" in everything we do would seem to be impossible. Even in art, the ideal eludes us: "I did not want anything to live except what wanted to come out of me all by itself. Why was that so difficult?"[2] The ideal of a completely spontaneous life remains remote because we are still convinced that we have to preside over the birth of every thought or action that arises. But if agency is an illusion, if there is no entity inside of us presiding over anything, is it not true that our experience already "comes out of us all by itself?" Is it not already spontaneous in the sense that Dinesen and Hesse want it to be? If it does not seem that way, might it not be because our beliefs about control and responsibility are getting in the way?

"But what about intentional behavior?" you ask. Artistic inspiration may come and go of its own accord while dreams too have a life of their own, but how can volitional acts such as decisions ever be spontaneous? Every day we are confronted with an endless string of choices: when to get up, what to eat for breakfast, what to wear to work, how fast to drive, where to park, and so on – all before we even get to work. At work, the choices become even more complex, more demanding of foresight and the ability to weigh alternatives. Those choices are critical in determining whether or not we ultimately get what we want. If we choose to work hard, success is more likely to come our way. Choosing foods for their nutritive value improves our chances of remaining healthy. Choosing to be thoughtful toward friends affects how much they care for us. Even the most ardent determinist will grant that our intentions, decisions, and choices make a difference in how we act.

The real question, the one which holds the key to a less desperate existence, concerns the origins of the choices themselves. Are they determined by a spiritual force or entity (the "true self") residing in but not physically attached to our brain, heart, or pineal gland? Or are they shaped by the circumstances of our birth, socialization, and current environment? Or is it sometimes one, sometimes the other? Our explanation of how choices originate is critical in determining the kind of responsibility we bear for our actions. If our choices originate in a spiritual self, our responsibility is moral or causal. If they originate in our genes and environment, we are only positionally responsible. Either way, the importance of the choices is beyond question: the issue is one of accountability.

What makes Dinesen's "ease of heart" so elusive and Thoreau's "quiet desperation" so common is our belief that, as free agents, we cause our own choices. If we fail at our careers, at love, or in finding peace of mind, we blame the agent within us, the *I* that could have made a different choice arise. If we succeed, it is because that same agent made the right choices arise. It is contrary to our belief in agency to acknowledge the importance of our choices and then attribute those choices to genetic and environmental circumstance. They would no longer be *our* choices, even though they arose here in this body. What makes the choices distinctively ours is the belief that our agent/I caused them.

This insistence on viewing ourselves as the causes of our own behavior accounts for much of our preoccupation with control. If all of our volitional comings and goings are determined by an inner driver, and that driver is who we really are, it follows that we risk our lives every time we relax our grip on the wheel. To let go even momentarily means turning our lives over to chance and the whims of other agents. In the end it is this fear of losing control, aroused by our belief in free agency, that obscures the spontaneity of life and consigns us to a quiet but unrelenting desperation.

This forced steering is not simply a poor strategy for getting things done, a case of more control than the situation requires; it reflects a fundamental distortion in our perception of how life works. It is a symptom of a deluded mentality. To see more clearly what I mean, consider the analogous situation of a passenger on a subway train who is convinced that, without his steering, the train will go off the track. Picture such a man entering the car and taking a seat. As the train begins to move, he grasps the back of the seat in front of him. Banking first one way and then the other, he successfully negotiates a small curve. As the train picks up speed, he responds by tightening his grip. If we look carefully, we can see his knuckles whiten. He is hunched over now, shoulder muscles taut, steering with both arms and legs. His tension is infectious; passengers who were smirking just moments ago are secretly steering along with him. A few more blocks of this and the whole train will slip into irreversible psychosis.

Having thrust a perfectly innocent man into this absurd predicament, let us see what we can do about extricating him from it. The conductor has been observing his strange behavior and chooses this moment to approach. Tapping him gently on the shoulder, he says, "Pardon me, sir, but all this steering is quite unnecessary. The train steers itself." The passenger is not easily taken in by so bizarre a remark, although the fact that it comes from someone who appears to know what he is talking about has a noticeably quieting effect. Without relaxing his grip, he turns and asks the conductor to explain himself. The conductor is aware that he is dealing with a disturbed man. Student of human nature that he is, he has waited for the auspicious moment to intervene. Experience has taught him that deluded passengers are least capable of hearing the truth when the train is going fast or when it is rounding a curve. Here on the straightaway with the train slowing down there is a chance that he can get through.

He begins by explaining that the seat which the passenger is gripping so desperately is unattached to the axles and thus has no influence over what happens to the wheels. He goes on to point out (inviting the passenger's own investigation as he proceeds) that the position of the wheels and thus the direction of the train is determined rather by the layout of the track. Patiently he leads the passenger through the simple mechanics of how the train steers itself. He asks the passenger to take nothing on faith but instead to examine more carefully than ever before his perceptions of how the train actually works.

Those fellow travelers who have been following the conversation with nervous interest notice that the passenger is starting to relax. His arms are not so stiff now, blood is returning to his knuckles and he has dropped his shoulders. Although his hands are still gripping the seat in front of him, he seems less obsessed with steering. The more convinced he becomes of what the conductor is saying, the more he lets go. It is only a beginning but the seed has been planted. He has had his first taste of surrender.

It demands an extraordinary kind of openness to consider the possibility that, like the passenger on the train, we are all deluded. For most of us, the idea that life steers itself is simply too strange to bother exploring. Even for those who are willing to make the effort, fear of what will happen if they stop straining may abort the investigation. Straining and desperation are so deeply etched into our everyday experience that we find it difficult to imagine life without them. We rarely question where they come from, preferring to accept them as unfortunate but unavoidable aspects of the human condition. It simply does not dawn on us that they are unavoidable only so long as we cling to our belief in agency.

Our desperation usually manifests itself as straining either to produce the outcomes we want or to prevent those we do not want. In this chapter I would like to focus on the former, leaving the latter for the next chapter. Merriam-

Webster defines straining as any "violent effort to influence events." Our efforts are most likely to become violent when we try to force outcomes. Our minds fill up with anxious thoughts and lose their clarity. Our movements lose their natural grace and efficiency. As a result, much of our energy gets wasted in worry, tension, and misdirected action.

Although we take straining for granted in the West, there is no reason why we have to do so. Effort, Lao-tze reminds us, can be both vigorous and sustained without being violent. He uses the term *wu-wei* (literally non-doing) to call our attention to a more natural, non-violent kind of effort; "it is what we mean by going with the grain, rolling with the punch, swimming with the current, trimming sails to the wind, taking the tide at its flood, and stooping to conquer."[3] Natural effort is flowing, unforced, and unpanicked even when it is intense. As Lao-tze put it, it obeys the principle by which "The Tao abides in non-action, yet nothing is left undone."[4]

Straining arises from a variety of sources, one of which is our view of ourselves as causal agents. In mapping out our goals, we are typically guided by the belief that, if we are to get what we want, it is up to us as causal agents to make it happen. We may start realistically enough with the assumption that, whether it is money we want, or an interesting career, or many friends, success depends on both ability and effort. Our delusion lies in assuming that we as agents can alter how much of each arises, particularly how much effort. Straining typically occurs in situations where the amount of effort we perceive to be required is not forthcoming naturally. We take it upon ourselves to force the issue. Our trying becomes exaggerated, violent, desperate, insincere and inevitably, painful. The symptoms are familiar to all of us: nervousness, irritability, defensiveness, fear, impatience, anger, depression, backaches, headaches, nausea, high blood pressure, and insomnia – the precise combination being determined by heredity and conditioning.

The undeluded way to view the same situation is to understand that there is no interior agent standing outside the chain of cause and effect that can "summon" an increase in effort. It is our genes, history of reinforcement, and present environment that determine how much effort arises in a given situation. The feeling that we as agents are free to choose whatever level of effort we want is an illusion arising from our lack of awareness of all the forces operating on our behavior. Whenever a decision to change our level of effort arises, we can assume that it is arising out of previous conditions. If our present level of exertion is insufficient for achieving a goal, awareness of that fact may trigger a more intense burst of energy. The proximate cause of that increase is the awareness that the situation requires more energy; the more remote causes are bound to be less clear but can be assumed to lie with our genes and early socialization. Whatever happens to our energy level, we need not assume an inner agent causing the change.

All levels of effort are determined by circumstance, even those unnatural, forced efforts we call straining. While straining arises from a whole matrix of factors, one of the most important variables is our *belief* in agency. Even though there is no agent there making us strain, the illusion of such an entity, in conjunction with our genes and training, has the power to trigger a forcing of effort. We strain because we are convinced that we as agents can cause our own effort. However vivid the call to extend ourselves, the proximate cause of our straining is still not a real agent; it is only the illusion of one.

In cases where even a strong, unforced effort proves inadequate to the task, it might be more sensible to give up or at least modify our goal instead of straining. To anyone raised to the tune of, "If at first you don't succeed, try, try again," this may seem suspiciously like surrender. And well it should. It is a surrendering to what feels natural, whether that be a mild, intermittent endeavor, or an intense, sustained one.

When we give up our belief in agency, we give up the feelings that go with straining. First and foremost that means anxiety. In any endeavor where the outcome is both important and uncertain, we are bound to feel anxious, whatever our beliefs about agency may be. What agency adds to that basic concern is the fear of moral evaluation. The belief that we have the power to cause our own behavior arouses a new apprehension independent of our concern with the outcome itself. "How good am I?" "Will others praise me for what I have done?" "Will I feel proud of myself when I have finished?" More often than not, it is this fear of agent-evaluation, both internal and external, that triggers the onset of straining.

Recognizing agency as an illusion has the power to change our feelings. Seeing that all experience and behavior arise out of circumstance relieves us of any responsibility for making them happen. We remain positionally accountable and will have to take the consequences, but we no longer feel burdened with moral responsibility for "our" role in the process. While we hope that our genes and conditioning are adequate to the task at hand, we realize that, if they are not, there is no agent within us that can do anything about it. So, while we may go on worrying about the final outcome, we stop worrying about our moral responsibility for making it happen.

As we learn to relax our grip on agency, we may also experience a change in attitude toward the outcomes themselves. Goals continue to arise but their attainment seems less urgent. Although it may not be initially obvious, believing that we cause the behavior necessary for achieving valued outcomes actually feeds our desire for them. Assuming that an objective is at least somewhat desirable to begin with, the belief that we control the thoughts, feelings, and actions required for attaining it makes the goal safer and, in turn, increases our efforts to achieve it. Without a belief in causal autonomy, we are forced to view all outcomes as a function of circumstance, even when our own behavior plays a mediating role. Whether or not we eventually reach our goal (e.g., becoming president of the company) depends on a causally-linked chain of events in which free agency plays no role at all. While desire is certainly possible under those conditions, it is less likely to become urgent.

Descartes had a similar theory of the relationship between control and desire in mind when he wrote:

> My third maxim [for self-guidance] was to try always to conquer myself rather than fortune, and to alter my desires rather than change the order of the world, and generally to accustom myself to believe that there is nothing entirely within our power but our own thoughts . . . and I believe that it is principally in this that is to be found the secret of those philosophers who, in ancient times, were able to free themselves from the empires of fortune, or, despite suffering or poverty, to rival their gods in their happiness. For, ceaselessly occupying themselves in considering the limits prescribed to them by nature, they persuaded themselves so completely that nothing was within their own power but their thoughts, that this conviction alone was sufficient to prevent their having any longing for other things.[5]

My only quarrel with the position taken by Descartes and the philosophers to whom he alludes is the qualification that "nothing was within their own power *but their thoughts* . . ." I fail to see why "the limits prescribed to them by nature" should not include their thoughts as well as their bodies and sensations. To make an exception of thought implies the existence of an agent (a thinker) who does the thinking and has the power to change it. In the long run, the reduction of "longing for other things" comes from seeing that *all* experience and behavior are determined not by an inner self, but by nature.

Buddhists have contended for centuries that craving represents the primary cause of our suffering. They believe that the only way to relieve craving and the suffering to which it gives rise is to become enlightened, i.e., to discover the fundamental unity behind all distinctions. Among other things, this implies transcending the distinction between subject and object, where subject refers to both agent *and* person. My own experience tells me that giving up the illusion of agency is sufficient in and of itself to take much of the urgency out of desire. While it cannot eliminate all suffering (loved ones still die, careers still fail), it reduces the power of everyday events to make us anxious and depressed.

Giving up the illusion of causal autonomy moderates our desires while reducing our temptation to engage in violent effort in order to achieve them. One of the primary effects of that changed attitude is a reduction in anxiety. The less urgent our wanting is, the less frightening is the prospect of not getting. The anxiety which remains after giving up agency is a response to the uncertainty inherent in wanting anything at all. Even without a feeling of moral (causal) responsibility, we may get anxious as we study for an exam, interview for a job, advertise for customers, make investments, await a baby, plan a party, or undergo surgery. What is strikingly new without agency, however, is the peace of mind arising from the knowledge that life is unfolding on its own. While we realize that our future depends on the behavioral choices which arise *here*, we are aware that all choices are shaped by a matrix of past and present events. Our serenity comes from recognizing the causal necessity of whatever arises.

My own approach to goals and the process of attaining them has changed radically. Life remains as uncertain as ever, but most of the melodrama is gone. I find it hard to imagine becoming obsessed about any goal or working myself into a frenetic lather to achieve it. I can see the change most clearly when I compare writing this present book with a book on experimental attitude research I wrote more than twenty years ago. That previous effort was saturated with agency. My desire to win the approval of my colleagues was urgent enough to keep my anxiety at fever pitch for two years running. My efforts to achieve positive research results were so violent that they blinded me to the artificiality of the experimental design I was using. When friends hinted that my results might be spurious, I refused to listen. I was too concerned about succeeding to worry about questions of validity. What I remember most about the experience was how anxious I felt about being evaluated. I recall little joy in either conducting the research or writing up the results, which is not strange given how little interest I had in the subject matter itself.

This present effort seems very different. I spend little time wondering what people will think of me when they read it, or what I might think of myself if no one bothers to. At the risk of exaggerating a subtle difference, I would say that the book does not feel as much "mine" as the earlier one, in the sense of my serving as its prime creator. It still feels personal, but more in the fashion of something which is happening *in* me. Whenever I stop to observe myself, I see ideas breaking on the surface of consciousness like bubbles; I see sentences forming, words being selected, and fingers typing. From this vantage point, I am reminded that the whole operation is arising spontaneously and that there is no agent inside of me that can alter what is happening. As a result I rarely feel anxious about my role in the process. On days when the ideas stop exciting me or the sentences fall flat, a decision to go for a long walk usually arises. My effort does not feel at all "violent," even though I usually put in ten or more hours a day at the computer. Writing is still intense work, but it is no longer the draining activity it once was. The quiet desperation I felt twenty-four years ago when I believed that I was responsible for completing the book has given way to a quiet buoyancy which I attribute, rightly or wrongly, to a new awareness that the whole process is happening on its own.

One of the things that goes along with this new freedom from anxiety is a willingness to be surprised by life. I find that as my grip relaxes, I spend less time worrying about achieving my goals and more time simply enjoying whatever comes up. I am certainly not indifferent to what arises here, but I am aware of a new openness to life. I feel that, for the first time, I can afford the luxury of being curious about the future, about this book, about what I am going to do next for a living, about meeting new friends and lovers, and so on. My psyche is no longer riveted to what I want that future to be. While plans and hopes continue to arise, I take them all less seriously than I used to. And taking them less seriously has the effect of creating the space in which curiosity and wonder flourish.

In a culture where being "driven" is admired as a sign of strength, and straining is tolerated as the price of success, all this talk about curiosity and freedom from anxiety may suggest a passivity which is at odds with our basic Western values. I don't think passive is an appropriate description of what is arising *here*, but I am aware that an important shift in motivation has taken place. Unlike my earlier book which was spawned almost exclusively by a desire for approval, this present effort comes out of a love for the ideas and a desire to communicate those ideas to others. As far as I can see, the anticipation of approval plays a very minor role in the process. It follows that, if I were less fascinated with working out the idea of non-agency and employed at a university where I had easy access to people interested in the same issue, the book might not have gotten written.

And perhaps this is the key point. When we give up agency, the anticipation of praise loses much of its power to move us. In many situations, concern with evaluation may make the difference between activity and passivity, between writing and not writing a book, or between painting a landscape and simply enjoying it. According to Ernest Cassirer, Voltaire considered the desire for acclaim a sine qua non of civilization itself.

> Voltaire says in his *Treatise on Metaphysics* that without the passions, without the desire for fame, without ambition and vanity, no progress of humanity, no refinement of taste and no improvement of the arts and sciences is thinkable: "It is with this motivating force that God, whom Plato called the eternal geometer, and whom I call the eternal machinist, has animated and embellished nature: the passions are the wheels which make all these machines go."[6]

While it is undoubtedly true that Voltaire was speaking for himself, it is fair to assume that he was also speaking for many others. How many fewer poems would John Keats have written in his brief twenty-six years if he had not been so concerned with fame? Would Wagner have undertaken the Ring cycle if he had not been so hungry for admiration? Or Michelangelo the Sistine Chapel? Would we have Hume's Treatise today if he had not been so eager to make a name for himself (a move which he later regretted)? Would Watson and Crick have broken the DNA code when they did if it were not for their anticipation of a Nobel prize?

If agency is only an illusion, it is nevertheless an illusion which has "animated and embellished" our lives with beauty and understanding. It has prompted thousands of artists and scientists, not to mention political leaders and activists, to extend themselves beyond their normal limits. It has motivated physicians to risk their health, shopkeepers to keep their doors open late, and parents to sacrifice homes and vacations so that their children could go to college. As Vaihinger might have put it, it may be only a fiction, but it is a very practical fiction, one on which our whole civilization seems to depend.

But, if that is true, why am I writing this book? Why should I bother if I am unconcerned (mostly) about how people are going to judge me as author? As far as I know, I am doing it primarily for the excitement I feel in working out an idea that has important implications for the way we all live. Although there may be other motives involved (e.g., attracting students), that excitement is sufficient to call up all the energy I need to finish the book. Even if I were to conclude from responses to query letters that the manuscript is never going to be published, I would want to finish it. As frustrating as it might be to give up the prospect of meeting other people who are attracted to the idea of non-agency, the pleasure of figuring out what non-agency implies and converting that understanding into words would be more than enough to sustain me.

There are other non-moral rewards with the power to motivate us. Money is certainly one of them, attention another. Receiving attention for what has arisen within us need not imply anything about agent causality. In a world without agency, it means simply that we are the body/minds where the behavior being evaluated arose. When we show a new painting at a gallery, for example, we are the ones people flock to see; we are the ones at whom they smile, over whom they hover, and to whom they pay their money. We are not required to interpret these rewards as judgments on us as creators of the painting, even when they are clearly intended as such by well-wishers who continue to believe in agency. Since there is no agent available for judging, the only thing actually being judged is the painting and the skill and effort that gave rise to it. Because of our intimate "association" with the painting, we stand to benefit from any positive judgments directed to it. The anticipation of those non-agency rewards may play a critical role in our efforts to complete the painting.

While the joys of creating and the anticipation of money and attention all have the power to bring forth great mental and physical effort, it is clear that the anticipation of moral (causal) judgment represents a very important additional inducement. Before concluding, however, that giving up agency leads inevitably to less art and science and, thus, to a decline in civilization, we should consider the possibility that any losses in output will be offset by gains arising from the transfer of energy from the self as creator to the product being created. Without agency, there is less for a creative person to worry about. All the energy typically invested in anticipating moral judgment is available for investment in the canvas or book. Whether or not that transfer is made depends, of course, on the personality of the individual. Once freed from a belief in agency, some artists would find the process of creating more exciting and satisfying than ever. Those who were particularly wary of moral judgment might be willing to invest more of themselves in their work, since they would have less to lose by doing so. Others, however, would undoubtedly find that something important had gone out of their work. Without the anticipation of acclaim and pride, they might consider that the painting, the symphony, or the experiment was no longer worth the effort involved.

It seems too simple to predict that a giving up of the agency illusion will lead to a shrinking of artistic and scientific output. More realistically, there will probably be a shift of "cathexis," as the Freudians say, from agent to output. Some artists and scientists will produce more, others less. As a result of their freedom from moral judgment, artists might become more heterogenous in their output. While composers, for example, continue to influence each other through innovations in harmony and orchestration, they will be less constrained by the opinions of colleagues and critics. As a result, we can expect them to become more experimental, less wedded to the fashions of the day.

Science, by contrast, is accumulative by nature and cannot tolerate the same degree of diversity. Even here, though, lifting of the agency illusion should have a freeing effect on the imagination. In considering that prospect, I am reminded of an extremely ambitious psychologist who devoted almost all of his evenings and weekends to research. Although he turned out articles at two or three times the rate of the average professor, at age fifty he still had not won a tenured appointment. The answer was obvious to anyone who bothered to follow his career. All of his research was limited to a single narrowly defined field and consisted exclusively of case studies devoid of any theoretical speculation. His concern for detail and avoidance of controversy both seemed to be colored by the same fear which confined him to what he knew best. As a result of that fear, his work remained meticulous but timid and, despite its quantity, unnoticed by his peers.

Even if we were to grant, that, without a belief in agency, people will work less hard, there is the possibility that they will become more effective at what they do. The anticipation of judgment can distract us from what we are doing and, while it probably emboldens some, it clearly intimidates others. In an interpersonal situation it is particularly easy to see how the desire for approval can interfere with effectiveness. It does so by setting up a hidden agenda in which blaming, avoiding blame, and jockeying for credit interfere with work on the overt task. Competition for approval may affect the way group members think as well as the way they appraise each other's opinions. Without acknowledging the fact, they may use their judgments as a means of repaying past snubs or rejections. Managers may be tempted by their own concern for causal approbation to make decisions based on pride or vindictiveness. And it is not unknown for subordinates to rebel against that authority on equally non-rational grounds.

It seems reasonable to conclude that our belief in agency has a mixed impact on how hard we work and how effective we are at what we do. It probably has the same effect on how we feel about our work. When we give up agency, the admiration of others and our own pride of accomplishment lose much of their meaning. For some, that loss may be more than compensated for by a new peace of mind and a new freedom to pursue ideas independently of others' judgment. Whether or not we see that as a fair exchange depends on a number of things, including how much anxiety and guilt our belief in agency has caused us.

My own experience with giving up that belief has been overwhelmingly positive, so positive, in fact, that more than once I have found myself in the position of straining to let go further. That predicament is certainly not original with me. Alan Watts talks about it in some detail in *The Way of Zen*.[7] When we come out of a past filled with anxiety and straining, as I have, our first few tastes of surrender are often heady enough to arouse a longing for more. From that new vantage point, it seems that, if we can just make ourselves let go more, we can have even more peace, more freedom from anxiety. My own "violent efforts" to accelerate the surrendering process took the form of writing down my thoughts every time I started to let go so that if the feeling threatened to slip away, I could bring it back by rethinking my original thoughts. It didn't work. For months, I alternated between periods of contentment devoid of all ambition and periods of high anxiety spent obsessing over how to recover that contentment. I was on a see-saw, blindfolded, with no idea of who or what was on the other end. When down, I strained to remember what it was like being up. When up, I worried about falling down.

What I failed to see was that letting go has to arise on its own, just like everything else. Initially I could not accept the fact that something this desirable was determined by factors beyond *my* control. Although my initial surrendering seemed to have emerged spontaneously, the feeling continued to arise that I could make the letting go return whenever it vanished. That lingering illusion, of course, was what kept the experience from lasting. What I could not yet accept was the truly spontaneous nature of the letting go. Superficially, I was convinced of the spontaneity of all experience, but my continued steering and clinging indicated that I did not yet believe it completely.

In those see-saw days, I could not see that if letting go is a relinquishing of the feeling that we have to make things happen, trying to let go is the equivalent of trying not to try. Obviously it cannot be done. The very attempt to let go creates a kind of mental and physical tension which guarantees that no real letting go will occur. It is well within the capacity of many of us, however, to try anyway, quite oblivious to the trap we have set for ourselves. And yet, getting out of the trap, Watts reminds us, requires only that we wake up to the fact that all actions, including our trying to let go, are spontaneous.

> As soon as I recognize that my voluntary and purposeful
> action happens spontaneously "by itself," just like breathing,
> hearing, and feeling, I am no longer caught in the contradiction
> of trying to be spontaneous. There is no real contradiction,
> since "trying" is "spontaneity." Seeing this, the compulsive,
> blocked, and "tied-up" feeling vanishes. It is just as if I had
> been absorbed in a tug-of-war between my two hands, and
> had forgotten that both were mine. No block to spontaneity
> remains when the trying is seen to be needless.[8]

There may be activities like reading, meditating, and exposing ourselves to certain people or places that will facilitate our letting go. But there is no agent within us with the power to make any of these things happen. Paradoxically, letting go is precisely what happens once the truth of spontaneity sinks in. And there is no better place for that sinking-in process to begin than with straining itself. Watts is telling us that straining is just as spontaneous as anything else in life. It arises out of heredity, the kind of training we received as children, and the circumstances of our present life. Once we begin to see our straining as a product of events rather a creation of agency, we are unlikely to condemn ourselves for it. We can begin to accept it as a result of what has gone before. But even that act of acceptance, if it is to arise, must arise spontaneously out of its own matrix of circumstances. Once it arises, however, it automatically sets in motion a whole new process, the end result of which is that straining in any form is less apt to arise. The key lies in accepting whatever arises. It is to that idea that I would like to turn in the next chapter.

REFERENCES

1. Dinesen, I., *Out of Africa*, New York: Random House, 1937, p. 91.
2. Hesse, H., *Demian*, quoted in Kaufmann, W., *Discovering the Mind*, New York: McGraw-Hill, 1980, vol. II, p. 206.
3. Watts, A., *Tao: The Watercourse Way*, New York: Pantheon Books, 1975, p. 76.
4. Lao-tsu, *Tao Te Ching*, translated by Gia-Fu Feng and Jane English, New York: Vintage Books, 1972, ch. 37.
5. Descartes, R., *Discourse on Method* in *The European Philosophers from Descartes to Nietzsche*, (ed) Beardsley, M.C., New York: Modern Library, 1960, pp. 20-21.
6. Cassirer, E., *the Philosophy of the Enlightenment*, New Jersey: Princeton University Press, 1951, p. 107.
7. Watts, A., *The Way of Zen*, New York: Vintage, 1957, Part II, chs. 2 & 3.
8. Watts, A., *The Way of Zen*, p. 144.

10

GOING GENTLE INTO THAT GOOD NIGHT

If I am aware of straining and want to report that perception to a friend, the rules of English grammar force me to say, "I am straining." That manner of speaking suggests the existence of two different things, an entity which serves as subject or actor and the straining in which that entity is engaged. And yet introspection reveals no agent standing apart from my straining or any of the other thoughts and actions arising *here*. Watts echoes Nietzsche's complaint when he reminds us that:

> There is not something or someone experiencing experience! You do not feel feelings, think thoughts, or sense sensations any more than you hear hearing, see sight, or smell smelling. "I feel fine" means that a fine feeling is present. It does not mean that there is one thing called an "I" and another separate thing called a feeling, so that when you bring them together this "I" *feels* the fine feeling. There are no feelings but present feelings, and whatever feeling is present is "I." No one ever found an "I" apart from some present experience, or some experience apart from an "I" - which is only to say that the two are the same thing.[1]

I *am* my feelings. I am also this body, these thoughts, these images and so son. The grammatical separation of subject from predicate creates the illusion that *I* am an autonomous agent that can change my feelings, or my thoughts, or my behavior. If the behavior is something undesirable, like straining, the illusion invites me in my role as autonomous agent to try to stop that behavior. But if straining is part of who or what I am right now, how can *I* stop it? How can straining stop itself?

Straining to make things happen and straining to keep things from happening both thrive on the illusion of agency. They arise because we are taught to believe that we can divorce ourselves from our own experience and then use that new vantage point to alter who we are. The illusion of causal freedom implies not only that we *can* change the course of our lives, but that we are morally responsible for doing so. It is up to us to use our freedom to become the persons we want to be. And that is what produces straining. Our efforts become forced because we are convinced that, if we don't make things happen, they won't happen at all. And so, when a desire to stop straining arises, we find ourselves trapped. The belief that it is up to us as agents to make the straining stop ends up having precisely the opposite effect. It keeps the straining going.

The only way out of this trap, and others like it, is to accept what is arising. To accept straining means, cognitively, to realize that there is no autonomous agent in a position to change the experience; emotionally, it means to stop fighting the experience. Acceptance implies the awareness that, at least for now, we *are* this straining. That may not be to our liking, but the only way for it to change is for something else to arise in its place. The fact that we recognize our straining as such increases the probability that something will arise to take its place. But our awareness that we are straining is not sufficient by itself to trigger any real letting go. It may serve to make us more observant of when, where, and how we strain – all of which is essential for integrating any new perspective into our everyday experience. For any deep and lasting letting go to happen, however, a new view of ourselves must arise – a view in which we see ourselves as body/minds emerging spontaneously out of circumstance. If and when that new perspective arises, letting go will follow automatically.

The opposite of acceptance is protest. While acceptance leads to the end of straining, protest usually has the effect of keeping it going. Life is full of experiences we would prefer to avoid. Some of them, like straining, may be going on right now; others (e.g., the death of a loved one) may have already happened. Still others represent possibilities for the future, e.g., the loss of money, property, reputation, or health. While adversity of any kind is difficult to accept, we make the task harder than it need be by viewing ourselves as causally (and, thus, morally) responsible for who we are. It is that view of ourselves that makes gods of us all and which, by extricating us from the causal chain that links all events, keeps us from accepting life "just as it is."

Clinging to what we already have is a form of protest, a refusal to accept the possibility of loss. Because loss occurs so often in life, that protest adds significantly to our pain. Like craving, clinging springs from an urgent desire fed by a belief in agency, in this case, a desire to hang on to what we already have. Agency enters into our clinging by fostering the illusion that we can, at will, leave the stream of our own experience long enough to prevent its taking an undesirable turn. In clinging, for example, to our homes, our belief in agency may lead us to take unnatural measures (make violent efforts) to prevent loss. Because we don't trust the unforced, rationally inspired efforts which arise, we second-guess ourselves, checking and double checking, forever wondering if we are really on top of the situation. The illusion of control demands endless vigilance about locks, alarms, strangers, fire, storms, insurance, new highways, and the threat of undesirables moving into the neighborhood. The belief that we are not only positionally but causally responsible for what happens to our home has the power to induce a state of sustained desperation that makes enjoyment of our property impossible.

An undeluded person living in the same house might take all the same basic precautions of locking doors, setting alarms, and buying adequate insurance, but would not waste time worrying about any of them. Such a person would do all the things that are rationally required, but no more. He or she would never count on anything, knowing that all events, including remembering to lock up, arise out of circumstance. Not counting on anything implies being ready for everything while obsessing over nothing. Being ready for fire, theft, or storm damage means accepting the possibility of their arising despite all the precautions taken or, in certain cases, because the precautions failed to arise. To accept the possibility of their arising means to take whatever happens in stride, to say yes, to yield to its causal necessity. When that acceptance is genuine, there is no room for panic or compulsive worrying.

It is in the nature of life that some of the possibilities for disaster actually materialize. Business ventures, for example, fail far more often than they succeed (by one count they fail eighty-five percent of the time). Acceptance, then, becomes a matter of dealing with a concrete, irreversible reality. When we as owners see all our plans, hopes, family savings, and years of hard work disappearing into thin air, our immediate response is usually to protest, all the more so if we believe that it was our fault. To the extent that we believe in agency, the failure of the business becomes a reflection on our worthiness as entrepreneurs, providers, and members of the community. Unless we can point to extenuating circumstances, accepting the failure of the business means having to accept our failure as agents.

To the undeluded person, such a conclusion makes no sense at all. True acceptance comes out of the realization that the original idea for the business, all the decisions made along the way, and all the consequences of those decisions have been determined by circumstance. That includes the circumstances of our genes, our socialization, our formal education, the people and ideas to whom we have been exposed, shifts in the demand for our product, the state of the economy as a whole, and the actions of our competitors. Accepting the failure of the business means recognizing the causal necessity of everything leading up to that failure. The problem may have been in the basic concept or perhaps in the way that concept was implemented. Either way, accepting the failure means taking it for what it is, knowing that given all the circumstances of heredity and environment, it could not have been otherwise.

When a business fails, the possibility of starting another may make acceptance a little easier. The death of a close friend or relative leaves no room for such hopes. While most of us eventually come around to accepting even the most painful loss, that acceptance is made more difficult by our belief in agency. There are a number of reasons why that is true. In the first place, the belief that we can almost always choose otherwise implies that the deaths of all but the elderly need not have happened when they did. If the young boy had not chosen to go swimming, he might not have drowned. If the teenage girl hadn't had that extra drink, or driven too fast, or been in that lane at that particular time, she might still be alive. If the patient in Room 15 hadn't smoked so heavily for most of his life, he might not now be dying of lung cancer. As long as we believe that we are free to make choices other than the ones we actually make, we are compelled to anguish over our unchosen choices. Accepting the finality of another's death must often wait until we have reviewed, with excruciating thoroughness, all the theoretically possible paths not taken.

Of course, even without a belief in agency, it is still possible, although rarely useful, to reflect on what might have happened "if the choice to go swimming had not arisen there" or "if the decision to try that first cigarette had not arisen there." Agency makes acceptance more difficult by creating the illusion that choices are self-caused. It is easier to accept our own and others' decisions, however tragic, when we view them as causally necessary than when we see them as a product of free will. It is the difference between thinking, "If only the choice to drive so fast had not arisen there," and "If only he hadn't chosen to drive so fast." While there is still room in the former case for anguishing over "alternative realities," the problem is not so acute because the possibilities are not as real. Viewing the choice to drive fast as part of a stream of behavior arising systematically out of past events makes it easier to acquiesce in the death which follows. In a deterministic view of the world, there is no agent capable of circumventing the chain of cause and effect. Given all the parameters of the situation, it is understandable that driving fast is the choice that arose, and death the outcome that followed. Accepting the past as past becomes easier, even in the case of death, when we interpret events as causally necessary.

I said earlier that our belief in agency affects our ability to accept death in several ways. In addition to creating the illusion that the victim was free to choose his or her behavior, agency invites us to blame ourselves for our complicity in what happened.

> I am thinking of the ashes, the torn clothes, the veil, the Klage Weiber of the old days – they are all means to ask you to take pity on them, the mourners, and are expressions of sorrow, grief, and shame. If someone grieves, beats his chest, tears his hair, or refuses to eat, it is an attempt at self-punishment to avoid or reduce the anticipated punishment for the blame that he takes on the death of a loved one.[2]

Besides punishing ourselves for the death itself, we exacerbate our pain by blaming ourselves for not having done enough to make the deceased's life a happier one. If only we had been kinder; if only we had not been so critical. Whatever form our self-torture takes, it is sustained by the belief that we are morally responsible for our behavior and any consequences that behavior might have for those around us.

Kubler-Ross writes that most terminal patients go through a series of stages (denial, anger, depression) before reaching that point of acceptance which allows them to die in "peace and dignity."

> There are a few patients who fight to the end, who struggle and keep a hope that makes it almost impossible to reach this stage of acceptance. They are the ones who will say one day, "I just

cannot make it anymore," the day they stop fighting, the fight is over. In other words, the harder they struggle to avoid the inevitable death, the more they try to deny it, the more difficult it will be for them to reach this final stage of acceptance with peace and dignity. The family and staff may consider these patients tough and strong, and they may implicitly communicate that accepting one's end is regarded as a cowardly giving up, as a deceit or, worse yet, a rejection of the family.[3]

Family members can play a powerful role in helping the patient to find acceptance, but, because of their own fears, may be equally instrumental in delaying it.

When we talked with her a few days later under more favorable circumstances, it was obvious that she was increasingly tired and ready to die. . . She asked to be allowed to die in peace, wished to be left alone – even asked for less involvement on the part of her husband. She said that the only reason that kept her still alive was her husband's inability to accept the fact that she had to die. She was angry at him for not facing it and for so desperately clinging on to something that she was willing and ready to give up.[4]

While the patient had accepted her death and was moving toward detaching herself from her surroundings, her husband continued clinging to his hopes for a recovery, unable to comprehend how someone who loved him could surrender to their irrevocable separation. Her own need to detach had nothing to do with her husband. It arose out of a need to shift her focus from husband and family to life itself, to her life, to the meaning of all life, to what might lie beyond life. Once she accepted death, her primary need was to prepare for it. And there was no room in that preparation for anyone else's clinging.

In one of the best known English poems of this century, Dylan Thomas limns the pain and anger he felt at his father's dying.

And you, my father, there on the sad height,
Curse, bless, me now with your fierce tears, I pray.
Do not go gentle into that good night.
Rage, rage against the dying of the light.[5]

The poem draws its power from the cultural injunction to approach death as we would an enemy, resisting with all the will, courage, and faith we can muster. In Western societies, giving in to death without a fight indicates a lack of moral fiber, a flaccidity of spirit at odds with the belief that, if we want something badly enough, we can make it happen by sheer dint of will.

When Thomas begs his father to "rage, rage against the dying of the light," he is speaking for all those who equate acceptance with capitulation. Acceptance exposes our impotence in the face of death; the poem's call to protest dying draws its appeal from its ability to mask that impotence. As rage against our own dying wells up within us, we are unlikely to see that the attempt to defy death, particularly when that death has been long in coming, represents another kind of straining. Like all violent efforts, raging arises out of the illusion that we are the causes of our own behavior. We rage because we are convinced that dying, like living, is shaped by will rather than circumstance. Once it arises, that raging may actually have the effect of postponing death. Any extra time gained through straining, however, will have to be paid for with the serenity that most of us seem to need in preparing ourselves for death.

Years later, in a final poem (Elegy) which he did not live to finish, Thomas returned to the same subject.

> ....Oh, forever may
> He lie lightly, at last, on the last, crossed
> Hill, under the grass, in love, and there grow
>
> Young among the long flocks, and never lie lost
> Or still all the numberless days of his death. . .[6]

The second poem has a different tone. The poet continues to protest, but his protest has lost its edge. It is no longer his father's dying that he faces, but the fact of death already come. His call to "burn and rave at close of day" has softened to "and there grow young among the long flocks, and never lie lost or still. . ." But he still cannot accept what has happened. Later in the poem he pleads, "Let him find no rest but be fathered and found," even though it was this very rest the father wanted:

> Above all he longed for his mother's breast
> Which was rest and dust, and in the kind ground
> The darkest justice of death, blind and unblessed.[7]

The poet's attempt to deny his father the rest for which he longed makes little sense unless we assume he is protesting death itself, not simply the loss of his father. And that is what touches us so deeply. The poem articulates our inability to accept that our own end is coming. When that day approaches, who among us will not "rage against the dying of the light"; who among us is willing "to lie lost or still, under the grass, in love?"

It is easiest for us to accept our own impending death, as well as that of someone close to us, when we are convinced of its causal necessity. Death becomes causally necessary when we see that all its parameters – time, place, and precipitating cause – are determined by genetic and environmental conditions. Death is simply another event in the stream of things arising spontaneously out of circumstance. The illusion that we can pull ourselves out of the stream long enough to change its course, e.g., by postponing death, is itself another event in that stream. As one of the many events in that stream, however, the illusion of agency may affect other events, including the time of death. As I mentioned earlier, the illusion of control may lead us to rage against death, which, in turn, may lead to a temporary postponing of death. This proves nothing, however, with respect to the existence of an agent that is free to alter the course of the stream. It proves simply that some events in the stream, if and when they arise, have the power to influence other events. Everything in the stream – the illusion of agency, the raging, the postponing, the dying – are all determined by other events in the same stream.

If the time and place of death are causally necessitated by other events in the stream, can we say that they are *inevitable*, meaning "incapable of being avoided or evaded?" For that matter, can we say that, since all events are causally necessary (at least at the atomic level or higher), they are all inevitable? In arguing against this "false elision of determinism and inevitability," Dennett reminds us that inevitability leaves no room for deliberation while determinism does. In the case of inevitability, the individual is

> temporarily *and tacitly* detached from nature, permitting the imaginer a relatively stationary viewpoint from which to experience the brute flow of causation – the sort of detachment with which one can contemplate the local fatalism of an impending sneeze or ejaculation.[8] (original italics)

To say, on the other hand, that an event is determined still leaves room for deliberation, even though the thoughts and ultimate choices making up that deliberation are all causally necessary. A decision that emerges out of a careful weighing of alternatives may be determined by antecedent conditions, but it is not, says Dennett, inevitable in the same sense as the daily rising and sinking of the sun. To say that an event is inevitable means that no amount of deliberating will make a difference. It is unavoidable, unstoppable, fated to happen. And this is simply not true of most human behavior.

> The depressing imagery of local fatalism does not belong in the background of anyone's thought about *what it would be like* to be a deterministic thinker in a deterministic world. And to the extent that one's distaste for determinism is colored by such imagery, one is simply failing to think carefully about the matter at hand.[9] (original italics)

Dennett's distinction is a useful one. Just because all behavior is causally necessary, it does not follow that it is all inevitable in the sense that, given a certain set of parameters, only one outcome is possible. What does follow from the assumption of causal necessity is that all causally autonomous agents are illusions – and this is what makes a difference in our emotions. What matters is that there is no agent inside of us that could have kept a given outcome from arising. Seeing that all outcomes unfold out of circumstance or chance initiates the process of acceptance – and all the changes of feeling that flow from that acceptance. When we lose a friend through death, for example, our pain is eased by acknowledging that neither of us had the power to make different behavioral choices arise. From that perspective, there is no room for regret, second guessing, or *if only* thinking. While it may not be accurate to say that the other's death *had to* happen when and where it did, since it is possible to conceive of acts which, if they had arisen in time, could have altered the outcome, it *is* accurate to say that there were no causally free agents that could have intervened in the process to prevent what happened.

Accepting our own impending death is made easier by a similar acknowledgement that, even though wiser choices (e.g., not smoking) might have prolonged our existence, the choices which arose and gave shape to our lives were all determined by the circumstances of heredity and environment. That generalization applies to other experiences as well. It makes no difference whether a particular outcome arose out of deliberate thinking or out of impulse, whether we planned it exactly the way it happened or whether it was entirely fortuitous. Nor does it make any difference whether or not we wanted it to happen. What makes acceptance easier, however distasteful the outcome, is the awareness that all events flow from other events and that there are no free agents that could have changed the outcome by choosing otherwise.

Does this make us all passive victims of fate? Not if we mean by fate, "the principle or determining cause or will by which things in general are believed to come to be as they are or events to happen as they do" (Merriam-Webster). That definition suggests a single governing Cause which accounts for all outcomes. Without evidence pointing to any such Cause, it makes more sense to conceptualize existence as a chain of cause and effect in which all events in the universe are connected. All human events represent links in this chain of causality. That includes death and all those factors such as age, genetic inheritance, smoking behavior, food intake, exercise, and personality which might be causally lined to it. It adds nothing, and is, in fact, misleading, to collapse all these specific causes into a single Cause and give it the name of Fate.

It is equally important to remind ourselves that, even though our wishes, choices, intentions, and effort are all determined, they continue to affect what happens to us.* The fact that there is no agent making them arise does not make them any less essential for our well-being. Without wise choices and sustained effort, we are unlikely to have much success in getting any of our needs met. That remains true even after we have given up our belief in agency. What changes with a surrendering of agency is the conviction that we are capable of making ourselves wise and energetic. Recognizing that our choices and effort are determined by circumstance relieves us *as agents* of the need to make them happen. It does not, however, make them any the less important because of that fact.

While non-agency does not imply becoming fatalistically passive about

---

* "A fatalist thinks that there is no point in my doing anything, as the future will be as it will be, regardless of what I do. This is a silly view, whether or not determinism is true. It has the consequence that I may as well drive when drunk, since, if there is going to be an accident, nothing I decide can make the slightest difference. In a determinist world, outcomes are the result of earlier causes, and there is no reason why my decisions and actions should be excluded from those causes." Glover, J., I: The Philosophy and Psychology of Personal Identity, London: The Penguin Press, 1988, p. 183.

life, it does imply learning to accept our lives as shaped by a combination of circumstance and chance. But does not that acceptance suggest a kind of resignation? In the strictest sense, to be resigned means "to give oneself over without resistance," and that comes close to what I have been trying to convey by the term acceptance. The problem with resignation, however, is that it usually implies giving oneself over to something negative. Can we say we are resigned to joy? Not without explaining carefully what we mean. So, acceptance would appear to be broader than resignation. I would define it as giving oneself over without resistance to whatever arises, where resistance implies either straining to make something happen, or, as with the death of a friend, protesting that which has already happened. To accept an event is to say yes to it, regardless of how painful it might be. Saying yes does not mean that we approve of the event, or that we enjoy it, or that we even understand why it happened. It means that we acknowledge it as a spontaneous expression of either circumstance or chance. Saying yes is the equivalent of saying, "I acquiesce in the causal necessity or randomness of what has happened. I realize that there is no causally autonomous agent that could have changed the course of events."

It is possible to acquiesce in the causal necessity of a situation and work to change it at same time. Just because something is arising on its own now does not mean that it has to go on arising forever. If I am having trouble with my spouse, accepting the situation does not imply giving up all attempts to improve it. Acceptance means, first of all, acknowledging that the situation has evolved spontaneously out of a combination of genetic and environmental conditions. I can accept what has already arisen, however, without concluding that this is the way it has to be permanently. My feelings about the relationship represent one of the most important conditions of all. And those feelings are capable of changing in response to their own set of past and present circumstances.

For me, accepting the present situation includes saying yes to my own desire to make changes in that relationship. . . and to any solutions that present themselves, whether or not they are ultimately adopted. Acceptance implies not lunging after a solution, not straining to make things better. It implies a patience fed by the awareness that answers to problems arise on their own out of circumstance in the very same way as the problems themselves. The solutions might involve hard work and deliberate thinking, but they are no less spontaneous because of that. Our patience comes from knowing that there is no agent within us that has the power to force a solution into arising.*

In the sense I am using the word here, it is possible to "accept" a marital situation and still choose to leave it. Staying in the relationship might require that kind of "violent effort" which in the long run can only make matters worse. Either way, acceptance of the situation implies not straining either to make something happen or to keep something from happening. It is a surrendering to the whole flow of events which includes my personality, my spouse's personality, our mutual blindness, our wisdom, our common history, the help of therapists and friends, and any decision that might arise about staying or leaving. What makes surrender possible is seeing not only that the process is happening on its own, but that we are a part of that process. We are whatever is happening here – including our attitude toward that what is arising. Although our language forces us to think of surrendering as something we do *to* the situation, the truth is that, in surrendering to what is arising in and around our bodies, we are really surrendering to who and what we are.

If my next physical reveals that I have cancer, I will probably seek the best medical treatment available. Accepting the fact that I have cancer does not imply sitting idly and allowing it to grow unchecked. What it implies for me is not panicking, not getting depressed, not blaming myself for all those years of smoking, not blaming the doctors for their failure to detect the tumor earlier. Ideally, the reminder will arise that there is no agent within me that could have generated a different set of choices and decisions. From that perspective

---

* This is a situation ripe for rationalization. For all its power to transform our lives, non-agency can be misused by those seeking to legitimize an unwillingness to make changes, particularly those changes that involve risks – such as leaving a loveless relationship. The logic behind the rationalization proceeds something like this: "I don't like where I am, but since this is what is arising at the moment, I will accept it. I realize that whatever happens *has* to happen. If I am ever to move on, that event, like any other, will have to arise on its own. There is no agent/I inside of me that can make it happen." This point of view is incomplete in that it fails to acknowledge that a desire to leave the present situation is also arising on its own out of circumstance. There can be no accepting of the situation as a whole unless that desire too is recognized and accepted. Accepting the rest of the situation (e.g., the bad marriage) while denying the desire to leave is simply a way to avoid taking action. What makes that avoidance particularly insidious is the ease with which it can be misinterpreted as evidence of a highly developed capacity for acceptance. It is not true acceptance, but rather fear disguised as acceptance. When acceptance is genuine, there is no denial, no repression, no rationalizing, no defenses of any kind. All desires, fears, ideas, and perceptions are free to compete for expression.

I can view the tumor as something that has emerged spontaneously out of the genes inherited from my parents, out of my training, my emotional state, the air I breathe, the food I eat, all the behavioral choices that have arisen here in the past, other people's behavior, my doctor's wisdom or lack of it, and the state of medical knowledge in the latter part of the twentieth century. When I come to see the situation that way, I am less likely to protest what has happened. What will probably arise instead is a readiness to go along with whatever happens – which includes the cancer, the treatment, and the outcome of that treatment, no matter what it is.

Accepting racism implies recognizing it as an inevitable consequence of certain economic and cultural circumstances. By itself, acceptance says nothing about approval or disapproval. It is simply an acknowledgment of causal necessity. There is still room in this acceptance for sustained, intense effort to eliminate an abhorrent practice. There is no room in acceptance, however, for either bitterness or moral outrage. Acknowledging the causal necessity of racism changes the emotions surrounding our desire to eliminate it. It makes us more tolerant of those who do not share our own ardor; it also makes us less self-righteous in pursuing what we feel is just. Accepting racism's past as we set out to eliminate it from our future gives us a quieter, more patient strength which is free of hatred and, in the long run, probably more effective for that very reason.

The same can be said for our efforts to avoid nuclear war or to prevent further damage to soil, ozone, water supply, and wildlife. Learning to view all events, even those we loathe, as part of a causal stream flowing spontaneously out of the past changes the way we go about making changes. Without a belief in agency, we are less likely to be distracted by moral judgments. We are also less likely to feel the unforgiving anger that goes with the making and receiving of those judgments. Hating the enemy may raise our energy level and heighten our threshold for sacrifice and pain, but, by flooding our minds with vengeful feelings, it also impairs our ability to think rationally.

In the long run, we improve our chances for survival as a species by learning to accept those who aggress against us – even as we make war against them. Viewing our attackers deterministically makes us less hot-headed. It makes us pause before asserting ourselves. It dampens our eagerness to punish, to torture, and to humiliate. Once we are unburdened of the need to avenge ourselves on agents who could have chosen otherwise, we can break out of that vicious circle in which aggression, moral outrage, and the desire for revenge perpetuate themselves.

The most effective long-term strategy for dealing with aggression is to change the environment that caused it. While passionate calls to resist aggression may stimulate our adrenalin and produce dramatic results in the short-run, they rarely confront the source of the problem. Moral fury not only fails to address the determinants of evil; it obstructs any rational assessment of what is needed to prevent the recurrence of that evil. In the long-run, the pivotal step in changing an abhorrent situation is learning to view it as part of a chain of cause and effect – learning to see it as a product not of agency but of circumstance. Once we adopt an objective point of view, we can proceed to identify what needs to be done to change the situation. Objectivity leads to acceptance, even when the situation involves aggression against us. To an observer accustomed to violent rhetoric and rash deeds, the patriot who accepts his enemy's behavior may seem unimpassioned in his defense of freedom. But the commitment remains. It has simply been shorn of its moral fervor.

Situations which we find repugnant offer the best opportunities for learning acceptance. It requires no special grace for a wildlife enthusiast to accept the creation of a new national park, or for an opponent of nuclear energy to accept the closing of a nuclear plant. Nor are we apt to learn much personally from accepting a promotion, a tax refund, or the chance to go to bed with someone we find attractive. The crunch comes when we are faced with a situation not to our liking. And it is precisely here that the work of assimilating non-agency into our everyday thoughts and feelings needs to be done. I speak of work, and yet there is no point in *trying* to accept the situation, as if acceptance were a moral virtue which we should cultivate. Acceptance arises on its own from the realization that all events are caused by circumstance. That realization itself is part of the stream of events flowing spontaneously out of previous conditions. All events are part of that stream, even the strained attempt to find a position outside of the stream from which to divert the flow of events. Acceptance arises automatically when we realize that we *are* the stream, that we *are* the ideas, emotions, memories, choices and biochemical processes flowing through *this* point in space and time.

Giving up our self-image as agents who can create our own experience has a concrete impact on the kinds of thoughts and feelings that arise within us. Without a strong sense of causal autonomy, fewer thoughts about either the future or the past come up. There is less scheming and plotting, less fantasizing about where we want to be next month, next year, or twenty years down the road. Most fantasies about jobs, money, houses, friends, and family draw their support from our view of ourselves as autonomous agents who, to a significant degree, give shape to our destinies by making choices we are free not to make. With the fading of that illusion, our fantasies lose much of their attractiveness. Plans still have to be made, but few require the time and energy we ordinarily give to them. The same is true of our fantasies about what might have happened in the past if only we or someone else had chosen differently. Accepting the past eliminates anguishing over how we should have behaved on those occasions when we were insulted, berated, or otherwise attacked. On a grander scale, it sweeps away all those idle, yet painful, speculations about "roads not taken."

With the giving up of agency, speculating about either the past or future becomes less interesting. We are drawn more intimately into the present and all the things going on around us right now. In the process, our perspective of how we are related to the world changes. Seeing ourselves as links in a chain of cause and effect has the effect of reconnecting us with the world. Of course, we have never been unconnected to that world. It has only seemed that way because of our identification with an entity standing off to the side looking at the world or listening to the world, but never entering into it.

When we give up straining either to bend the world to our will or to prevent it from taking away the things we love, we can experience what it is like to live *in* that world. Because our wishes are less urgent and our efforts less violent, we no longer feel pitted against the world. Every event, at least in hindsight, appears necessary. When those events involve us, we feel more accepting of whatever outcomes arise *here*. We not only feel more accepting of them; we find ourselves identifying more and more with them. We begin to see ourselves as a stream of outcomes arising here and that awareness, more than anything else, is what makes us feel connected to the rest of the world. As a stream of outcomes, we are at the effect of a million past and present events: our genes, our education, friends we have made along the way, the house we live in, our boss's mood, the mail we get, the weather, and even the food we eat. At the same time, through our own mood, our ideas and perceptions, our looks, our personality, and our physical movements, we represent the causes to which other events must respond. This feeling of connectedness, while more superficial than the Oneness of Buddhist enlightenment, has the power to dissolve the paranoia which arises from our view of the world as alien and resistant to our will. As Watts puts it,

> . . . the discovery that both the voluntary and involuntary aspects of the mind are alike spontaneous makes an immediate

end of the fixed dualism between the mind and the world, the knower and the known. The new world in which I find myself has an extraordinary transparency or freedom from barriers, making it seem that I have somehow become the empty space in which everything is happening.[10]

REFERENCES

1. Watts, A., *The Wisdom of Insecurity*, New York: Vintage, 1951, pp. 85-86.
2. Kubler-Ross, E., *On Death and Dying*, New York: Macmillan, 1969, p. 4.
3. Kubler-Ross, E., *On Death and Dying*, p. 114.
4. Kubler-Ross, E., *On Death and Dying*, pp. 115-116.
5. Thomas, D., "Do not go gentle into that good night" in *Collected Poems*, New York: New Directions, 1971, p. 128.
6. Thomas, D., "Elegy" in *Collected Poems*. pp. 200-201.
7. Thomas, D., "Elegy" in *Collected Poems*, p. 200.
8. Dennett, D., *Elbow Room*, Cambridge: MIT Press, 1984, p. 129.
9. Dennett, D., *Elbow Room*, p. 129.
10. Watts, A., *The Way of Zen*, p. 144.

11

THE WILL TO POWER

The discovery that mass is equivalent to energy reveals the universe as pure process devoid of any underlying *stuff*. We humans play our parts in that process as concentrations of energy in an infinite energy field, alternately influencing and being influenced by other configurations. The power we feel to move, think, speak, and create arises out of our connections with other event-clusters in the field. What we think of as *our* power is really the power or energy of the system as a whole, pulsating through *this* particular point in time and space. While we are unique as individual constellations of energy, we are not the sources of our own power.

Our belief in free agency, however, implies that we are. It implies that, as souls, we can create thoughts and actions by willing them into existence. If we ask where the soul gets its power, we shall be told either that it is in the nature of souls to generate their own (which is no explanation), or that it comes from God (which simply postpones the explanation). The illusion of agency leads us to imagine ourselves erroneously as discontinuous pockets of will capable of acting independently of other forces in the system. Our power is thought to lie ultimately within ourselves, not in our connections with the sun, the earth, plants and animals, and our fellow human beings. Much of the time, in fact, we experience our will as a force directed *against* the rest of the world. It is our will against everyone else's will, our power against the forces of gravity, time, and death. Life is a struggle in which success lies in overcoming the opposition.

This view of life as a contest between wills, or between will and circumstance, cuts each of us off from the world and sets the stage for self-doubt. As isolated centers of will, we are constantly making free choices and being evaluated for the choices we make. How can we be sure that we are using our freedom wisely? In most things we do there are no absolute standards to which we can turn. The best and many times the only way to prove our worth as free agents is to compare ourselves with others. To confirm our wisdom, strength, intelligence, knowledge, and moral virtue, we must show that we are superior to others. We must assert ourselves *over* others, and, given the vagaries of public opinion, we must do it over and over again.

The struggle to dominate constitutes a major theme in the lives of most higher animals. Among most species of fish, birds, and mammals, establishing a superior position vis-à-vis rivals is critical for obtaining food, mating partners, and the territory that makes each of those outcomes possible. For humans, dominating rivals pays off in a variety of ways – including money, authority, mates, property, and recognition. But the expectation of such tangible rewards cannot account for all the energy we typically invest in promoting our own cause. It cannot explain the hours we spend, privately and publicly, boasting, blaming, and, in general, elevating our own status at the expense of others. We obviously want more than the material benefits superiority brings. We want recognition as superior agents; we want to be seen as superior think*ers* and act*ors*. Gaining ascendance over other members of the species represents, above all else, a quest to prove our worthiness as causal agents.

NIETZSCHE'S WILL TO POWER

Nietzsche was so impressed by the ubiquity of this desire that he adopted it as the centerpiece of his psychology and called it the "will to power."

> Wherever I found the living, there I found the will to power.
> Only where there is life, there is also will: not will to life
> but . . . will to power. There is much that life esteems more
> highly than life itself; but out of the esteeming itself speaks
> the will to power.[1]

In Nietzsche's hands, will to power becomes the fundamental drive in all human thinking, feeling, and behaving. It is the drive to prove our superiority – by winning fame and glory, conquering enemies in battle, overcoming obstacles in nature, excelling in competition, dominating partners sexually, getting "one-up" on colleagues, and solving the mysteries of nature. Nietzsche saw the will to power in every nook and cranny of human existence, even in the way we express gratitude. Showing our appreciation, he argued, removes the sting of having allowed others to help us. It equalizes the relationship by eliminating our indebtedness. More subtly, it conveys the message that we have deliberately allowed the other person to help, that we have really been in control of the interaction all along.

Given the central role of will to power in Nietzsche's philosophy, his admiration for strong men like Caesar, Napoleon, and Cesare Borgia comes as no surprise. In *The Will To Power* and *On the Genealogy of Morals* he directs some of his most acerbic comments to those Christian moralists who preach humility and would have the strong feel guilty about their strength. The strong man, Nietzsche argues, is not accountable for being strong. He is not free to be anything other than what he is. The insistence that he could be something else if he chose to be is based on the illusion of an inner "doer" who can choose freely to be either strong or weak. Nietzsche says that the assumption of such a doer (our agent/I) is simply a maneuver on the moralists' part to take away the strong person's strength, to emasculate him, to make him feel guilty for being strong.

> To demand of strength that it should *not* express itself as strength, that it should *not* be a desire to overcome, a desire to throw down, a desire to become master, a thirst for enemies and resistances and triumphs, is just as absurd as to demand of weakness that it should express itself as strength. A quantum of force is equivalent to a quantum of drive, will, effect – more, it is nothing other than precisely this very driving, willing, effecting, and only owing to the seduction of language (and of the fundamental errors of reason that are petrified in it) which conceives and misconceives all effects as conditioned by something that causes effects, by a "subject", can it appear otherwise. For just as the popular mind separates the lightning from its flash and takes the latter for an *action*, for the operation of a subject called lightning, so popular morality also separates strength from expressions of strength, as if there were a neutral substratum behind the strong man, which was *free* to express strength or not to do so. But there is no such substratum; there is no "being" behind

doing, effecting, becoming; "the doer" is merely a fiction added to the deed – the deed is everything. . . . No wonder if the submerged, darkly glowering emotions of vengefulness and hatred exploit this belief for their own ends and in fact maintain no belief more ardently than the belief that *the strong man is free* to be weak and the bird of prey to be a lamb – for thus they gain the right to make the bird of prey *accountable* for being a bird of prey.[2] (original italics)

Nietzsche sees the agency principle as an illusion which the moralists have exploited for the purpose of controlling the strong men of the world. By promoting the fiction of an inner agent that is "free to express strength or not to do so," they seek to make the powerful morally responsible for their actions, thereby bringing them under the control of the more timid majority. Despite the elegance of his critique of agency, Nietzsche failed to see that the fiction of a "doer" can work both ways. In his eagerness to counter the moralists' attempt to emasculate the strong man by making him accountable for his strength, he overlooked how important that same belief in accountability may be to the strong man himself. Not all strong men are born with an instinct for strength. Many *become* strong – and they do so, in part anyway, because they are trying to prove something about themselves. From that perspective, the doctrine of moral responsibility represents more than a Christian ploy to control strong men. It constitutes a primary factor in motivating men and women to become strong – and then to demonstrate to the world just how strong they are. If the will to power is as universal as Nietzsche contends, it is at least partly due to our widespread belief that we are morally responsible for our behavior – for making ourselves strong, weak, or whatever we may appear to be.

My own experience suggests that much of our striving to gain ascendance over one another is prompted by the belief that we are free to create ourselves. What makes it so important to establish our superiority or to avoid being thought inferior is the belief that we are causally responsible for who we are. Given the assumption of free will, everything we do reflects our adequacy as creators. Superior mental or emotional strength vis-à-vis others points to a superior agent/self. By the same token, indecisiveness and timidity suggest an inferior agent/self. Our need to *make* ourselves strong owes much to the assumption that we are free to be either weak or strong. Recognizing the importance of beliefs does not rule out the influence of heredity. It simply means that any predisposition to aggressiveness we inherit at birth is likely to be exaggerated by the desire to prove our worth as causal agents.

Once we see that there is no inner agent (Nietzsche would say "doer") that can in any way add to or subtract from our strength, we are less likely to "thirst for enemies and resistances and triumph," or to find satisfaction in "throwing down our neighbors." Our strength may still express itself in vigorous physical activity or assertive speech, but it will no longer be driven by a fear of moral judgment. We may still delight in elevating ourselves at the expense of others (e.g., in work and sports) and gathering the tangible rewards that accompany such success, but, without a belief in agency, those efforts are apt to be less burdened by desperation, anger, and cruelty. Without a belief in agency, the strong man's will to overwhelm his neighbor can be expected to shrink to a healthy assertiveness free of any need to prove his efficacy as free agent.

Conquering Nature

The belief in agency which drives us to prove our superiority over each other fuels much of our obsession with conquering nature as well. Climbing mountains, navigating fast rivers, crossing oceans, and pursuing dangerous animals draw much of their appeal from what Nietzsche called the joy of overcoming. Part of that appeal would appear to come from proving our superiority over nature itself, part of it from demonstrating our skill and daring to our fellow human beings. Agency contributes to both by attaching a new meaning to success. To the believer in free will, climbing a mountain successfully says more than, "I am in good physical shape" or "I am technically knowledgeable about climbing." It demonstrates that he possesses a powerful will. His joy in succeeding may come from a variety of sources, but prominent among them is the fact that he has confirmed his efficacy as causal agent.

That kind of joy makes little sense when we view nature as a field of energy in which we, as clusters of energy ourselves, are connected directly or indirectly to every other cluster in the field. When we are no longer deluded by agency, we look at mountains and rivers less as challenges to our spirit than as related forms of energy fascinatingly different from our own. From that perspective, the satisfaction of climbing a mountain lies not in the prospect of conquering it and bragging about that achievement afterwards, but in gaining a more beautiful view or the chance to discover what kinds of rocks and vegetation exist at the top. When we are no longer deluded by agency-inspired thoughts of dominance and submission, our interest in nature becomes more purely inquisitive and aesthetic. We begin to sense the mountains, rivers, and ourselves as alternative expressions of a single, basic energy. With that sense of oneness comes a feeling of power that transcends any momentary exhilaration we might experience as a result of proving our superiority over the rest of the world.

AVOIDING DOMINATION

The fear of being dominated plays as critical a role in our motivation as the desire to dominate. Among nonhuman animals, being forced to submit can lead to critical losses in territory, food supply, mates, and nesting sites. Comparable losses for humans may take the form of physical injury, slavery, theft, business failure, or loss of a mate. Our view of ourselves as causally autonomous agents raises the stakes in any struggle for power by giving new meaning to the experience of being dominated. In the context of free agency, being beaten implies not only the loss of material goods and relationships, but the loss of moral approval as well. Given a belief in agency, insult does not have to be added to injury; it is already built in. Being forced to submit implies humiliation, ridicule, and shame. Unlike the wolf or elk, we cannot afford to take physical defeat in stride. An assault on our bodies represents an assault on our worthiness as causal agents – and, thus, on our dignity, pride, and self-esteem.

The threat of being overpowered physically has been acutely painful for me ever since early childhood when, as the smallest person in my class, I experienced repeated defeat at the hands of my peers. In the years following, the fear and anger generated by those defeats gave rise to what seemed like hundreds, maybe even thousands of dreams and daydreams in which I was attacked by a group of sadistic adolescents whom I ultimately managed to defeat with the help either of friends or superior weapons. Those dreams continued arising without any loss of intensity throughout five years of intensive Zen meditation and another ten years as a practicing psychotherapist. They stopped arising (for the most part) about two years ago – some five years after I launched my bid to give up all belief in agency.

Long before that time, I remember seeing a film called The Seventh Seal in which a small band of travelers, including a knight returning from the latest crusade, sought to escape the plague sweeping Europe. Among them, only a young juggler and his family were spared, an event presumably bearing testimony to God's special interest in the innocent of heart. In the scene I remember best, the juggler entered a tavern where he was first taunted and then physically threatened by a much larger, coarser man. What amazed me, given my own experience, was the juggler's total lack of defensiveness. He was neither unsettled by the rude remarks directed at him, nor especially frightened by the physical confrontation. He simply refused the invitation to fight, accepted the jeers of the other drinkers, and left - *without* bad feelings about himself or thoughts of retaliation against his tormentor. He seemed free of all the burdens of agency: fear, anger, defensiveness, humiliation, and the need to redeem his pride. I remember envying him his freedom, and yet being repelled by what seemed to be his lack of courage.

Years later I felt the same ambivalence after coming across the following lines in the Dhammapada (Sayings of the Buddha):

> Look how he abused me and beat me,
> How he threw me down and robbed me.
> Live with such thoughts and you live in hate ...
> Abandon such thoughts and you live in love.[3]

Again, I felt attracted to the freedom implied by a surrendering of pride and just as keenly diminished at the thought of giving up my hard-won man-hood. While the key to resolving that ambivalence continued to elude me, I sensed that it lay somewhere in the words with which that collection of sayings begins:

> We are what we think.
> All that we are arises with our thoughts,
> With our thoughts we make the world.[4]

According to this ancient text, all I needed was a change of thought, a new way of interpreting old experiences. But how was I to go about changing the meaning of something so painful as to occupy my dreams for the better part of a lifetime?

From the perspective of late middle age, I continue to see the problem as a cognitive one, but one whose roots lay much deeper than I had suspected earlier. What has changed the meaning of defeat in my own life over the past few years has been a shift in the way I conceive of personal responsibility, both my own and that of any potentially threatening adversary. In the past, the assumption that I was free to cause my own behavior had the effect of escalating threats upon my body into threats upon me as causal agent as well.

The possibility of being judged as author of my physical ineptness aroused feelings of humiliation, shame, bitterness – all of which made acceptance of defeat impossible.* Those feelings continued to arise until a shift in beliefs about agency changed the meaning of such confrontations by reducing them to their simpler, physical dimensions. If I am threatened now, I may still choose to fight back if something concrete, e.g., avoiding injury or loss of property, is to be gained by doing so. I have less reason to fight, however, since there is less to be defended, less to be lost by giving in. Without the burden of agency, I feel freer to respond according to the exigencies of the situation. Because there is less anxiety and anger arising within me, I find myself in a better position to think clearly and do the most efficient thing to get out of the situation intact.

CONQUERING OURSELVES

Through Nietzsche's eyes, history becomes the story of power and its expression in war, ideas, and art. At the most primitive level, the will to power expresses itself in the barbarian's torturing of his neighbor; in its most highly evolved form, it appears as the ascetic's torturing of himself. The lofty status accorded asceticism in Nietzsche's hierarchy of values testifies to the importance he assigned to what he called *self-overcoming* (Selbst-Uberkommen). In his meta-psychology, all power over others or over nature originates in the experience of overcoming pain and weakness in ourselves. The more suffering we overcome, the more powerful becomes our will.

> *I assess the power of a will by how much resistance, pain, and torture it endures and knows how to turn to its advantage.* I do not account the evil and painful character of existence a reproach to it, but hope rather that it will one day be more evil and painful than hitherto.[5] (original italics)

The emotionality of the language suggests that Nietzsche had more than a little personal investment in his view of will as spiritual accomplishment. This should not be surprising given his life-long struggle to overcome the pain

---

* For years I had trouble understanding what was so funny about comedian Jack Benny's response to the stick-up man who demanded: "Your money or your life." Benny, as anyone who grew up in the forties knows, replied that he needed time to think about it. To me, the response seemed quite reasonable.

of both mental and physical disease, conditions which eventually led to his insanity and premature death.

The concept of *self-overcoming* implies a belief in free agency, although Nietzsche never endorsed that premise explicitly.* Self-conquest of any sort suggests a splitting of the personality into two antagonistic camps, that which seeks to impose its rule and that which does its best to resist. But there is only one camp, the person, which consists of *both* the pattern of behavior to be changed (e.g., the overeating, oversleeping, or tabooed desire) and the determination to make changes in that behavior. "Overcoming" a bad habit is not a matter of an autonomous spirit imposing its will on a recalcitrant body/ mind, but a matter of one spontaneous, fully determined impulse successfully competing with another. A desire to change is just as much determined by circumstance as a desire to go on eating or sleeping. There is no free agent involved in either and thus no victory for will power when the desire to change prevails. The only thing victorious is the desire itself, a fact of considerable importance, however, in that it increases the likelihood that further attempts to change behavior will arise there in the future.

The way we view the process of self-change shapes both how we approach that process and how its outcome affects the rest of our lives. When we see self-change as a battle between a causally autonomous agent and a resistant body/mind, the lure of pride and threat of guilt tempt us to strain – with a predictable increase in worry and tension. Our effort becomes rigid and forced, as when we try to transcend sexual desire through self-mortification. When we approach the process of self-change, instead, as a competition be- tween two equally spontaneous impulses, it becomes easier to accept both the undesirable behavior (e.g., laziness) and the wish to change it. What makes the laziness easier to accept is the realization that it is the necessary result of thousands of social and genetic circumstances operating upon us in both the past and present. And if that laziness is causally necessary, so is our desire to change it. Recognizing the necessity of both sides of the conflict makes it

---

* "In view of the passages already cited, it hardly need be said that Nietzsche is not re-pudiating free will in favor of determinism. Rather he considers the popular notion of causality untenable and is convinced that that assumption of free will depends on it. . . . The crucial point is that Nietzsche – occasional polemical antitheses or popular expressions notwithstanding – did not deprecate consciousness in favor of physiological processes, but did criticize the conception of consciousness as a separate 'thing,' as an 'entity' apart from the body, as a 'spiritual cause.'" W. Kaufmann, *Nietzsche*, Princeton: Princeton University Press, 1974, p. 266.

possible to weigh the costs and benefits of changing without the distraction of self-love or self-loathing. The process is simpler, less tense, more rational.

Alcoholics Anonymous (AA) draws its power from a similar spirit of acceptance. As paradoxical as it might seem to outsiders, the first step toward recovery in AA involves accepting the fact that one is powerless over alcohol. There is no call at any time to conquer one's drinking through an exercise of will. On the contrary, the call is to surrender the illusion that one has any control over drinking at all. Abstinence is still the goal, but it is not a goal to be achieved by "overcoming" the desire for alcohol. Members learn to abstain not by asserting their wills, but by turning control of their addiction over to each other - and to a higher power. For many it works. Accepting their own powerlessness and turning to God and other AA members for help leads to the very control that eluded them earlier. They stop drinking and stay stopped. For a significant minority, however, abstinence is only temporary. After months or even years of sobriety, they begin entertaining the idea that they are now ready to become normal, social drinkers. At this point, they try to take control again. Typically they begin drinking moderately but within a matter of months increase their intake to a level exceeding that of the period just before they entered the program. Another breakdown follows and the process of surrendering control has to start all over again.

Given the fact that many never resume drinking, we must ask why admitting one's powerlessness over alcohol should increase one's ability to abstain from drinking. The answer has at least two parts. For one thing, the illusion of causal autonomy arouses fear and anxiety which feed the craving for a depressant like alcohol. Accepting our powerlessness over drinking reduces that tension and self-doubt by reducing the area over which we think of ourselves as exercising causal autonomy. At the same time, accepting our powerlessness as agents allows us to draw on the power of a group (the AA community) which *does* have the power to change our behavior.

Admitting that we have no power over our use of alcohol represents a step in the direction of non-agency, but only a step. While AA manages to strip the agent/I of much of its putative power, it never questions that reality of that agent as an entity in its own right. AA's success demonstrates, nevertheless, that even a partial giving up of the illusion of causal autonomy can lead to significant self-changing.

Religious conversion experiences offer us further evidence of how the relinquishing of power can precipitate dramatic changes in feelings and behavior. In *The Varieties of Religious Experience* William James states that, self-surrender has been and always must be regarded as the vital turning-point of the religious life, so far as the religious life is spiritual and no affair of outer works and ritual and sacraments.[6]

Martin Luther stated the case for self-surrender in its most uncompromising form:

> For so long as a man is convinced that he can do something for his own salvation, he retains his self-confidence and does not completely despair; for this reason he does not humble himself before God, but asserts himself, or at least hopes and wishes for opportunity, time, and work in order finally to attain his salvation. But he who never doubts that all depends on the will of God, despairs completely of helping himself, does not choose us, but awaits an act of God; he is nearest to Grace and salvation.[7]

James cites several cases of conversion which document the kind of salvation to which Luther is referring. I pick just one, that of French Protestant Adolph Monod:

> "My sadness", he says, "was without limit, and having got entire possession of me, it filled my life from the most indifferent external acts to the most secret thoughts, and corrupted at their source my feelings, my judgment, and my happiness. It was then that I saw that to expect to put a stop to this disorder by my reason and my will, which were themselves diseased, would be to act like a blind man who should pretend to correct one of his eyes by the aids of the other equally blind one. I had then no resource save in *some influence from without*. I remembered the promise of the Holy Ghost; and what the positive declarations of the Gospel had never succeeded in bringing home to me, I learned at last from necessity. Renouncing then all merit, all strength, abandoning all my personal resources, and acknowledging no other title to his mercy than my own utter misery, I went home and threw myself on my knees, and prayed as I never

prayed in my life. From this day onwards a new interior life began for me: not that my melancholy had disappeared, but it had lost its sting. Hope had entered into my heart, and once entered on the path, the God of Jesus Christ, to whom I then had learned to give myself up, little by little did the rest."[8] (original italics)

According to James, a surrendering of control to a higher power plays the key role in most conversion experiences, the specific object of that surrender being secondary. While in our culture it is God to whom we usually relinquish our power. ("Not my but Thy will be done"), it could just as easily be Circumstance or Causal Necessity or Chance. The secret, as Alcoholics Anonymous has long claimed, lies in "turning it over." For most individuals, what follows from that surrendering of will (or, more accurately, the illusion of will) is

the loss of all the worry, the sense that all is ultimately well with one, the peace, the harmony, the *willingness to be*, even though the outer conditions should remain the same. . . . A passion of willingness, of acquiescence, of admiration, is the glowing centre of this state of mind.[9] (original italics)

At what James calls the "glowing centre" of the conversion experience is a kind of power, but it is far cry from the power of which Nietzsche speaks, the power to overcome either oneself or others through the exercise of will.* It is, if anything, the very opposite. It is the power which comes from seeing oneself as the instrument of a higher will or, in less theistic terms, as a vessel through which the energy of the universe is passing. It is the power of powerlessness, the power that comes from giving up all pretense of authorship,

---

* Despite his fascination with self-surrender, James remained faithful to the concept of free agency in his personal life: "Hitherto, when I have felt like taking a free initiative, like daring to act originally, without carefully waiting for contemplation of the external world to determine all for me, suicide seemed the most manly form to put my daring into; now, I will go a step further with my own will, not only act with it, but believe as well; believe in my individual reality and creative power. My belief, to be sure, can't be optimistic – but I will posit life (the real, the good) in the self-governing *resistance* of the ego to the world." Kallen, H.M, *The Philosophy of William James*, New York: The Modern Library, 1925, p. 29. (original italics)

all aspiration to divinity. In ordinary circumstances, powerlessness implies impotence and frustration at not being able to control events. The powerlessness of which James is speaking, however, is that of someone who sees that no straining is necessary. It contains no "violent effort," no desire to dominate, no frustrated need to prove one's superiority. The self that has been converted or reborn is emptied of all trace of will and stands ready to experience that transcendent power we usually identify as divine, but which can just as easily be conceptualized as the power of Circumstance. However described, such power is never experienced as one's own; it belongs to the whole field of forces of which the experiencer is but a part. For that reason, it is not something in which one takes pride. It is simply that which is arising *here*, something for which one is more apt to feel grateful than proud.

REFERENCES

1. Kaufmann, W., *Nietzsche*, Princeton: Princeton University Press, 1974, p. 206.
2. Nietzsche, F., *On The Genealogy of Morals*, New York: Vintage Books, 1967, p. 45.
3. *The Dhammapada*, trans. Thomas Byrom, New York: Vintage Books, 1976, p. 4.
4. *The Dhammapada*, p. 3.
5. Nietzsche, F., *The Will To Power*, New York: Vintage, 1968, Section 382, p. 206.
6. James, W., *The Varieties of Religious Experience*, New York: Penguin, 1982, p. 210.
7. Luther, *On the Enslaved Will*, quoted in Cassirer, E., *The Philosophy of the Enlightenment*, Princeton: Princeton University Press, 1951, p. 140.
8. James, W., *The Varieties of Religious Experience*, pp. 243-244.
9. James, W., *The Varieties of Religious Experience*, p. 248.

12

EMOTION: TORRENTS OF THE SOUL

Our human world is emotional beyond anything else seen in nature. Other animals scream, growl, jump for joy and even occasionally shed tears, but their lives lack the intense, sustained emotionality that colors human existence. This appears to be true of our closest primate relatives, the chimpanzees and gorillas, as well as more remote mammalian species like dogs, cats, and hoofed animals. It is not only the intensity but the duration of our emotions that sets us apart. Most animals are capable of becoming angry, even explosively so, but rarely for more than a few minutes at a time. Under the right conditions human rage can smolder for years, as can human sadness, bitterness, and despair. We are also capable of a much broader range of emotions. Beyond anger, fear, elation, jealousy, bewilderment, and grief – which many other species appear to experience – we alone seem capable of feeling guilt, pride, contempt, humiliation, scorn, vengefulness, self-hate, self-love, gratitude, resentment, indignation, smugness, and self-pity, to name but a few.

All these uniquely human feelings share a cognitive complexity not found in the simpler, more widely distributed emotions like anger and fear. But there is more to their uniqueness than complexity. To varying degrees they rest on the belief that we have the capacity to cause our own behavior. That belief has powerful emotional implications whether the putative agent is one's own (as in guilt, pride, self-hate, indignation, and smugness) or is thought to reside inside the other person (as in contempt, gratitude, and resentment). A belief in agency amplifies emotions by exposing self and other to moral judgment.

Believing that we cause our own behavior frees us from the chain of cause and effect and, in so doing, sensitizes us to judgments concerning our use of that freedom. Many of our strongest and most uniquely human emotions arise out of the experience of judging and being judged.

From this perspective, Nietzsche's characterization of emotions as "impetuous torrents of the soul" needs modification. Emotions are not inspired by an invisible, spiritual entity presiding over our thoughts and actions. They may be inspired, however, by a *belief* in such an entity. The belief that we cause our own behavior – and others theirs – intensifies our emotional reaction to events by changing the meaning of those events. When we interpret behavior as freely willed, we are forced to consider the possibility that the agent responsible for the action could have willed something different. That possibility – whether it refers to someone else's behavior or to our own – has a direct impact on our feelings. In the case of all of the primary emotions – anger, fear, sadness, and joy – viewing behavior as freely willed rather than determined intensifies our emotional response. It makes us angrier, sadder, more frightened, and more joyous. A brief review of these four responses will make the connection between belief and emotion clearer.

ANGER

A belief in agency escalates our anger by transforming comments on our behavior into judgments on us as authors of that behavior. Through a slight but powerful shift in thinking, disapproval of "that which has arisen here" is transmuted into rejection of the self that made the behavior happen. Our frustration increases accordingly and, thus, the intensity of our anger. We make the same emotional conversion when we transform our disapproval of another's behavior into contempt for the agent thought to have caused that behavior. The key to our reaction lies in our assumption that the agent/other could have chosen to behave differently. What escalates our frustration and in turn our anger is the belief that if he had really wanted to, he could have caused a different kind of behavior to happen. The possibility that he could have chosen otherwise implies not only that another kind of behavior was possible, but that the agent within the other was free to make that alternative behavior happen.

Believing in agency introduces a potent, new character into the human drama – a semi-divine entity with the miraculous power to create choices out of nothing. If we humans have a penchant for hate, bitterness, and murder unduplicated by any other species in nature, it is at least partly due to the fact that we insist on taking the fiction of the homunculus seriously. Because of our putative freedom to cause our own choices, no behavior of either self or other is ever completely necessary. When we say something to offend another, we are causally responsible for the decision not to say something different. When the other responds with a counter jab, he too is acting independently of predisposing forces. Without intending to do so, we transform mildly frustrating events into highly emotional, even violent ones by ascribing them to quasi-spiritual entities that do not exist.

This is not to argue that anger is purely a matter of distorted cognition. Life offers countless opportunities for frustration and anger independently of what we believe to be true about the causes of either our own or other people's behavior. Like many other animal species, we become angry when protecting ourselves, when driving intruders from our territory, and when competing for scarce goods. All of these situations are capable of causing frustration and provoking anger whether we believe in agency or not. At the same time, their potential for generating anger can be greatly affected by such a belief. By postulating an agent inside the other person and then identifying that agent as the sole cause of the offending behavior, free will increases the probability that we will respond with anger. Conversely, viewing the offender simply as part of a situation unfolding out of circumstance makes us less angry than we might otherwise be.*

Anger ordinarily accompanies blaming even when that blaming is positional rather than causal. For example, having our car rammed by another is bound to be aggravating and, in turn, anger-arousing even when we see the driver's behavior as arising out of circumstance and chance. Without the assumption, however, that the ramming was caused by an agent free to choose otherwise, that anger is apt to be brief and short-lived. To accept the offending behavior as a spontaneous expression of circumstance, it is not necessary that we know exactly why it arose when or where it did. It is sufficient to realize that, given the various aspects of the situation, the accident was highly

---

* Given the connection between agency and anger, some of us may be tempted to use a belief in non-agency to rationalize our inability to express angry feelings. A flaw in emotional development can thereby be passed off as evidence of cognitive change. The refusal to act on angry feelings, however, or to acknowledge that such feelings even exist, suggests a fear of moral judgment rather than a lack of emotion. When the uprooting of agency is genuine, little resistance remains to accepting all our feelings, whether we act on those feelings or not. If the liberated person shows little anger, it is not because he or she is unwilling to acknowledge angry feelings, but because little anger is arising.

probable. What happened arose by itself out of circumstance. It was causally necessary.

ANXIETY

Psychologist Aaron Beck summarizes the difference between anxiety and anger as follows:

> For the arousal of anxiety, the salient feature is *danger*: The person is concerned primarily with the possibility of being hurt and with his perceived lack of coping devices to deal with the noxious stimulus. In the case of anger, he is more concerned with the violation of rights, rules, and principles and with the blameworthiness of the offensive agent, and less so with the danger to himself.[1] (original italics)

Like anger, anxiety can be found throughout the animal kingdom. It occurs, as Beck suggests, whenever the organism feels itself threatened. Among humans, the number of situations capable of arousing anxiety is infinite, ranging from the physically dangerous to the socially intimidating to the merely uncertain. As Beck's definition implies, a situation is likely to make us anxious only if we *perceive* it to be dangerous. There are many factors giving shape to that perception, one of which is what we believe to be true about ourselves. On one level, this takes the form of beliefs we have about our ability to cope with threat. At another, deeper level, it involves our beliefs about who we are. By changing the meaning of events, particularly the meaning of being evaluated by others, our belief in agency has the capacity to heighten our perception of danger and thereby affect our level of anxiety.

Of all the everyday events in life that have the power to make us anxious, being evaluated for the way we act is one of the most common. Some of our fear arises from a realistic perception of what negative evaluation implies for the loss of power, support, credibility, money, or other tangible goods. That fear needn't involve our belief in agency. It commonly does, however, for the simple reason that, once we identify ourselves with our agent/I, we become concerned not only with the way others evaluate our behavior, but with the way they evaluate us as *authors* of that behavior. Being evaluated as authors of our behavior raises the stakes in what might otherwise be an innocuous or only mildly threatening situation. By imputing to us the freedom to cause our choices and decisions, agency changes the meaning of negative judgment.

When viewed from the perspective of agency, disapproval indicates more than a rejection of our particular behavior; it conveys the message that we are unworthy as causal agents. Understandably, the anticipation of such judgment heightens our perception of danger, and, in turn, our experience of anxiety.

JOY AND SADNESS

A belief in agency intensifies the highs and lows of life by adding the dimension of authorship to our personal triumphs and tragedies. At least some of the joy we feel in achieving a long-sought goal comes from the conviction that we as agents have made it happen. While we may be glad for the outcome itself – the promotion, the graduation, the finishing of the book – our joy is made sweeter by the belief that we have played a causal role in its happening. We feel proud. We feel good not only about the outcome but about ourselves as authors of that outcome.

The belief in agency that heightens our joy when we succeed is the same belief, of course, that deepens our grief when we fail. We feel bad not only about the outcome itself but about the part we as agents have played in that failure. It is our fault. We could have worked harder or acted more wisely, but we failed to make either happen. Because the failure is of our making, it implies that we are less worthy of respect as causal entities. Such thoughts deepen our sense of failure and, in so doing, intensify our feelings of sadness and self-blame.

In the economy of agent-inspired emotions, guilt, grief, and regret represent the mirror image of pride, joy, and self-satisfaction. If much of life seems to be marked by an abrupt swinging back and forth between these polar opposites, it is due in great part to the myth of causal autonomy and what that myth implies for moral responsibility. For anyone who takes it seriously, the belief that we cause our own choices can transform life into an emotional roller coaster. And, of course, most of us do take that belief seriously – with the predictable result that life perpetually alternates between feeling high and feeling low, with only rare moments of serenity in between. For most people, life *is* this series of ups and downs – the warm rush of a compliment, the cold, sinking sensation of a snub, the thrill of watching a son or daughter graduate from college, the despair of being passed over for a promotion. Those peaks and valleys are so much a part of life, in fact, that we have a hard time imagining what our days would be like without them.

For most of us, the prospect of a life without constant ups and downs strikes us as devoid of something quintessentially human. Despite the pain associated with many of our emotions, we remain deeply attached to them. But attachment notwithstanding, are these emotions really essential to being human? Will we abandon our true nature if we learn to take disappointment in stride without becoming angry or depressed? Will we forfeit our special place in nature if we learn to accept success with a contented smile instead of proud elation? We typically see life as a series of peaks and valleys, but this perception may say more about our beliefs than it does about human nature. We can acknowledge the roller coaster nature of our experience without leaping to the conclusion that it has to be that way. In inferring that it must, we may be confusing what we have created with what is biologically given.

Getting Off the Roller Coaster

Nietzsche, who was as enamored of passion as he was of power, would not have responded warmly to the argument that human emotionality has its roots in an illusion. As convinced as he was that the "doer" behind every deed was only a fiction, he never considered what giving up that fiction might imply for the world of emotions. His overriding concern was to defend passion against those moralists who would sacrifice our character to the purification of our souls.

> Affect, desire, the passion for power, love, revenge, possessions – the moralists want to extinguish and uproot them, to "purify" the soul of them. The logic is: the desires often produce great misfortune – consequently they are evil, reprehensible. A man must free himself from them: otherwise he cannot be a *good* man. This is the same logic as: "If thine eye offend thee, pluck it out." In the particular case in which that dangerous "innocent from the country," the founder of Christianity recommended this practice to his disciples, the case of sexual excitation, the consequence is, unfortunately, not only the loss of an organ but the *emasculation* of a man's character. And the same applies to the moralist's madness that demands, instead of the restraining of the passions, their extirpation. Its conclusion is always: only the castrated man is a good man. Instead of taking into service the great sources of strength, those impetuous torrents of the soul that are so often dangerous and overwhelming, and economizing them, this most shortsighted and pernicious mode of thought, the moral mode of thought, wants to make them dry up.[2]

While Nietzsche would have us restrain our passion, he is careful to distinguish between the harnessing of impulses and their outright repression. In the process of self-overcoming, he says, we can learn to take our potentially dangerous aggressive and sexual impulses "into service" by sublimating them into good and beautiful works. Suppression for the sake of morality, on the other hand, dries up our juices; it prevents evil by emasculating our character. Our restraint is thus no longer a virtue but an expression of impotence. There is more hope, he argued, for a powerful albeit evil man like Cesare Borgia than for a good but passionless man like Parsifal.

> Nietzsche believed that a man without impulses could not do the good or create the beautiful any more than a castrated man could beget children. A man with strong impulses might be evil because he had not yet learned to sublimate his impulses, but if he should ever acquire self-control, he might achieve greatness. In that sense, there is more joy in heaven over one repentant sinner than over ninety-nine just men – if the latter are just only because they are too feeble ever to have sinned.[3]

According to Nietzsche, our impulses, dangerous though they may be, provide the fuel for our creative genius; they are the prime movers of art, science, and military greatness – the makers of our civilization. Violence, sexual passion, pride, jealousy, the desire to dominate, the desire for revenge – these are natural impulses given to all of us in some measure and, to a few, in abundance. For Nietzsche, not only the greatness of our civilization but our very survival as a species depends on our ability to harness these natural passions just as we have learned to harness the wind, water, and lower animals.

In arguing his case, Nietzsche is making two questionable assumptions – first, that violence, jealousy, the need to conquer, and the desire for revenge are "natural: and, secondly, that their sublimation is necessary for civilization. The universality of passionate behavior is thrown into doubt by cultures like that of the Hopi of the American Southwest in which expressions of intense emotion are rare. In his eagerness to censure the moralists for trying to make us all eunuchs, Nietzsche overlooked the possibility that our emotions are shaped as much by our beliefs and values as by our genes. Culture serves as more than a set of restraints on our biologically given nature. What we are taught to believe about ourselves has a direct effect on what we feel quite apart from the way we express those feelings. The passions that Nietzsche takes for granted - and cautions us against repressing – are intimately tied to our beliefs about who we are. Much of the love for power, dominance, and glory which Nietzsche attributes to our biological nature owe their strength to the illusion that we are the authors of our own behavior.

If that is true, it follows that Nietzsche, who would have us "harness" our destructive impulses, and his antagonists, the moralists, who would have us repress them, have both missed the point. Without an agent/I to stand in judgment over our behavioral choices, our emotions are apt to be less intense, less dangerous to others, and thus less in need of either harnessing or repressing. It does not seem to have occurred to Nietzsche that the leading role in most of our melodramas is played not by instinct but by an imaginary homunculus. Without the agent/I and its vulnerability to moral judgment, there would be far less shouting and screaming, less wailing and gnashing of teeth, fewer tears of joy, fewer tears of sorrow, more serenity, and probably more sustained happiness.

According to Nietzsche's second assumption, civilization thrives on the harnessing of destructive impulses. If those impulses were repressed by the moralists or vitiated by a dispelling of the free will illusion, art, science, technology, and military greatness would all decline. The argument is unconvincing because it fails to consider both sides of the issue. If there are fewer destructive impulses to sublimate in a non-agency world, there may be more impulses of a constructive nature. What evidence do we have to suggest that great art *has* to originate in the desire to conquer, to hurt, or destroy? Beethoven, it must be admitted, looked and wrote as if he were capable of violence, and both Verdi and Wagner went so far as to promote revolution, but what about Mozart? Is there any reason to believe that the Magic Flute, Don Giovanni, and Cosi Fan Tutte had their roots in dark, anti-social impulses or that the magnificent piano concerti were inspired by a need to conquer? The energy I hear in Mozart's works strikes me as neither sexual nor aggressive but aesthetic – a personal expression of *joie de vivre*. Bach, Haydn, Schubert, Chopin, and Mendelssohn all testify to the possibility of great art without any apparent wish to destroy or overwhelm.

Art would certainly be different without those "impetuous torrents of the soul" of which Nietzsche was so fond, but there are no grounds for assuming that it would be inferior. Without a belief in free will, scientists too might be less motivated by the desire to *wrest* secrets from nature or to *conquer* disease – but that need not mean the end of curiosity about the world. In the world of politics, leaders would be less anxious to build empires or prove their superiority on the battle field. Wars might still be fought, but they would be fought less often over national pride or out of a desire to dominate one's neighbors. In general, the world of a non-agency would be less passionate and violent, more objective and peaceful. In terms of Ruth Benedict's typology, it would be less Dionysian, more Appolonian.

REACTIVE ATTITUDES IN THE WORLD OF NON-AGENCY

Philosopher Peter Strawson is convinced that while it may be possible to change our belief in free will, it is unlikely that a simple change in belief will eliminate the "reactive attitudes" that presently dominate interpersonal life (attitudes such as resentment, indignation, and gratitude). Such attitudes, he claims, are so thoroughly embedded in our bio-social nature that they are impervious to cognitive influence. On occasion, he admits, we may be capable of temporarily suspending our reactive attitudes, i.e., of becoming "objective" about other people's behavior, but it is not a position we can sustain. To be objective in an interpersonal situation implies excusing others for their offensive behavior because of what we know about the causes of that behavior. Ordinarily, according to Strawson, we reserve that objectivity for the mentally ill, for young children, or for someone "peculiarly unfortunate in his formative circumstances."

> We have this resource [our objectivity] and can sometimes use it: as a refuge, say, from the strains of involvement; or as an aid to policy; or simply out of intellectual curiosity. Being human, we cannot, in the normal case, do this for long, or altogether. If the strains of involvement, say, continue to be too great, then we have to do something else – like severing a relationship. But what is above all interesting is the tension there is, in us, between the participant [reactive] attitude and the objective attitude. One is tempted to say: between our humanity and our intelligence.[4]

By an objective attitude Strawson means one in which all events are seen as either caused or random. There is no room in that objectivity for spiritual agents operating according to rules other than those of cause and effect or chance. There is no room, therefore, for free will. It would seem to follow, then, that as we become persuaded of the illusoriness of agency, we will adopt more objective and less reactive (emotional) attitudes toward others. While Strawson agrees, in theory, that such a shift should follow, he remains convinced that

> it is, for us as we are, practically inconceivable. The human commitment to participation in ordinary interpersonal relationships is, I think, too thoroughgoing and deeply rooted for us to take seriously the thought that a general theoretical conviction might so change our world that, in it, there were no longer any such things as interpersonal relationships as we normally understand them; and being involved in interpersonal relationships as we normally understand them precisely is being exposed to the range of reactive attitudes and feelings that is in question. . . . A sustained objectivity of interpersonal attitude, and the human isolation which that would entail, does not seem to be something of which human beings would be capable, even if some general truth were a theoretical ground for it.[5]

If Strawson is right in arguing that it is impossible to sustain an objective attitude in the face of all the fears, frustrations, and disappointments that mark our encounters with each other, how do we account for that fact? What makes it so hard to be objective with other people? Are we bound to our reactive attitudes because of something in our nature, something carried in our genes? Should we assume that, in the course of evolution, reactive attitudes proved to have greater survival value than rational, objective ones? Perhaps so. But if those reactive attitudes are inherited, what do we do with the fact that, when they are aimed at another individual, they are implicitly directed to an entity within that person for which no evidence can be found? Perhaps we are born with a predisposition to resentment and have concocted the illusion of free agency in order to justify that instinctual reaction. Or does it makes more sense to turn the hypothesis around. Has the internalizing of the agency illusion predisposed us to attitudes like resentment and indignation for which we have concocted a genetic explanation? A third and more reasonable alternative is that resentment, indignation, spite, bitterness and all the other reactive attitudes are rooted in both our inheritance and our training. If we have learned anything at all from generations of nature-nurture research, it is that no psycho-social phenomena can be traced exclusively to either our genes or our environment. If this is so, it means that our reactive attitudes are, to some degree, dependent on our conditioning and are thus amenable to change.

Despite his obvious sympathy for a more objective social order, Strawson seems convinced that it is out of our reach. Since he cites no evidence for his pessimism, it seems likely that he is generalizing from personal experience. While I share his observation that most interpersonal relationships are saturated with pride, resentment and other reactive attitudes, I am not convinced that those attitudes are impervious to cultural influence. The pervasiveness of resentment in our culture would seem to say at least as much about our beliefs and values, i.e., our socialization, as it does about our genes. My own experience over the last eight years has convinced me that reactive attitudes and agency go hand in hand. As our belief in an originative self is replaced by a view of experience and behavior as self-arising, our reactive attitudes give way to more objective ones. During the changeover, the lingering presence of reactive attitudes can be used to identify those areas where the ghost of agency still reigns. Later in the book, in the course of spelling out a strategy for exorcising that ghost, I hope to show that the very attitudes Strawson sees as indelibly etched into human character represent the key to learning how to live without the illusion of free agency.

Eliminating resentment, forgiveness, and vindictiveness from our lives does not imply a life without feeling. It implies a less passionate world, a world in which our relationships are no longer driven by agency-inspired emotions. Although he uses a different terminology, English philosopher Jonathan Glover comes to essentially the same conclusion.

> But it is wrong to say that the only responses to people in a hard determinist [non-agency] world will be coolly scientific. Reactions which presuppose desert will have to be given up. But a whole range of reactive attitudes are not desert-based. Consider the aesthetic-cum-sexual responses we have to people's appearance, or to their style and charm. We have aesthetic responses of another kind to people's intellectual qualities: to their being imaginative, independent, or quick on the uptake. These responses are not desert-based. We do not think people are attractive, or quick on the uptake, because of praiseworthy efforts they have made. On the contrary, these seem very clear cases of features owing a lot to luck. Perhaps

this is one reason why we think of our responses to them as aesthetic rather than moral.[6]

Glover makes the further point that such "aesthetic" responses play an important social control function.

> These aesthetic responses could be conveyed to other people. And, just as people want to be thought physically attractive, rather than ugly, so people would care about aesthetic responses to their character. Desert-based attitudes, like blame, would have to be renounced. But unfavorable aesthetic responses to character as revealed in actions might function like blame. They might be just as effective in putting pressure on people to change their behavior.[7]

Non-moralistic or aesthetic responses, the author continues, can also be directed *inward* – as in the case of what I have previously referred to as positional self-blame and self-credit.

> And giving up pride, guilt, and other desert-based responses to our own actions would not eliminate all reactive attitudes to ourselves. Aesthetic responses parallel to the old desert-based ones could grow up. I could regret being selfish or dishonest in the way I regret having no talent for music or sport. I could judge my actions aesthetically as admirable or appalling, and these thoughts could be charged with feeling.[8]

Glover's argument that in a non-agency world aesthetic feelings would replace desert-based feelings fits my own experience over the last eight years. While anger, pride, and despair have continued to arise, I find that they arise less frequently than before and when they do, they rarely last very long. As a result, I feel less buffeted about, more stable, less given to either elation or sadness. I still feel very much alive, perhaps even more alive than before, but not because of anything melodramatic going on in my life. While it is true that I experience a more muted emotional life, I am aware of a new sensibility to beauty and a keener curiosity about the world. Both responses have an aesthetic rather than passionate quality about them; each comes with its own quiet joy unshaken by intense emotion of any kind.

Of all the changes that have taken place over the last eight years, the one I appreciate the most is the virtual disappearance of anxiety. I speak as someone whose adult life, from mid-twenties to mid-fifties, has rarely been free of anxiety. If I try to explain this change in conventional psychological terms, e.g., as a result of growing self-confidence or a more supportive social environment, the evidence is not there. I am not aware of feeling any more confident or of receiving any more support from friends and family. What feels new is a less urgent need to prove myself. Energy which once went into worrying about my career flows instead into thinking about philosophy and psychology. The soaring quality that once lifted my ambition to neurotic heights is still there, but it is more apt to come out now as intense curiosity about the world.

For all the leveling off that has taken place in my emotional life, I do not consider myself a vegetable or robot (although I have occasionally been accused of the latter by colleagues whose own behavior is highly passionate).* While desire continues to spark much of my behavior, my most intense moments of pleasure no longer come from winning approval but from creating objects of beauty and meaning. Once freed from the burden of fame and glory, my intellectual interests have grown to the point where they literally fill my life. I wake up thinking about the issues in this book – or those I hope to cover in the next one. In between stints of research consulting, I write, hike, take photographs, read, compose, turn wooden vases, and go to concerts and plays. I can't think of anything else I would rather be doing, not because of any benefits these activities promise for the future, but because what I am doing feels good right now.

Aside from having to go to work when I would rather stay home and write books or music, there is very little in my life that I would change – and

---

* "We're afraid that without feelings we will be inhuman, cold, insensitive, robot-like creatures, so detached from this world that we might as well be dead. Needless to say, there is no truth in this view at all; it is just another myth created out of fear of the unknown – where all myths come from. Nevertheless, to explain what life is like without this system is not easy because it must be lived to be understood, and any description of it only gives rise to an unending chain of philosophical arguments. All that need be said here is that it is a dynamic, intense state of caring; caring for whatever arises in the now-moment. It is a continuous waking state in which the physical organism remains sensitive, responsive, and totally unimpaired. When the journey is over, nothing is found to be missing or wanting. It is only in the encounter with other selves that a self or affective system is seen as a continuous reminder of what was." Bernadette Roberts, *The Experience of No-Self*, Boston: Shambhala, 1984, p. 179.

nothing at all that I find especially hard to accept. Events may change without my blessing, of course, but I have little reason to expect the acceptance to stop arising. Nietzsche would appear to be saying something very similar when he writes:

> My formula for the greatness of a human being is *amor fati:*
> that one wants nothing to be different – not forward, not
> backward, not in all eternity. Not merely bear what is neces-
> sary, still less conceal it . . . but *love it.*[9]

At first glance, he appears to be recommending acceptance, but the final phrase makes it clear that it is still passion that he admires. To *love* whatever happens goes beyond simple acceptance – so far beyond, in fact, as to be unrealistic. Can we really learn to love sickness and accidental death? As our child lies dying, can we truly say that we would want "nothing to be different?" True to his view of life as power and passion, Nietzsche wants to be able to love every moment, every event, just as it happens.* From what I have observed of life, this is simply not possible. What we *can* do is learn to accept the world at every moment.

William James demonstrated a similar predilection for rash judgment when he wrote:

> He who, with Marcus Aurelius, can truly say, "O Universe, I
> wish all that thou wishest," has a self from which every trace
> of negativeness and obstructiveness has been removed – no
> wind can blow except to fill its sails.[10]

James' romantic ideal of uniting desire with reality, like Nietzsche's, obscures what seems to me to be the deeper truth that we remove every trace of negativeness and obstructiveness and unfurl our sails to the wind when we start accepting the world just as it is. The key lies not in loving every moment or wishing for every event but in accepting whatever arises. When we do so, our sails stand ready to catch the wind whenever and wherever it blows.

---

* Nietzsche appears slightly more reasonable elsewhere when he calls for "a Yes-saying without reservation, even to suffering, even to guilt. . . This ultimate, most joyous, most wantonly extravagant Yes to life represents not only the highest insight but also the *deepest.* . . . Nothing in existence may be subtracted, nothing is dispensable. To comprehend this requires courage and, as a condition of that, an excess of strength . . ." *Ecce Homosexualis*, p. 272.

REFERENCES

1. Beck, A., *Cognitive Therapy and The Emotional Disorders*, New York: New American Library, 1976, p. 75.
2. Nietzsche, F., *The Will To Power*, New York: Vintage, 1968, #383.
3. Kaufmann, W., *Nietzsche*, Princeton: Princeton University Press, 1974, p. 224.
4. Strawson, P., *Freedom and Resentment*, London: Methuen & Co., 1974, pp. 9-10.
5. Strawson, P., *Freedom and Resentment*, pp. 11-12.
6. Glover, J., *I: The Philosophy and Psychology of Personal Identity*, London: The Penguin Press, 1988, p. 191.
7. Glover, J., *I: The Philosophy and Psychology of Personal Identity*, p. 192.
8. Glover, J., *I: The Philosophy and Psychology of Personal Identity*, p. 192.
9. Nietzsche, F., *Ecce Homo*, New York: Vintage Books, 1969, p. 258.
10. Kallen, H., *The Philosophy of William James*, New York: The Modern Library, 1925, pp, 148-149.

13

LOVE AND SEXUALITY

If thoughts do not go so far as to make the world, as Buddha claimed they do, they at least influence the way we feel and act. The thoughts which affect us the most are the basic metaphysical assumptions we make about the way the world works. Free agency is one of those basic assumptions. We should not be surprised, therefore, to see its influence manifested throughout the full spectrum of human experience and behavior. As we have already seen, that spectrum includes blame, credit, pride, guilt, sin, virtue, defensiveness, anger, anxiety, despair, straining, craving, clinging, and the will to power. In light of that diversity, it would be strange to find that agency had no implications for love. Our beliefs about ourselves, in fact, imply a great deal for love, but, as this chapter will show, what they imply depends very much on the kind of love we are considering.

ROMANTIC LOVE

Most of us growing up in a Western culture have either known romantic love directly or participated in the experience vicariously through literature and film. While being in love tends to be a relatively brief experience, counted more often in months than years, our fascination with it rarely ceases altogether, even in old age. It comes as something of a shock, therefore, to learn that the non-Western world of Asians, Indians, Africans, Polynesians, and Eskimos knows little of romantic love. A phenomenon we have always thought of as a *human* experience is limited primarily to Western and, to a lesser degree, Near Eastern culture.* Strange as it must seem to someone nurtured on *Romeo and Juliet, Gone With the Wind,* and *Love Story,* it appears that, before we can fall in love, we must be educated to the *concept* of romantic love. La Rouchefoucauld put it simply when he said that "... few people would fall in love had they never heard of love."[1]

Before asking why romantic love is so rare outside of Western culture, we need to ask what makes it different from other kinds of love. To see romantic love in its purest form, we must go back to one of the earliest and most famous love stories of all times, that of Tristan and Iseult. In that thrice-told twelfth century tale, we find all the essentials of romance – irresistible desire, idealization of the beloved, the impossibility of fulfillment (Iseult is betrothed to Tristan's uncle), short periods of bliss, long periods of torment, and the only ending possible for true passion – death for both lovers.

According to Denis de Rougemont, at the heart of Tristan's and Iseult's passion is a surrendering of self, not to the other, but to the experience of love itself.

> Passion means suffering, something undergone, the mastery of fate over a free and responsible person. To love more than the object of love, to love passion for its own sake, has been to love to suffer and to court suffering all the way from Augustine's *amabam amare* down to modern romanticism.[2]

That which gives romantic love its intense, unreal, soaring quality is the very thing that dooms it to non-fulfillment. The lovers are not in love with each other but with love itself. The other person is simply an excuse for being

---

* While Japanese literature has for centuries reflected a fascination with romantic love, romance has always remained peripheral to the family: "The Japanese set up no ideal, as we do in the United States, which pictures love and marriage as one and the same thing. We approve of love just in proportion as it is the basis of one's choice of a spouse. 'Being in love' is our most approved reason for marriage. ... The Japanese judge differently. In the choice of a spouse the young man should bow to his parent's choice and marry blind. He must observe great formality in his relations with his wife. Even in the give and take of family life their children do not see an erotically affectionate gesture pass between them. 'The real aim of marriage is regarded in this country ... as the procreation of children and thereby to assure the continuity of the family life. Any purpose other than this must simply serve to pervert the true meaning of it.'" Ruth Benedict, *The Chrysanthemum and the Sword,* Boston: Houghton Mifflin Co., 1946, pp. 184-185.

in love, the passion being "tasted and savoured for its own sake, in a kind of indifference to its living and external object."[3]

"Indifference" is an interesting choice of words. The truth to which it points is that lovers sustain their passion by projecting ideal images onto the shadowy forms they take to be each other. When they fall in love, it is with their own projections rather than anyone real. The relationship is actually an emotional fiction which survives reality by remaining distanced from it. It follows that the greatest threat to romance is not physical separation but too much closeness. Passion is doomed to fade when frequent interaction forces the lovers to confront each other as real persons, as they eventually must if they choose to live together. In literature, the two favorite endings to love stories are death and marriage. While the latter is the happier of the two, it is usually no less final as the end of romance.

If the essence of romantic love is unfulfilled longing for an idealized other, why has it come to play such a central role in Western culture and only a peripheral one elsewhere? Rougemont explains it as a hedonistic reaction against Christianity on the part of "people whose spirit, whether naturally or by inheritance, was still pagan."[4] Christianity, he argues, demands the repression of egocentric, erotic love in favor of agape or "loving thy neighbor as thyself," the latter sentiment being best expressed in marriage. The "pagan" reaction, according to Rougemont, consists of breaking through that repression and asserting passion over marriage.

While romance is certainly erotic, is it not possible to rebel against Christian moralism without going to the extremes of that "sickness of the soul" we call romantic love? Pre-marital and extramarital sex can both be enjoyed without either party's falling in love. Conversely, it is possible to fall in love without rebelling against Christianity or without being a Christian at all. And there is another problem. If romantic love is a reaction against Christian repression, a relaxing of Christian sexual standards should lead to a shrinking of interest in romance. Here in the latter part of the twentieth century those standards *have* been relaxed, but Western interest in romantic love remains as strong as ever. It would seem, then, that if we are to explain the appeal of "unfulfilled longing for an idealized other," we must look beyond Christian morality and the antagonism to it which arose in the late Middle Ages.

Of the many beliefs and values which make Western culture unique in the world, a concern for the dignity and rights of the individual is certainly one of the most important. Such a concern was already stirring in the late

Middle Ages and erupted full-blown in the Renaissance. The Reformation, eighteenth century rationalism, and modern political libertarianism have all elaborated on that basic regard for the sanctity of the individual, a regard rarely found outside of the West. Is it possible that romantic love, while compatible with more than one kind of culture, has a special affinity for Western individualism? Is there something about our concern for the individual that makes the experience of falling in love more plausible? The close historical development of the two lends support to that hypothesis, as does the fact that in American culture both romantic love and individualism are probably more highly prized than anywhere else on earth.

At the heart of our concern for the rights and freedom of the individual is a belief in free will. If romantic love has thrived especially well in the Western world, it may owe its success at least partially to the belief that we are all free, autonomous, morally responsible agents. Rougemont provides the conceptual link when he suggests that passion consists of the "mastery of fate over a free and responsible person." If so, its appeal must lie in the *surrendering* of freedom and responsibility. Romantic love offers an escape from the (illusion of) isolation imposed by our belief in free will. That perspective makes sense, of course, only if we can assume that there is significant pain involved in believing oneself to be a free, autonomous agent.

Some of that pain, we have already seen, arises out of the fear of being judged for one's choices. There is a still deeper discomfort, however, associated with the image of oneself as an autonomous agent. I refer to what might be called the pain of differentiation, the pain of being separated from the rest of the world. That pain is not limited to free agency. It is the price we pay initially for leaving the womb and then pay again in the early years of life as we struggle to separate ourselves emotionally from our mothers. The universal pain of becoming an individual is intensified, however, when we are taught to identify ourselves as causally autonomous agents endowed with freedom of choice. As free agents we are not only separate from everyone else physically; we are separate spiritually, separate as souls, separate as centers of will and moral responsibility. The more highly a culture values this spiritual separateness, the greater will be the pain of differentiation and, thus, the greater the appeal of a kind of love that promises to overcome all separation through a merging of selves.

According to this alternative hypothesis, the widespread appeal of romantic love in Western culture draws much of its power from our view of ourselves as autonomous agents. Easterners, many of whom are inclined to look upon romance with disdain, are more apt to find their basic identity in the Tao, the Buddha-nature, the Brahman, or whatever it is that transcends subject and object, the ultimately nameless One. They view free will and moral responsibility as expedient illusions, necessary for survival in the samsaric world, but meaningless in the nirvanic world of no-form. For the un-westernized Easterner, all autonomy is ultimately illusory. The world is One and all seemingly separate objects and selves participate in that Oneness. If differentiation appears painful, it is because we do not yet see beyond the illusion of form.

Our Western belief that individual souls remain separate throughout eternity, in heaven as well as on earth, creates a sense of personal isolation unknown elsewhere in the world. This isolation heightens the appeal of returning to a less differentiated state through a surrender of the agent/self to passion. As Rougemont points out, romantic love is not a surrender of the self to another person, but to love itself. Surrendering to another person may ease the burden of individual responsibility, but it does not erase the boundaries of the agent/I. Romantic love goes further. By shutting out everyone else, it reduces the world to "me and thee" and then holds out the promise of further dissolution into oneness. To the lovers it may not be clear or may not even matter whether that is the oneness of union or the oneness of death. What matters is the dying of the agent-self, the surrendering of autonomy, the return to an undifferentiated unity.

From his Christian view of romantic love as a pagan (erotic) rebellion against the ideal of charitable love, Rougemont concludes that, for the sake of our psychological maturity and spiritual well-being, we must say no to passion and romance, and yes to marriage and commitment. If my own analysis is valid, any such attempt to replace eros with agape is likely to founder on the illusion of agency. Romantic love has its roots not so much in "pagan hedonism" as in the escape from free will, a concept which Christianity itself staunchly defends. It follows that there will be no outgrowing of our obsession with romance until we outgrow our obsession with free will and the false sense of isolation that illusion creates. Ironically, in defending free will, Christianity may be postponing the day when Westerners lose interest in romance.

If giving up agency implies losing interest in romance, it also implies gaining freedom from attachment. The essence of that freedom lies in never becoming desperate about losing oneself in another – not because we fear rejection, but because the pain of differentiation is no longer as intense.

We can continue to enjoy another person both sexually and non-sexually, but without the longing and despair that typically go with being in love. In this new world, relationships do not *have* to work. Our freedom from craving allows us to be less demanding and less anxious about pleasing the other person. Consequently, we might not try as hard to save relationships if they become less satisfying. On the other hand, because our desire is less compulsive, we can be afford to be more patient in exploring relationships to their fullest extent.

This is not the first time I have referred to that paradox in which surrendering a belief in freedom of will leads to greater freedom of action. Non-agency gives us more options in sexual relationships just as it does everywhere else in life. Over the last few years I have come to experience this personally as the freedom to approach relationships without needing anything in particular to happen. After four major romances and several minor ones, all marked to different degrees by intense sexual desire, possessiveness, jealousy, and fear of rejection, I feel relieved to be able to enjoy intimacy without the burden of being in love. For me, loving a woman without being *in love* with her means being able to enjoy long stretches of time apart; it means not idealizing her, not obsessing over her, and not trying to possess her. As some of my recent partners have hinted, it is also possible that I am simply worn out from all those years of pursuit. While there may be some truth in that conjecture, the freedom I feel is too similar to what I experience elsewhere in my life to be explained solely in terms of a shrinking libido.

The whole romantic syndrome of hyper-sexuality, possessiveness, and idealization has a great deal in common with ambition, at least as I have experienced the two over the past thirty years. As I know them, romance and ambition share a common urgency, compulsiveness, irrationality, insatiability, and detachment from reality. Whether by coincidence or design, they both began fading from my life at the time my belief in agency began to weaken. What feels new to me is the capacity to enjoy both work and relationships without obsessing over approval or affection. Some of the excitement is gone, particularly in relationships, but I feel more than compensated by the peace and clarity of mind that have arisen in its place.

SEXUALITY

What we believe to be true about ourselves affects the way we express our sexual feelings. That generalization can be verified by reminding ourselves how easily our concern with being liked or admired can influence the way we approach other people sexually. Our view of ourselves as free agents introduces an additional agenda into love-making. At its worst that agenda can turn the bedroom into a stage where the giving and receiving of pleasure become incidental to winning approval. Falling into that trap is made easier by the fact that our bid to be seen as desirable or potent tends to be woven into gestures and words in such a way that we are only subliminally aware of the game we are playing.

Some of this concern with evaluation has nothing to do with agency; it arises out of a desire to please the other and thereby increase the probability of going to bed again. What is driven by agency, particularly for a man, is the need to perform – a need that is furthered by the conviction that one serves as the cause of one's own sexual efficacy. A belief in agency also finds its way into love-making by way of the need to dominate and possess. For a man, "taking" a woman forcefully gains added significance when he feels the need to prove his adequacy as a free agent. Human males are not alone, of course, in their eagerness to dominate and possess, suggesting that testosterone may have as much to do with dominance as does culture. What seems to be uniquely human, however, is the use of sex to demean and negate, as in the case of rape. As with most violence, the impulse to rape receives its strongest impetus from doubts about one's power as a causal agent.

If our beliefs about ourselves affect the intensity of our emotional responses to other people, we should not be surprised to find them affecting the intensity of our sexual desire as well. I have already argued that romantic love has its roots in our view of ourselves as causally autonomous soul/agents. To the extent that agency exaggerates our separateness from each other, it heightens the ecstasy of surrendering. Since orgasm provides the physical means for the surrendering of self, it tends to be most intense when we are romantically attached to our partners. To women, this surrendering seems to express itself in the sensation of being filled or completed – being taken up into another, being consumed. To men, the surrendering of self in orgasm is more apt to be experienced as a relinquishing of control, a giving up of the need to manage. In either case, it is the yielding of autonomy that gives orgasm its other-worldly quality and which has earned it the nickname of "the little death."

Without a belief in agency, there is less autonomy to yield, thus less urgency in love-making. There is also less self-consciousness, less eagerness to look good in the eyes of the other. Being less concerned with evaluation makes it easier to stay in the moment and accept whatever arises – or whatever doesn't. Without the constant self-monitoring that so often accompanies a belief in agency, we can afford to be more playful. When we go to bed without any fixed idea of what *has* to happen, love-making becomes more spontaneous. We remain open to more possibilities. Sex becomes less of a performance and, as a result, more interesting, more fun, and, strangely enough, more intimate. It is more intimate both because our attention is focused on what is actually happening rather than what we think should be happening, and because we see each other as real persons rather than as projections of internalized ideals.

MARRIAGE

If giving up our belief in agency means giving up romantic love, what does it imply for marriage? According to Rougemont, romance is a threat to marriage. In his eyes, the pervasiveness of adultery and divorce in modern Europe and America constitutes a sign of our refusal to give up the quest for romance. We are stuck on a treadmill, he says: we fall in love, get married in hopes of securing that love, discover that romance and marriage are incompatible, and leave marriage to find passion in a new relationship. In the process, he laments, we never mature into adults who are capable of a giving, charitable love based on fidelity rather than passion. Romance does more than keep us young; it keeps us from growing up and accepting the constraints of marital life. According to this point of view, if we are to strengthen and, in time, perfect the institution of marriage, the way to begin is by giving up our attachment to passion.[5]

From this it seems to follow that, by diminishing the appeal of romantic love, a shift in beliefs away from agency will have the effect of strengthening marriage. But this may not be the case. For one thing, romance and marriage may not be as antagonistic as Rougemont makes them out to be. After all, many couples would never get to the altar if it were not for their romantic attachment early in the relationship. And, despite the high divorce rate, the majority of couples that get married stay married. Rougemont might argue, of course, that they stay married only because both partners accept the fading of passion and are too timid or tired to revive it through extra-marital affairs.

Whatever the relationship between passion and marital stability, there is another reason to question the conclusion that giving up our belief in agency will strengthen the institution of marriage. Marriage is, among other things, an alliance of spouses against the world and the appeal of such an alliance is certain to be affected by the way we perceive ourselves. Viewing ourselves as isolated, causally autonomous entities maximizes our vulnerability to judgment, thereby heightening our need for validation. One of the appeals of marriage is the promise of an ally who will take our side in our quarrels with the world and who will console and reassure us when we begin to doubt our efficacy as causal agents.

There are many reasons for getting married, among them financial security, the desire to raise children, the convenience of living with someone whose companionship we value, moral support, physical support during sickness, and care in old age. In the last century, many of these functions have been taken over by organizations outside the family. The state, for example, has taken over the function of educating children, a task once reserved for parents. Nursing homes provide much of the care for the elderly that formerly devolved upon relatives. Social security, pension plans, welfare, and medical insurance now provide the financial security formerly provided by the extended family.

Talcott Parsons has argued that, even though the family has lost many of its functions to other organizations, it remains critical for two basic activities, the early socialization of children and what he calls tension-management.[6] By the latter he means all the things that family members do for each other to relieve the tension generated by the outside world. They console and reassure each other when things go badly at work or school. They empathize with each other's feelings and invite the expression of emotions not permitted elsewhere. They praise achievements and forgive failures. They offer advice. They provide the individual attention which is impossible in a bureaucratic setting. It is no exaggeration to say, then, that the family serves as an asylum to which members can withdraw for emotional support and relief from the tension created by participation in the outside world.

Much of the tension generated at work and school involves matters of blame, credit, power, and emotionality – all of which are intensified by our belief in free agency. If giving up agency implies less tension in our lives, it also implies less tension for the family to manage. In particular, it means less need for emotional support. For anyone who has surrendered agency, there may still be compelling reasons for getting married, but the need for validation and psychic comfort is less likely to be among them. By reducing our need for an emotional alliance against the rest of the world, non-agency may diminish the value of marriage, and, thus, make living alone more attractive.

Non-agency also affects marriage by way of its impact on romantic love. Couples who are in love are apt to view marital commitment as a way of safeguarding their attachment to each other. Without those romantic feelings and all the insecurity to which they typically give rise, they might not feel so strongly about making such a commitment. At the very least, they would be emotionally free to consider other options, such as living together unmarried or living apart and seeing each other often. They may still choose, of course, to marry for non-romantic reasons, e.g., for the sake of raising children, or companionship, or financial security. Non-romantic marriages tend to be less burdened with idealizing and obsessing – and, for that reason, have a better chance of surviving than those fueled by romantic compulsion. Non-agency contributes to the stability of marriage both by minimizing romantic distortion and by reducing the amount of tension to be managed in the relationship. Although it diminishes our need to enter into emotional alliances, non-agency has a positive, stabilizing effect on relationships entered into for other reasons.

The role of agency in raising children deserves further consideration. When a prospective parent talks enthusiastically about wanting to teach or, even more bluntly, to mold a child, we can assume that agency is not far off. What is left unsaid, but clearly implied in such talk, is that the child is to be molded in the image of the parent. A strong desire to leave one's imprint on a child reflects an unwillingness to see that child as a separate person with a psyche of its own. Parents cross that boundary whenever they impose lifestyle preferences, career decisions, and personal values on their children. The narcissism implicit in such attempts stems from the belief that we are responsible for what we have done with our own lives. That belief makes it particularly flattering to watch our children make similar choices, or to be told by others that our child is a "chip off the old block." Being imitated by our children confirms the rightness of what we have done with our own lives. Our delight in that imitation, however, says less about our love for those children than it does about our concern with having made the right choices ourselves.

It is impossible to love children as long as we view them as opportunities for feeling proud of ourselves or as evidence of our own worthiness. To love them for who they are, we need to view them as persons with an emerging identity of their own. That means suspending our expectations and approaching them with curiosity. It means helping them to figure out what is arising within them, instead of burdening them with our own notions of what should be arising. Accepting our children for who they are becomes easier when we give up the view of ourselves as causal agents. Dispelling the illusion that we are the sculptors of our own personalities reduces our temptation to validate what we have created by molding the personalities of our children in our own image.

NON-ROMANTIC LOVE

Giving up agency makes a deeper love and intimacy possible in both marital and non-martial relationships, despite the fact that it reduces our dependence on others for emotional support. What appears to be a paradox is simply a matter of making up in quality what is lost in quantity. The quality of most relationships suffers from our preoccupation with ourselves. Thinking of ourselves as autonomous agents makes us less loving by making us more self-centered. By exposing us to blame and guilt, encouraging us to strain, and tantalizing us with the illusion of power, agency fills us with thoughts about ourselves. In conversation those thoughts demand attention, often at the expense of our interest in and concern for others.

Giving up the illusion of agency eliminates much of our self-preoccupation, thereby allowing us to listen more carefully and receptively to what others are saying. Without the burden of our own melodrama, we can more easily enter into other people's experiences. Self-forgetting lies at the very heart of non-romantic love (agape). It is true that in romantic love we also lose ourselves, but it is to the passion – to love itself – rather than to another individual. Losing ourselves to another individual does not mean that we cease to be a separate person. It means that we enter into his or her life without an axe to grind, without an agenda of our own. To be more accurate, it means emptying ourselves so that the other can come into us. Of all the things we can give to others, none is so basic as this gift of emptiness. To remain alert, caring, non-judgmental, and empty of self-concern allows the other to be himself while experiencing our acceptance. This is the essence of agape. Our belief in agency makes such emptiness virtually impossible. Except for those rare occasions when everything is going exactly the way we want it to, agency arouses too many needs of its own for us to give ourselves fully to anyone else.

Agency gets in the way of intimacy as much as it gets in the way of love. It is impossible to get close to another person without sharing our most serious feelings and thoughts. Without that sharing, relationships remain stuck at the surface of things – trading pleasantries, mutual complaining, story-telling, and having fun. By intensifying our fear of evaluation and in turn our defensiveness, agency makes intimacy more hazardous than it would otherwise be. Because of that fear, we have greater reason to conceal our true thoughts and feelings behind a wall of affability or reserve. No one is allowed in where they might discover how inadequate we really are – or how easy it would be to hurt us.

When both parties are engaged in the same defensive strategy, the wall is doubled, with results bordering on the absurd. Imagine, for example, two men who have known each other for years meeting on the street for the first time in months. Bill is coming out of a depression triggered by the news that his wife is dying of cancer. Jack is a businessman who has just filed for bankruptcy. Bill speaks:

"Well, Jack, how *are* you?"
"Good, how's yourself?"
"Oh, fair to middling. How's the family?"
"Just fine. And yours?"
"Couldn't be better. Helen had some stomach problems, but she's doing better. How's business?"
"Not bad. Certainly nothing to complain about. Hey, how did you like what the Celtics did to the Lakers the other night?"
"Terrific. Those guys really know how to win. Well, I've got to run now. Nice talking to you."
"O.K. Look, drop by some time."
"I will. Thanks. So long."

There can be little satisfaction for either party in such a strained and dishonest exchange. Their mutual fear of being judged has trivialized their relationship to the point where nothing of substance remains. And yet, this is the way many of us operate day after day, year after year. Perhaps we have one close relationship, a spouse with whom we feel free to let our guard down. But even here, communication is often indirect at best. With a highly guarded husband, for example, a wife may have to learn to read between the lines, to infer appreciation from a box of candy and anger from a slammed door. Because it is easy to make the wrong inference, such relationships tend to be precarious. If they last, it is usually because both parties have resigned themselves to silence and withdrawn into their own private worlds.

Giving up the illusion that we are morally responsible for who we are makes it easier to accept ourselves and to share who we are with others. It may also mean, however, that we have fewer emotions to share. If neither party feels any urgent need for support or any need to vent strong feelings or any need to brag about recent achievements, it might appear that little remains to be communicated – at least to those accustomed to viewing relationships in terms of agency. Such a view, however, obscures a more subtle kind of intimacy which is usually overshadowed by agency-driven concerns. It is the intimacy of shared perceptions and ideas. There is no end of things to share - the feel of a summer evening, the expression on a passerby's face, a book, a caress, a piece of music, a psychological insight, a political opinion, a photograph album. There are feelings to be shared as well – sadness at a friend's death, joy at the change of seasons, curiosity about the origins of life, frustration with politics, concern about losing a job – feelings which we may want to share for the sake of sharing itself, rather than for any consolation or validation we might gain by doing so. Without the emotionally charged agenda that agency introduces into relationships, intimacy becomes simpler. Being close still means sharing, but the neediness and urgency are no longer there. What continues to make sharing important is not so much the prospect of relief or reassurance, but a chance to experience the world, including the world of our own thoughts and feelings, through another consciousness.

However highly we value non-romantic love, it is not something that can be made to happen. Striving to be a more loving person is unlikely to succeed for the simple reason that the effort is driven by a concern for oneself. When we make love a spiritual goal, we are driven by thoughts of our own goodness or salvation rather than a genuine feeling for the other. Like every other experience, love represents a spontaneous unfolding of circumstance. The only thing we can do to increase the probability of its arising is to remove the obstacles to it and even that act must arise on its own. One of the primary obstacles to love is a belief in ourselves as creators of our own experience and behavior. Recognizing agency as an illusion empties our minds of defensiveness, pride, guilt, and moral anger. In that emptiness, love has its best chance of arising.

References

1. Quoted in Rougemont, D. de, *Love in the Western World*, New York: Pantheon, 1940 p. 173.
2. Rougemont, D. de, *Love in the Western World*, p. 50.
3. Rougemont, D. de, *Love in the Western World*, p. 152.
4. Rougemont, D. de, *Love in the Western World*, p. 74.
5. Rougemont, D. de, *Love in the Western World*, Bk. VII.
6. Parsons, T., Unpublished lectures, Harvard University, 1955.

JUST WHO DO WE THINK WE ARE?

IDENTITY AS A PSYCHOLOGICAL PROBLEM

Ever since Erik Erikson wrote *Identity: Youth and Crisis*, we have taken it for granted that a clear, coherent sense of self is critical to the normal functioning of the human organism. At the level of what Erikson calls "personal identity," this amounts to little more than an awareness that as persisting body/minds we exist in time and space and that our existence is recognized as such by others. In what he calls "ego identity," however, our awareness of self goes beyond the mere fact of existence. It is the

> . . . awareness of the fact that there is a self-sameness and continuity to the ego's synthesizing methods, the *style of one's individuality*, and that this style coincides with the sameness and continuity of one's *meaning for significant others* in the immediate community.[1] (original italics)

In the context of our own effort to spell out the implications of non-agency, it matters little whether we focus on personal identity or its more individualized counterpart, ego identity. Both forms of perceived self-sameness are presumably critical to our mental health. The question that needs answering is whether either sense of self requires the assumption of an agent/I. The importance of a clear subjective definition of who we are is undisputed. Psychologist Jack Engler describes it as a need for

> ...a cohesive and integrated self..., one that is differentiated from others and has a degree of autonomy.[2]

R.D. Laing goes further when he says that to be healthy the individual must

> ...experience his own being as real, alive, whole; as differentiated from the rest of the world in ordinary circumstances so clearly that his identity and autonomy are never in question; as a continuum in time; as having an inner consistency, substantiality, genuineness, and worth; as spatially co-extensive with the body; and, usually, as having begun in or around birth and liable to extinction with death. He thus has a firm core of ontological security.[3]

Traditionally we have assumed that what differentiates us from the rest of the world "so clearly that [our] identity and autonomy are never in question" is the unique spirit given to us at birth by God. It is this spirit that defines our deepest, most personal self. Behind all the empirical trappings of age, gender, and physical appearance, we are the spiritual creations of a heavenly Being. As souls, we are impervious to the vagaries of cultural conditioning and genetic inheritance. We are non-physical entities, unique, unchanging, and eternal – immune to the ravages of time, disease, and misfortune – even capable of transcending death itself. While most atheists reject the notion of a heavenly Being and immortality, they too define the root self in terms of a non-physical essence – the mental essence of subjectivity. In either case, our identity as separate, unified, boundaried selves is anchored in our existence as inner agents.

Does it follow, then, that we can expect to lose all sense of "selfsameness and continuity" if we decide that the soul/agent is nothing more than a flattering illusion? To the extent that we define ourselves in spiritual terms, the answer is yes. For the orthodox Christian, Muslim or Jew, giving up one's soul implies much more than a loss of identity. It means giving up one's humanity; it means regressing to the level of an animal. But the belief that personal identity is rooted in the soul is not limited to religious fundamentalists. Variations on that belief can be found throughout our culture, even in scientific circles. Witness neurologist Oliver Sacks' observations on a patient suffering from Korsakov's disease. The patient's amnesia was so severe, Sacks tells us, that he could not remember anything for more than a few seconds. The diary which Sacks had asked him to keep was limited to unconnected trivia ("Eggs for breakfast," "Watched ballgame on TV," etc).

> I had wondered, when I first met him, if he was not con-
> demned to a sort of "Humean" froth, a meaningless flutter-
> ing on the surface of life, and whether there was any way
> of transcending the incoherence of his Humean disease.
> Empirical science told me there was not – *but empirical sci-
> ence, empiricism, takes no account of the soul,* no account of
> what constitutes and determines personal being. Perhaps
> there is a philosophical as well as a clinical lesson here: that in
> Korsakov's, or dementia, or other such catastrophes, however
> great the organic damage and Humean dissolution, there
> remains the undiminished possibility of reintegration by
> art, by communion, by touching the human spirit; and this
> can be preserved in what seems at first a hopeless state of
> neurological devastation.[4] (italics added)

Science failed to provide a solution, Sacks would have us believe, because it took no "account of the soul, no account of what constitutes and determines personal being." And what made Sacks so sure of his diagnosis? One day he watched his patient in chapel and was profoundly moved,

> . . . because I saw here an intensity and steadiness of atten-
> tion and concentration that I had never seen before in him or
> conceived him capable of. I watched him kneel and take the
> Sacrament on his tongue, and could not doubt the fullness
> and totality of Communion, the perfect alignment of his spirit
> with the spirit of the Mass . . . There was no forgetting, no
> Korsakov's then . . . for he was not longer at the mercy of a
> faulty and fallible mechanism . . . but was absorbed in an act . . .
> which carried feeling and meaning in an organic continuity
> and unity . . . so seamless it could not permit any break.[5]

Like Sacks, we might attribute the patient's temporary remission to the operation of a soul which awakened only in a moment of spiritual concentration – or, taking our cue from Ockham ("Entities are not to be multiplied beyond necessity"), we can ascribe the remission more simply to the patient's heightened interest in his surroundings. What allowed him to regain a sense of continuity was his elevated state of arousal. We might go on to speculate that if he were moved deeply by a sunset, baseball game, or ballet, he might reveal a similar ability to concentrate. From a naturalistic perspective it seems both arbitrary and unnecessary to invoke a spiritual entity to explain changes in experience and behavior when there are simpler explanations already at hand.

Most contemporary psychologists and psychiatrists who write about identity avoid any reference to the soul. They take it for granted that we construct and change our identity according to gender, physical matura-tion, learned values and the vicissitudes of social contact. At the heart of the process is the ability to "step outside" of oneself and take the role of what G.H. Mead called "the generalized other." From that vantage point, the individual conceptualizes and evaluates himself. As Erikson describes it,

> . . . identity formation employs a process of simultaneous reflection and observation . . . by which the individual judges himself in the light of what he perceives to be the way in which others judge him in comparison to themselves and to a typology significant to them . . . [6]

Identity arises out of a process in which we judge ourselves through the eyes of others. But the process does not end with judging. Selfsameness re-quires the organizing of diverse and sometimes conflicting desires and values into a unified self-concept that brings consistency to our choices. Without a stable picture of who we are and who we want to be, we would find decisions of any complexity impossible to make. While this integrated concept of self leaves room for variation in mood, interest, and behavioral style – even for "sub-personalities," it neither requires nor permits the splitting of body/mind into independent identities.

Selfsameness gives structure and consistency to our choices but it does not imply that the self with which we identify is an entity existing apart from the perceptions, thoughts, and actions of which it is composed. The self is a concept, an abstract mental picture of a complex network of interlock-ing processes. Both the concept and the processes from which it has been abstracted arise spontaneously out of the interplay between organism and environment. For any given individual we can account for the arising of a unique identity without positing the existence of either a causal agent serving as the creator of that identity or an autonomous, substantive entity to which the identity refers.

The problem with contemporary developmental psychology lies not so much in anchoring personal identity to an eternal soul but in conceptualizing the self as an emergent entity capable of exercising autonomous power over experience and behavior. The error lies in inferring that if the organism is capable of thinking about its own thinking or perceiving the way it perceives, it must be a subject distinct from the experience it is "having." As we saw in chapter six, philosopher Daniel Dennett was led into a similar trap by his eagerness to demonstrate the feasibility of a morally responsible "self-made self." Developmental psychologists succumb to the same temptation when they refer to the evolution of a

> . . . self which maintains a coherence across a shared psychological space and so achieves an identity. This authority – sense of self, self-dependence, self-ownership – is its hallmark. In moving from "I am my relationships" to "I have relationships," there is now somebody who is doing this having, the new I, who, in coordinating or reflecting upon mutuality, brings into being a kind of psychic institution.[7]

Contrary to what Robert Kegan would have us believe, what has emerged is not a new entity which exercises control over "its" experiences but a new set of thoughts and feelings which take other thoughts and feelings as their object. Coordinating relationships and reflecting upon mutuality are still processes arising spontaneously out of genetic and environmental conditions. While they indicate an advanced level of sophistication and reflexive awareness, they do not imply the existence of an agent/self that has either made them happen or is engaged in having them. The only self to evolve is that which *consists* of new ways of thinking, feeling, and acting. The self which is thought to emerge *out* of experience and reflect back upon it is an illusion.

IDENTITY AS A PHILOSOPHICAL PROBLEM

Despite their insistence on reifying the self as agent, psychologists like Erikson, Piaget, and Kegan have helped to clarify the process of self-identification by reminding us that the way we define ourselves is constantly changing as we pass from infancy through childhood into adolescence and adulthood.

From the developmentalist's perspective, each stage of life presents a set of perceptual, cognitive, and emotional problems to which the stage-specific self represents a temporary adaptation. It should be added that the evolutionary process continues *within* each stage as well – although less dramatically so. Change may be slow at some times, rapid at others, but the process of changing in response to maturational or environmental circumstances is constant throughout life. Contrary to what our belief in souls would suggest, the self is not an entity that remains fixed from birth to death but rather a constantly evolving system of physical and mental processes.

That way of conceptualizing ourselves, however, raises some perplexing philosophical questions. If *I* am not an enduring soul/agent but a system of interlocking processes arising here right now, am I the same person as the one called Paul Breer who went to the store yesterday? Does it make sense to say that *I* was born in 1930? Do *I* even have a future?

If I identify myself as simply that which is arising here at this very moment, the answer to those questions must be no. But it is unrealistic for me to define myself that narrowly. It makes more sense for me to think of myself as a series of overlapping constellations of body/mind stretching backward and forward in time from this present moment. All the constellations in the series are part of the continuing person, Paul Breer, although they are not equally central to the person I perceive myself to be now. Those constellations that are closest to the present seem much more *me* than those I remember from twenty years ago or those I anticipate arising twenty years from now. Viewing myself this way is a bit like standing at the peak of a bell-shaped curve looking one way into the past and another into the future. As the curve drops away in both directions from my central point of awareness, the area under the curve (the area I define as *me*) diminishes. At the farthest points of the curve (the distant past and future) that area of *me-ness* vanishes altogether. It remains true, however, that while I have little hesitation in identifying points close to the present as *me* and those remote from the present as *not-me*, I cannot identify a specific point along that curve where the constellations become so alien that they stop being *me*.

Viewing myself as a series of body/mind constellations (symbolized by the bell-shaped curve) generates feelings that differ sharply from those I experience when I view myself as an unchanging soul (represented by a straight line starting at birth and ending either at death or extending into eternity). The way I define myself affects my feelings about past and future versions of the person called Paul Breer. It shapes my feelings about personal history, commitments, desert, security, and death. Such an identity influences my present experience and behavior through its impact on the meaning I assign to past or future events. Events (such as setting personal goals or making promises to friends) which I consider to be part of *me* have the power to alter my feelings and actions. Similar events that have arisen in a body/mind I no longer consider to be *me*, or which may someday arise in a body/mind I do not now identify with, have no such power over what I feel and do.

PB 1989 AND PB 1948

Consider the relationship between Paul Breer as he exists in 1989 and the Paul Breers of 1948 and 2000. From the perspective of PB 1989, PB 1948 seems almost like another being. For one thing there is the dramatic difference in looks, a difference so great that PB 1948's high school sweetheart failed to recognize PB 1989 at a recent reunion. There is also the matter of personality, values, and tastes. PB 1948 was 18 years old, a freshman at Harvard College, extremely ambitious, intent on making his name and fortune in the corporate world. Fresh from a life of basketball, fraternities, poker, and pop music, he was oblivious to the intellectual and aesthetic values that were to become central in the lives of later PB's. Most of his thoughts were about success – getting good grades, impressing his roommates, getting elected to the Jubilee Committee (which he didn't). Emotionally he was a callous adolescent. Intellectually he was unborn.

How does PB 1989 know all of this? Because he has direct memories of PB 1948 – as distinct from indirect memories that PB 1948's roommates might now have. PB 1989 remembers what it felt like to be PB 1948 – at least he has recollections of that experience which he believes to be similar to what PB 1948 actually experienced. Despite their faded, distorted, and highly selective quality, those memories give PB 1989 a unique tie to PB 1948. By virtue of those memories, PB 1948 remains a part of what PB 1989 considers his self. In the context of PB 1989's full identity, however, the tie with PB 1948 is no more than a peripheral one – comparable in genealogical terms to his relationship with a great nephew or second cousin once removed.

PB 1989's view of himself as a temporary cluster of body/mind only partially related to past and future clusters has the effect of weakening his connection with PB 1948 and all other PB's. One of the major effects of that weakening is that PB 1989 spends far less time than previous PB's in reviewing his past. Reflecting on "My Life" has become less interesting for PB 1989 than it was for his predecessors for two different reasons. For one thing, there is no single self for him to reflect upon, no essential *PB* that has endured years of waxing and waning fortune. Without a soul to tie all the different *PB's* together, he is less likely to look back with awe at how far *he* has come – or shudder at how far *he* has fallen. He has less of a history to consider, explain, justify, take pride in, or feel guilty about. Without a soul, the self that really matters encompasses a briefer span of time and includes fewer experiences.

Giving up my belief in agency also means that there is no agent/I that can be held causally responsible for what has happened *here*. If I am not the cause of my own experience and behavior, I am less likely to waste time applauding myself for my uncanny wisdom or berating myself for "roads not taken." Defining myself as a constantly changing constellation of body, thoughts, and actions draws attention away from me as author and thus away from the history of successes and failures which I supposedly have created. Energy that formerly went into evaluating what I have done with my life and what I hope to make of it in years to come pours instead into a heightened awareness of what is arising here right now. Emotionally, the effect is less regret, guilt, pride, and self-satisfaction – and more peace of mind.

The change in identity generated by giving up the agency illusion has implications for all thoughts and feelings that involve a connection between two temporally separated constellations of the same person. Giving up the illusion of a single, enduring PB, for example, has the effect of weakening the hold of any one PB's commitment on all later PB's. To see that concretely, assume for the moment that ambitious, corporation-bound PB 1948 has promised his dying father to carry on the family business. Assume further that by the time PB 1952 receives his A.B., his zest for making money has been replaced by a love for music and books. Is PB 1952 obligated to fulfill a commitment made by a PB whose values and preferences were very different from his own? What about PB 1962 or PB 1989 whose priorities are even further removed from PB 1948's? Intuitively, we are inclined to absolve PB 1989 of responsibility for a promise made forty-one years ago, but where do we draw the line? If there is no soul or agent linking PB 1948 to later PB's, are we justified in holding *any* PB responsible for PB 1948's commitment to his father?

There would appear to be no non-arbitrary way of deciding at what point a commitment is no longer binding. In fiscal matters, we simply assume that a legally liable person endures throughout a lifetime. If PB 1948 borrowed money from the bank to finish college, *all* PB's (and their heirs) would be legally responsible for paying that money back. In money matters, perhaps, it is obvious that the social order would crumble if we did not agree that all PB's constitute an enduring if changeable person. Criminal matters are less clear. If PB 1948 had committed a felony which remained unsolved until 1989, would we automatically (the statute of limitations notwithstanding) hold PB 1989 responsible for that crime? It might depend on how heinous the crime was. It might also depend on our perception of how different the two PB's were. Our moral wrath and desire to punish PB 1989 could be weakened, for example, by the discovery that he is a law-abiding, mild-mannered recluse, quite unlike his profligate namesake of forty-one years ago. Despite our belief in an enduring soul and a legal system founded on that belief, we intuitively acknowledge that people sometimes change so radically that it is no longer appropriate to treat them as the same sort of person they once were.

Non-agency formalizes that intuition by anchoring it to a new way of viewing identity. Without the veil of "soul-sameness" to obscure the flux of human existence, each of us is revealed as a series of changing body/mind "configurations," no one of which constitutes our *real* self. Defining ourselves as constellations in flux rather than permanent souls affects the way we view positional responsibility. While non-agency stops short of providing specific answers to questions of criminal responsibility (Is PB 1989 responsible for PB 1948's felony?), it invites us to approach such questions with an open mind. At the very least, it raises the possibility that we may not be positionally responsible for acts that have arisen in a previous body/mind which is continuous with but not qualitatively identical to the present one.

PB 1989 AND PB 2000

If PB 1989 turns his attention to the future, he is faced with a different dilemma. Should he put money into a pension or a savings account so that PB 2000 (if there should be one) won't have to go hungry in his old age? As he confronts that question, PB 1989 is aware of the possibility that PB 2000 will prove to be as different from him as he is from PB 1948. PB 2000 may turn out, for example, to be a fully domesticated old man who is only too happy to give up pondering the universe for the pleasures of indulging his grandchildren. From PB 1989's non-agency perspective, the question is this: should I set aside thousands of dollars for the upkeep of such a changed and potentially alien self or spend it now on me? There is more at issue here than whether or not to delay gratification (Should I spend the money now or save it for the time when I retire?). The issue of *when* to seek gratification assumes that there is but a single self to be gratified, whether that experience occurs now or later. Having already given up his belief in "soulsameness," PB 1989 is addressing the more elusive question of what is implied in identifying himself as a series of different but connected body/mind constellations. He is asking: Will PB 2000 be the same sort of person as me? How much overlap is there between me and the person who will be PB 2000? Is there enough overlap to warrant putting money in the bank now for his/our benefit?

Since I *am* PB 1989, I can answer that question directly. Yes, there is enough overlap. I feel enough physical and psychological continuity with PB 2000 to make some sacrifices on his/our behalf. This should not be surprising since there is only an eleven year difference in age. PB 2000 will certainly be grayer and more wrinkled than I am but not so different that if I saw him now I would fail to recognize him as me. While his interests may be quite different from mine, he will almost certainly have *some* of my interests. Unless he suffers from some kind of dementia, he will also have many memories of me – as well as other PB's like PB 1948 of whom I too have memories. All in all, it seems reasonable to assume that if anyone is going to look out for PB 2000's welfare, it should be me. Moreover, since PB's 1990, 1991, 1992 etc. will probably identify even more closely with PB 2000 than I do, there is good reason to believe that I will not have to shoulder this responsibility alone.

What about commitments to other people? If we are not eternal souls but evolving constellations of tissue, thought, and action, what does it mean for us to commit ourselves to another person "until death do us part?" What does it mean, for example, for PB 1955 to stand up in church and commit himself to caring for QZ 1955 for the rest of his life? Given the possibility of personality change in both PB and QZ, it could be argued that it means little or nothing at all. PB 1955 is in no position to know how future PB's are going to feel about future QZ's. All he can be sure of is that *he* loves QZ 1955 and wants to be an integral part of *her* existence. Does he really have the right, we might ask, to commit all future PB's to caring for all future QZ's?

All commitments based on emotional attachment are compromised by the possibility of change. We continue to make them anyway because we assume that the person taking the vow and the person on whom that vow is meant to be binding will remain more or less the same. That assumption, in turn, is grounded in the belief that, despite surface changes in body and personality, we retain the same fundamental essence throughout life. But what if that "essence" is an illusion? What if the spiritual thread we count on to unite our empirical selves is no more real than the collective soul our Indian forbears believed to unite all buffalo?

It does not follow that, without that thread, we are relieved of all commitments. Learning to view ourselves in non-agency terms does, however, call into question the wisdom of making long-term promises in the name of future selves whose values may be very different from our own. We do not remain the same body/minds from year to year. While the short-run differences are often minor, they are additive and eventually grow to the point where commitments made by one self are often perceived as alien and no longer binding by subsequent selves. At that point, without a soul to unite our disparate selves, the very notion of commitment may break down altogether and lose its power to shape behavior.

Non-agency and Death

In exploring the impact of non-agency on our attitude toward death, it is useful to distinguish between fear of losses that attend death and fear of non-being itself (". . . fears of what death brings rather than fears of being dead").[8] My fear that I will never get to finish this book or go hiking in Nepal or compose music on a synthesizer is different from my fear of extinction. For one thing, I don't have to die to be deprived of one or more of those valued experiences. It could happen, for example, if I become senile or arthritic or if I am banished to an island without electricity. The two fears are different as well in that my present fear of losing out on future satisfactions is rational and consistent with my view of myself as a series of body-mind constellations extending over a period of time ordinarily counted in years. I can legitimately fear the loss of future activities like writing, hiking, or composing because the desire to do those things is already part of who I am and is likely to continue. My 1989 concept of myself includes PB's extending both backwards in time through memory and forward in time through intention. The possible loss of PB 1995's chance to go hiking in Nepal because of deteriorating health or death is *my* loss just as PB 1986's breaking up with a close friend remains *my* loss. As PB 1989, I can be harmed by both previous and anticipated losses to the extent that they frustrate my current desires.

It is not rational and consistent with my self-concept, however, for me to fear what is going to happen after I die. As Epicurus argued 2500 years ago, the fear of extinction is irrational in that it assumes a subject capable of experiencing its own non-being.

> So death, the most terrifying of ills, is nothing to us, since so long
> as we exist, death is not with us; but when death comes, then

we do not exist. It does not then concern either the living or the dead, since for the former it is not, and the latter are no more.[9]

The series of PB's of which this present self is a part ends with the death of the last PB body/mind. Beyond that point there will be no PB's to experience either the loss of goods attendant upon death or death itself. It would be foolish, then, for me or any subsequent PB's, to worry about what it will be like being dead. As Rorty puts it, "While one can regret and sometimes fear that there will be a time when one will not have whatever the goods of life may be, one cannot regret that one will be harmed by not having them after one is dead."[10] Rorty goes on to suggest that the fear of "being dead" persists despite its irrationality because it serves to make us more conscious of danger and, thus, more likely to avoid life-threatening situations.

The question before us is this: what does giving up the illusion of agency imply for our attitude toward death. From what I have said thus far, it would seem to follow that if non-agency has any effect it all, it is limited to allaying our fear of non-being rather than our fear of the losses attendant upon death. In my own personal experience, however, I am aware that both fears have abated with the giving up of a belief in agency. Even though it is logically possible for a believer in non-agency to fear losing out on life's goods, giving up agency appears to diminish that fear as well as the fear of extinction itself. Non-agency makes all kinds of acceptance easier. My willingness to accept the possibility of not finishing any of my current projects is part of a greater readiness to accept whatever arises here. While I still want to finish them all or at least experience the joy of working on them, much of the old urgency is gone. There are very few things left that I "have to" do. When I saw myself as the causal agent behind these projects, I felt more proprietary about them and more alarmed at the possibility that I might not finish them. Now that I am beginning to view all ideas, insights, and bursts of energy as gifts of circumstance, I find it less painful to acknowledge that those gifts may be withdrawn at any time.

The lessening of my fear of extinction seems even more directly related to a change of beliefs about agency. There was a time not too many years ago when I simply could not comprehend death. I could not grasp the idea that something as precious as human consciousness could exist for years – loving, thinking, creating new meaning and beauty – and then vanish forever. It didn't matter whether it was the death of people I had known personally or those I knew only by their music or writings. What seems different today is the meaning I ascribe to death. I no longer view *me* or *you* as all-or-nothing entities. I see us rather as constantly evolving configurations of body/mind that die and are reborn every moment. I am aware that the boundaries I use to define myself are a matter of personal choice and are influenced by my need for a stable identity. I am aware that in conceptualizing myself as a series of past, present and future PB's, I am glossing over the fact that each individual constellation making up that identity constitutes a unique, temporary configuration of flesh, thought, and behavior which lasts for but a moment before giving way to a slightly different configuration.

This is very different from thinking of myself as a soul or spiritual agent that has remained unchanged from conception or birth. When I consider the question of how this change in self-concept has affected my fear of non-being, the first thing to come to mind is that I am already familiar with a certain kind of death. As I said earlier, the ambitious, corporate-bound PB 1948 "died" some time ago. PB 1955, the one who rashly committed himself to caring for QZ 1955 forever, can be considered dead for all practical purposes. Also gone are PB 1960-66 the college professor, PB 1967 the nature poet, PB 1969-74 the Zen novice, and PB 1975-84 the psychotherapist. The awareness that so many PB's have already passed away makes the prospect of my own non-being less frightening. Unlike agents which constitute all-or-nothing entities and whose extinction is total and final, body/mind constellations come and go. Viewing myself as a series of such constellations makes it easier to accept my finitude. It also makes it easier for me to take in the wisdom of Epicurus' insight that there will be no *I* around to experience my own non-being.

I am not alone in feeling this way. English philosopher Derek Parfit claims that giving up his belief in agency (he calls it ego) has dramatically altered the way he thinks about his own death. In *Reasons and Persons*, tells us that viewing himself as a soul left him feeling imprisoned.

> My life seemed like a glass tunnel, through which I was moving faster every year, and at the end of which there was darkness. When I changed my view, the walls of my glass tunnel disappeared. I now live in the open air.[11]

The author goes on to explain how redefining himself in non-agency terms changed his attitude toward death.

> When I believed the Non-Reductionist View [when I believed in agency], I also cared more about my inevitable

death. After my death, there will be no one living who will be me. I can now redescribe the fact. *Though there will later be many experiences, none of these experiences will be connected to my present experiences by chains of such direct connections as those involved in experience-memory, or in the carrying out of an earlier intention.* Some of these future experiences may be related to my present experiences in less direct ways. There will later be some memories about my life. And there may later be thoughts that are influenced by mine, or things done as the result of my advice. My death will break the more direct relations between my present experiences and future experiences, but it will not break various other relations. This is all there is to the fact that there will be no one living who will be me. Now that I have seen this, my death seems to me less bad.[12] (italics added).

According to Parfit, if I die in 2000, all it means is that there will be no more experiences after that which are connected through memory to what I am experiencing now or what PB 1948 experienced forty-one years ago. This is very different from saying that as of 2000 *I* as soul/agent will no longer exist, a statement which assumes that "continued existence is a deep further fact, distinct from physical and psychological continuity, and a fact that must be all-or-nothing." Parfit would agree that our delusion lies in making too much of ourselves to begin with. We are not essences that span a lifetime and die in one fell swoop. We are overlapping links in a chain of feeling, thinking, and breathing; as such, we give way to new links at every moment. The physical death of the last PB in this chain does not involve the death of all previous PB's – a final inferno in which every PB that ever lived is consumed. If I, PB 1989, were to die right now, the only thing to perish (as far as I am concerned) would be the series of PB's I presently include in my definition of who I am. While this constellation of flesh, thought, and action – this self – includes memories of recent PB's and plans for future PB's (particularly those of the next few years), it is only tenuously connected with earlier PB's. Approaching extinction from this viewpoint – the viewpoint of my present self rather than that of all PB's – gives me less to fear for the simple reason that there is less of me to die. The earlier PB's have already passed away.

The way I define myself also affects my fear of death through what it implies about my ties to the rest of the world. As an *eternal* soul, I have little to fear from death other than divine judgment and the temporary loss of my body. My true home is in heaven with God and the angels. As a free but *mortal* agent, however, I am cut off from the rest of the world; I am an uncaused cause, a spiritual entity removed from the chain of cause and effect that connects all material things. Death represents the obliteration of everything *I* am – the end of the unchanging, unchangeable essence that from birth I have taken to be *me*. The price of my semi-divinity is that I am isolated from everything else on earth. As an unmoved mover, I have no ancestors, no descendants. I am a spiritual entity whose boundaries prevent me from establishing a connection with anything in the physical world.

As a constellation of body, feelings, and behavior, on the other hand, I am intimately connected to the rest of the world through cause and effect. I am a rivulet in a larger stream of events, a stream that includes parents, children, teachers, students, clients, friends, the New England weather, twentieth century American culture – everything that has directly or indirectly shaped my life or been shaped by it. As an aspect of that larger stream, my existence changes drastically with the death of this body-mind but does not end completely. I continue on so long as the stream lasts. While I remain PB 1989 on a personal level, it is this stream of events linked by cause and effect with which I ultimately identify. That identification arouses diffuse feelings of caring for all that has evolved over the past fifteen billion years and all that is yet to come. In one sense, I *am* all of it. Knowing that now makes my own immediate physical death less "terminal." Some part of me has always been here and will continue to be here as long as a single atom of hydrogen exists.

B.F. Skinner reminds us that the threat of non-being is most acute for the individual who believes in free agency and identifies himself exclusively with it.

> One of the great problems of individualism, seldom recognized as such, is death – the inescapable fate of the individual, the final assault on freedom and dignity . . . Some religions have made death more important by picturing a future existence in heaven or hell, but the individualist has a special reason to fear death, engineered not by a religion but by the literatures of freedom and dignity. It is the prospect of personal annihilation. The individualist can find no solace in reflecting upon any contribution which will survive him. He has refused to act for the good of others and is therefore not

reinforced by the fact that others whom he has helped will outlive him. He has refused to be concerned for the survival of his culture and is not reinforced by the fact that the culture will long survive him. In the defense of his own freedom and dignity he has denied the contributions of the past and must therefore relinquish all claim upon the future.[13]

The heart of Skinner's argument against individualism and the myth of "the autonomous man" can be found in the last sentence. If we are free souls, our acts do not arise out of antecedent conditions but out of individual will. As causally autonomous agents, we owe the past nothing. For that very reason we cannot expect future souls who will be equally free to be indebted to us. By denying the contributions of the past, Skinner is saying, we forfeit our ability to influence the future. And without the capacity to influence those who come after us, we are forced to confront death as total extinction. By cutting us off from both past and future, free agency gives physical death a finality it otherwise would not have. When we give up the illusion of causal freedom, we reaffirm our connection with the stream of events from which we as individual body/minds arise and to which we ultimately return. It is that feeling of connectedness that makes our death as individuals easier to accept.

REFERENCES

1. Erikson, E., *Identity: Youth and Crisis*, New York: W.W. Norton, 1968, p. 50.
2. Wilbur, K., Engler, J., & Brown D., *Transformations of Consciousness*, Boston: Shambhala, 1986, p. 39.
3. Laing, R.D., *The Divided Self*, New York: Pantheon Books, 1960, p. 43.
4. Sacks, O., *The Man Who Mistook His Wife for a Hat*, New York: Harper and Row, 1970, pp. 35-39.
5. Sacks, O., *The Man Who Mistook His Wife for a Hat*, p. 37.
6. Erikson, E., *Identity: Youth and Crisis*, p. 22.
7. Kegan, R., *The Evolving Self*, Cambridge: Harvard University Press, 1982, p. 100.
8. Rorty, A., "Fearing Death," *Philosophy*, 58, 1983, pp. 175-188.
9. Epicurus, "Letter to Menoeceus," in Bailey, C., *Epicurus*, Oxford: Clarendon Press, 1926, p. 85.
10. Rorty, A., "Fearing Death," p. 175.
11. Parfit, D., *Reasons and Persons*, Oxford: Clarendon Press, 1984, p. 281.
12. Parfit, D., *Reasons and Persons*, p. 281.
13. Skinner, B.F., *Beyond Freedom and Dignity*, New York: Ballantine Books, 1971, p. 201.

DISPELLING
THE FREE WILL
ILLUSION

A STRATEGY FOR GIVING UP THE GHOST

In the first chapter I quoted a passage from Marvin Minsky's *Society of Mind* in which the author grants that free agency is only an illusion, but defends its continued acceptance on the grounds that our social stability and mental peace require it.

> No matter that the physical world provides no room for freedom of will: that concept is essential to our models of the mental realm. Too much of our psychology is based on it for us to ever give it up. We're virtually forced to maintain that belief, even though we know it's false – except, of course, when we're inspired to find the flaws in *all* our beliefs, whatever may be the consequence to cheerfulness and mental peace.[1] (original italics)

Before we can give up our belief in free agency, Minsky argues, we must wait until we are inspired to expose all of our illusions. Apparently we have not yet reached that point. Despite three centuries of scientific thinking, we are still not ready to look at the world and ourselves objectively. According to Minsky, a scientist himself, the psychic consequences of attempting to live without illusion are simply too dire to contemplate.

If the arguments presented here are valid, however, giving up the illusion of agency is more likely to enhance than detract from our "cheerfulness and mental peace." In fact, the most striking of all the changes that can be expected to follow from giving up agency is a growing serenity and "ease of heart." This raises the possibility that the negative consequences of giving up other illusions have been similarly exaggerated – and the gains similarly underestimated. Consider, for example, what some believe to be one of our most obvious illusions – the illusion that moral codes are divinely inspired. Will giving up that belief lead to social chaos, as our religious leaders suggest? My own guess is that, if it leads to anything at all, it will be a greater tolerance for cultural differences – and thus a greater stability in relationships among nations.

If we were to accept Minsky's challenge to identify the flaws in *all* of our beliefs, whatever the consequences, we could not choose a more strategic place to begin our search than with the illusion of free agency. There are few other cultural premises that so directly affect the way we feel and act. It has been the purpose of this book to trace the impact of that belief on our everyday experience and, in the process, to document how much might be gained by giving it up. Assuming that a desire to exorcise the ghost of agency has arisen, what remains to be explored is the question of how to do it. It is the purpose of this final chapter to explain and illustrate the strategy that has arisen *here* over the past eight years.

In the long run, the most effective way to eliminate agency from our culture is to stop planting the illusion in our children. That is a process which, once begun, will take many generations to complete. In the meantime, we need a strategy for helping adults to *change* what they believe. Since all beliefs arise on their own, you may question whether a deliberate strategy to change what we believe is appropriate or even feasible. Does it make sense, you might ask, to draw up a plan for altering our belief in agency if all our beliefs – including changes in those beliefs – are determined by circumstance?

That question implies that, once we give up our belief in agency, all intention to change will stop arising. There is no reason why it should. While I accept the fact that all my future behavior will be determined by some interplay of genes and environment (or chance), my intention to change remains meaningful to me for the simple reason that it has a potentially critical role to play in that causal chain. At the moment an intention arises, I have no way of knowing how important it will eventually prove to be. As long as I am convinced that it *could* be part of a causal chain leading to desired outcomes, I will continue to experience it as meaningful.

As deliberate as the decision to embark on a course of self-change might appear, there is no need to assume the presence of an agent-supervisor at any step along the way. To see how such a sequence might unfold on its own, imagine that at a dinner party you meet someone who seems free of the anxiety you have experienced for years; that meeting triggers the thought that you could be free of tension yourself; a few days later, the decision arises (out of that realization) to enter a book store where you see a book called *The Spontaneous Self*; a combination of having been rewarded in the past for buying books and being interested now in finding something to help you change gives rise to a decision to buy the book; the concept of non-agency espoused in the book initiates a train of thoughts about the self-arising nature of all experience; over subsequent weeks, those thoughts give rise to a new interpretation of events at work and at home; as a result of that shift in perspective, events which previously aroused anxiety stop doing so.

There are many different decisions required in this process, but whether or not they arise is a function of circumstance. The process flows automatically from decision to decision without any agent standing outside the stream deciding whether or not to decide. The self-arising principle applies to deliberate choices as well as impulsive ones. A carefully thought out decision to embark on a program designed to implement the concept of non-agency is just as determined as the last-minute decision to go to a dinner party. Such decisions arise not because an uncaused causal agent decides to make them arise, but because genetic and environmental conditions happen to be ripe for their arising.

A Strategy For Dispelling the Illusion of Agency

Our goal is to replace a belief in agency with a belief in non-agency. The strategy involves two basic steps: first, the assimilation of arguments and evidence in favor of non-agency and, secondly, the use of emotions to identify situations where the belief in agency continues to operate. We should be aware before starting that the process of uprooting a belief planted early in childhood is bound to be a gradual one. The more central the belief, the longer that process is likely to take. In the case of agency, the uprooting process is made even more difficult by the fact that, in Western culture, the belief is nearly universal. It is a process, nevertheless, that builds momentum and, when practiced with patience, leads ultimately to a transformation of feelings and behavior.

The process of dispelling a belief in agency resembles a military invasion in which troops land on an enemy shore, establish a beachhead, and proceed to take the nearest city street by street. Resistance to that "invasion" is not only deeply entrenched in the individual psyche, but supported by a vast array of cultural institutions including schools, churches, the media, and the language we speak. That resistance, however, can be used to good advantage. Once we learn to read its signs, it can tell us where the enemy is located; it can tell us, in other words, where the illusion of agency continues to operate. That illusion can be counted on to show itself in a variety of ways – sometimes in behavior, sometimes in thought, but particularly in emotions. The basic strategy for eliminating agency from our thinking consists of looking for such signs of resistance and then using them, wherever found, to advance our belief in non-agency.

The very first step in that strategy is to repeat the experiment described in chapter three in which you searched your images, thoughts, and decisions for evidence of an agent/I. Continue repeating that experiment until you either find an agent (in which case notify me immediately) or conclude, as did Hume, that there is no one there. There can be no advancing until you have given whole-hearted intellectual assent to non-agency. This is the beachhead. Securing that beachhead is a rational process that can be facilitated by reading and talking to like-minded friends. Although it is unlikely by itself to change your life noticeably, it is the step that makes all subsequent steps possible.

Once you are at least partially convinced of non-agency, the next step is to extend that belief into all concrete aspects of your life. Given the strength of the resistance, that extension cannot be expected to progress automatically. At the outset you should not be surprised to find yourself assenting intellectually to non-agency while continuing to act as if agency were still true. My own experience suggests that non-agency sinks in not only slowly but unevenly, a fact of life which, at least in the short run, may produce anomalies puzzling both to you and your acquaintances. You may find, for example, that, while you have become less defensive about criticism at work, you remain as sensitive as ever to comments about your cooking. Such temporary disparities are likely to arise from idiosyncratic factors in your history, as well as unevenness in the depth of your awareness of what non-agency implies for different life situations.

The key to extending non-agency to all of your behavior is to identify those areas where the agent/I continues to operate. A belief in agency reveals itself in many ways: bragging, moral blaming, defensive anger, straining, guilt, jealousy, vindictiveness and so on. While a wide variety of thoughts, feelings, and actions show the influence of agency, emotions are usually easier to work with than other phenomena. It is easier for most people, for example, to identify what they are feeling (e.g., anger, anxiety) than what they are doing (e.g., defending, straining), although the two tend to arise and disappear at approximately the same time. In my own experience, emotions represent the clearest and most easily identified symptoms of agency that we have.

There are five basic emotions that can be taken as symptomatic of a belief in agency: anger, anxiety, sadness, pride, and guilt. This does not mean that they *always* indicate the presence of agency or that they arise only in conjunction with a belief in agency. It is part of the changing process, in fact, to learn how to differentiate emotional reactions that are shaped by agency from those which are not. I will assume at the outset, however, that agency is usually present to some degree when we experience one of those five emotions. Since these five are among the most common of human feelings, it follows that giving up agency carries the potential for transforming our emotional lives.

Step two has three parts. It starts with (a) an awareness that you are feeling angry, anxious, sad, proud, or guilty. Upon becoming aware of that feeling, you conduct a test (b) to determine whether or not agency is implicated. The test consists of translating the precipitating event into non-agency language. A significant reduction in emotion as a result of that translation can be taken as a sign that a belief in agency is involved. Once you are convinced that you have identified an area in which agency is operating, you proceed (c) to reinterpret the situation, assigning causal efficacy to circumstance rather than agency.

Awareness needs no special comment. Translation and reinterpretation are unique enough, however, to warrant further explanation. The purpose of translating events into a language devoid of agency is to see if changing our assumptions has the effect of changing our feelings. Conventional language repeatedly confirms the illusion of an inner entity that exercises causal autonomy over experience. The primary culprit is the personal pronoun. While it is theoretically possible to use the pronoun *I* in a strictly positional sense (i.e., as a way of referring to a particular constellation of body/mind), we ordinarily use it to mean both the body/mind *and* the agent presumed to dwell within that body/mind. The only way to form sentences without any reference to agency, then, is to adopt a syntax devoid of personal pronouns altogether.

The simplest way to speak of our experience without any suggestion of agency is to refer to events as *arising here*. In its entirety, translation into non-agency terms involves three changes: replacing the pronoun *I* with the adverb *here*, making each thought, feeling, or action the subject rather than the object of the sentence, and using some form of the verb *to arise* to indicate that the event is happening on its own. Thus, "I gave a terrible speech" gets translated as "A terrible speech arose here." The same logic applies to translating someone else's behavior into non-agency terms. For "here" we simply substitute "there." For example, "You said some very cruel things" becomes "Some very cruel things arose there."

If translating the event into non-agency terms brings about a noticeable change of feeling, we can infer that the situation requires reinterpreting. By reinterpretation I mean adopting a new perspective, a new way of understanding the same events. For someone who has already given intellectual assent to non-agency and is interested in expanding that belief, this means re-examining the situation in terms of a cognitive model which assigns causal power to circumstance. To re-examine the situation means to interpret the thoughts and actions making up that situation as effects of other events rather than as expressions of free will. It means extending a new and tentative assumption about life to a situation which has either never been examined from the perspective of non-agency or which has thus far managed to resist reinterpretation.

The purpose of the strategy is to deepen our belief in non-agency. It uses emotions for detecting when and where we are still acting as if our old belief in agency were true and then proceeds to a reinterpretation of those situations in the light of our new belief. Each situation that is successfully reinterpreted in this fashion represents a step toward eliminating agency from our thinking and extinguishing those emotions which tend to be associated with that belief. A gradual decline in anger, anxiety, sadness, pride, and guilt can, in fact, be taken as primary evidence of a shift away from an agency-inspired view of the world.

Throughout the process, of course, our behavior changes along with our emotions. Bragging, moral blaming, defending, straining, and self-punishing are just as indicative of a belief in agency as their emotional counterparts and can be expected to decline at the same time. If I have given priority to emotions in this strategy, it is only because I find emotions more reliable than actions for detecting the influence of agency. A few examples from each of the five domains will illustrate how well emotions lend themselves to the detection process.

Let us assume at the outset that you have read the previous chapters and have spent some time seriously considering the idea that all experience arises out of circumstance unaided by agency, an idea for which you have repeatedly found evidence in the workings of your own mind. At one level you are already convinced that the agent/I is an illusion and yet you continue to feel and act as if it were real. The determination arises within you to dispel the illusion altogether. You begin looking around for signs of where in your experiential world a belief in agency still seems to be functioning. As per instructions, you are especially mindful of your emotions – particularly anger, anxiety, sadness, pride, and guilt. You are aware that the recognition and reinterpretation process will have to be repeated many times before the illusion of agency begins to fade. This does not daunt you. The prospect of breaking free of agency and all its emotional constraints arouses your eagerness to begin.

ANGER

What makes anger so useful in detecting the presence of agency is the diversity of situations in which it can be expected to arise. It arises when we blame others for behaving offensively; it arises when we blame ourselves for errors and mistakes in judgment; it arises when we defend ourselves against moral blaming, when we strain to make good things happen, when we strain to prevent bad things from happening, and when we refuse to accept that which has already happened. It remains true, of course, that anger arises out of frustration. In tying anger to agency, I am simply suggesting that the degree to which we find events frustrating depends on the way we interpret them. Our belief in agency affects our level of frustration and, in turn, our anger by way of its effect on the meaning we attach to events.

To see how anger can be used to detect the presence of agency, imagine that for today you are the manager of a restaurant. Upon arriving at work this morning you find that one of the cooks is missing. You can't call him because he doesn't have a phone. When he still hasn't shown up a half an hour later, you start calling other cooks on your roster who might be able to cover for him. Five calls: three no's and two no answers. Meanwhile the cook who did show up is frantically trying to prepare for lunch, which now involves doing twice as much work as usual. His snarls are distinctly audible above the hissing of the gas burners.

Two hours later, just as the lunch crowd starts pouring in, the missing cook arrives. A token apology, an inarticulate reference to "too much dancing," and off he goes to change into his uniform. You follow him downstairs to the locker room where, in a loud voice, you begin confronting him with his delinquency. "Why did you stay up late last night when you knew you had to work this morning?" "Why didn't you at least call?" "Do you realize all the work you have caused the rest of us?" "How could you have been so thoughtless as to put us in this position?" By the time you get around to saying that his job is on the line, you have worked yourself into a real lather. As you leave, slamming the door behind you, your heart is pounding, your breathing rapid and shallow, your hands trembling.

You know that you are angry, but it is only after you are back upstairs and have had a chance to sit down that it suddenly occurs to you that your anger may be a sign of a continuing belief in agency. It is clear that you have been blaming, but is that blaming positional or moral? If your new belief in a deterministic world is valid, there is no agent inside the cook that made him go dancing last night and oversleep this morning, thus no one who can be morally blamed for his being late to work. The whole sequence of events simply arose on its own out of his genes, his previous training, and events of the recent past.

To test whether agency is implicated in your perception of the episode, you decide to recast your thinking in non-agency terms. "He chose to go dancing last night" becomes "The choice to go dancing arose there last night." "He didn't even have the decency to call us this morning and say he was going to be late" becomes "The decency to call us this morning and say that he would be late did not arise there." The first thing you notice as a result of this translation is that you don't feel as angry, a sign that you indeed have been acting on the assumption of free agency. With a simple change in language the whole edifice of moral blaming, self-righteousness, and rage begins to crumble. Gradually it dawns on you that, given the matrix of circumstances surrounding the cook's life, your life, the life of the restaurant and everyone else in it, what happened was causally necessary. As you proceed to reinterpret the situation in non-agency terms, what begins arising in the place of moral blaming, hesitantly at first but growing stronger with every thought, is acceptance. This is simply the way things worked out. There is no agent inside the cook or inside you that could have made events unfold any differently from the way they did. While you are still frustrated with what has arisen, you are no longer morally outraged at the cook for making it happen.

As you sit there, somewhat calmer now, you are reminded that, although the cook is not morally responsible for what has happened, he remains positionally responsible and thus subject to the consequences of his actions. It is entirely consistent with your new belief to fire him or to punish him in such a way that minimizes the probability of his being late again. Without the burden of moral rage, however, you are in a better position to approach that decision objectively.

Moral blame typically arouses defensiveness. Often, the most effective way to defend oneself against negative judgment is to blame the blamer. When both parties are simultaneously blaming and defending, a shouting match usually ensues. Imagine, for example, that while you are fuming at the cook in the locker room (before you calmed down), he starts fighting back, accusing you of inconsistency and favoritism. He cites the cases of other employees who have been late repeatedly but who have never been treated with anything more than a mild rebuke. This is an ugly truth which, up to now, you have been loathe to admit even to yourself. His incisive jab leads you to respond with an assault of your own, an assault on the most promising target of all his character, or, more precisely, his agent. You attack him for having made a mess of his life, citing this morning's tardiness as the latest in a long series of moral failings including alcoholism, several broken marriages, and financial delinquency. As you swing away verbally, you realize that the only way you can come out of this fight feeling good about *yourself* is to make sure that he ends up feeling bad about *his*. Since he, of course, is thinking the same thing and swinging away as wildly as you, you must alternate between impugning his agent and protecting your own.

What can alter the situation is the awareness on your part that the rage you feel in defending yourself is just as symptomatic of a belief in agency as the rage you felt earlier in morally blaming him for being late. That awareness is unlikely to arise, however, until you have cooled off long enough to translate the cook's accusation into non-agency terms. When you make that translation, his statement "You have been playing favorites" becomes "Playing favorites has arisen there." You may be able to see the difference even more clearly when you convert the two statements into questions about yourself. In that case, "Is it true that I have been playing favorites?" becomes "Is it true that playing favorites has arisen here?" If the second way of phrasing it makes you less defensive, chances are that your belief in agency has been contributing to your anger.

Assuming that to be the case, the translated version of the cook's accusation points the way to a different interpretation of the situation. Favoritism is not something that agents make happen; it arises out of circumstance. It is caused by other events, such as previous success in winning approval and avoiding rejection through dispensing favors. Viewing favoritism as an effect of previous conditions makes it easier to accept. You are not being asked whether you made the favoritism happen when you could have chosen otherwise, but whether circumstances conspired to produce this behavior in you. Reinterpreting the cook's accusation in this manner not only helps to dissipate your anger; it deepens your understanding of what it means to say that all events arise on their own out of circumstance.

As your rage abates, it becomes possible for you to look at the accusation more objectively. You see that, despite the cook's attempt to blame you morally, there is no agent within you to be blamed. This new awareness makes it easier to accept the fact that playing favorites has indeed *arisen here*. What follows may very well be an acknowledgment that the cook was right and a new determination to treat everyone fairly in the future. It is nevertheless consistent with your new objectivity to remain frustrated and at least mildly angry over the cook's failure to show up on time. While dispelling the illusion of agency changes the meaning of the cook's behavior and thereby makes it less upsetting, there remains a level at which the situation continues to be frustrating and thus conducive to anger.

Moral blaming and defending are just two of the many contexts in which anger arises. Perhaps the activity that most often evokes angry feelings is straining. Straining implies a violent effort to make something happen or to keep something from happening. Behind that forced effort lies the illusion of an autonomous agent that is free to impose its will on events. When that will is frustrated, as is the case at some point in practically every day of our lives, irritation or anger is almost certain to follow. How much anger arises depends to a great extent on how hard we strain which depends, in turn, on how we interpret the situation.

To see more clearly how agency encourages straining and how you can use straining-induced anger to detect a belief in agency, assume that you are still manager of the restaurant. On your way to work this morning you spend some time reviewing the things you want to get done during the day. First, there is the linen company that needs consulting with respect to the shortage of napkins last weekend. Then, a phone call to the wine salesman to see what can be done about getting in a better assortment of French whites, one of the owner's pet peeves. A talk with the radio station is mandatory in the light of evidence that recent ads are simply not working. A review of the kitchen payroll with the chef is also in order, as is drawing up a new house policy with respect to taking deposits for large-party reservations. It is clearly going to be a busy day, but your energy is high and there is good reason to believe that, if you work fast, you can get everything done.

Arriving at the restaurant, you are immediately greeted by a waiter who insists that he talk to you about a discrepancy in last week's paycheck. Reluctantly you agree and usher him into your office where you start looking around for last week's time cards. As you are going through the files, the phone rings. It's the cook you hired yesterday, saying that he has found a better job elsewhere and won't be coming in after all. This means you must find a replacement immediately.

As you reach for the stack of job applications, the waiter shifts his feet, just to let you know that he is still there. You drop the job applications and resume looking for his time card. Just as you find it, there is a frantic rapping at the door; it is the busboy with news that his sister, the lunchtime hostess who seats guests, woke up this morning with severe cramps and won't be able to make her shift. Your heart begins racing. The situation is rapidly getting out of hand. You feel anger rising but you are too caught up in the situation to know how to stop it. The vise will have to be tightened another turn or two before things come to a head.

One of those turns suddenly appears in the form of the owner who strides into the office, barely pausing to say hello, and demands to know why nothing has been done yet to revise the wine list. As you gasp for enough air to tell him that you haven't gotten to it yet, the waiter, who has grown visibly impatient, reaches over and grabs his time card out of your hand. THAT DOES IT. "Give me that card," you yell. "What's going on here," the owner asks. "I was cheated out of a day's pay last week," the waiter intrudes. "Is that true?," the owner demands, turning to you. "I don't know," you blurt out, "and I'm too pissed off to figure it out right now."

As the two of them leave, you slump into your chair, still clutching the contested time card. Out of the corner of your eye you suddenly spot the simple truth behind the waiter's claim that he lost a day's pay: he forgot to punch in on Tuesday. The ensuing scream of rage reverberates throughout the restaurant, striking terror into the hearts of cooks, waiters, and guests alike.

That evening, back in the privacy of your apartment, nursing a third martini, the thought occurs to you that your explosion earlier in the day might have something to do with a continuing belief in agency. You start by making some simple translations: "I didn't get time to review the wine list today" becomes "Time to review the wine list did not arise here today." "I never got around to calling the linen company" becomes "Getting around to calling the linen company did not arise here today." "I didn't get one important thing done today" becomes "Getting one important thing done did not arise here today." In each case the second way of stating the fact has the effect of reducing your frustration and, thus, your anger. From this you infer that agency has indeed distorted your perception of the day's events.

If I really believed that all events arise unaided by agency, you reason, I could have accepted the whole chain of events as something happening spontaneously. Given all the circumstances, that which happened had to happen. There is no entity inside of me or inside any of the others at the restaurant that could have made things unfold differently. I lost my temper because I interpreted events as a threat to my causal autonomy. My anger can be seen as symptomatic of a persisting belief that I have the power to make events conform to my will.

Giving up the illusion of causal autonomy means being ready for anything. It means entering each situation openly, with curiosity, knowing that whatever arises will be determined by past and present circumstances. Viewing life in these terms can actually catapult you into a different state of consciousness. When it happens, nothing can unnerve you. The phone may be ringing off the hook; you may be surrounded by people making outrageous demands; your well-thought out plans for the day may lie shattered at your feet, but you continue doing what you can, saying yes to this, no to that, always ready for whatever the next moment brings. Throughout it all there is no protest on your part, no tormenting frustration at not being able to make events conform to your expectations and thus no angry explosion. You may not like what is happening, but you find that you can live with that disappointment without losing your emotional balance.

It is a different state of consciousness in that your own notions of what *should* be happening are constantly subordinated to the causal necessity of the situation as it is. However unpleasant it might be, that situation has a reality about it that overshadows all considerations of what you might like it to be. What you are saying privately in this state of consciousness is: "Whatever happens has sufficient cause to be happening; right now, this is simply the way life has to be. That includes the waiter's intransigence, the owner's demands, the cook's decision to take another job, the hostess's cramps, and whatever behavior, thoughts, and feelings are arising within me. This is life, at least for now. It may not be what I had planned, and it is certainly not what I want, but I accept it. I recognize that, given all the antecedent circumstances involved, this is what has to be." This acceptance does not rule out the legitimacy of my desire to change the situation or weaken my resolve to implement that change. It does, however, eliminate straining to make events conform to my will.

Not all anger is driven by a belief in agency. If you apply the translation technique every time you get angry, you will find that some of the time it makes no difference in your feelings. When, for example, someone steps heavily on your foot in the subway, your reaction is likely to be an angry one, despite your awareness that the other person's behavior was precipitated by the lurching of the train. There need not be any agency involved, no assumption that he or she could have chosen otherwise, and thus no moral blaming. Your anger may be just simple, reflexive anger of the sort we would expect to find if one animal accidentally bumped into another.

On the other hand, your belief in agency *may* play a role in your emotional reaction. If, for example, you interpret someone's stepping on your foot as a sign of lack of respect, as an insult, or more simply as an act which the other could have chosen to avoid, you are likely to engage in moral blaming and, as a result, feel more anger than if you were to view the same event deterministically. The same can be said for getting mugged, losing a lover to a rival, or being turned down for a raise. They are all, to different degrees, frustrating and painful experiences, whatever our beliefs. A belief in agency simply makes them more threatening and, thus, more frustrating and more likely to arouse anger.

ANXIETY

Anxiety is as common as anger and equally affected by how we define ourselves. Once we identify ourselves as causal agents, every comment on our behavior becomes a potential judgment on us as authors of that behavior. Not surprisingly, the anticipation of such judgment heightens our perception of danger and, in turn, our experience of anxiety. Because of the link between belief and emotion, we can use that anxiety as symptomatic of a persisting belief in agency. This is not to say that anxiety always reflects the presence of agency or that believing in agency leads inevitably to feeling anxious. It means that, because a belief in agency is one of the primary causes of anxiety, we can use evidence of the latter as a possible sign of the former. Learning to discriminate between those situations in which anxiety is symptomatic of agency and those in which it is symptomatic of something else is also part of the strategy.

Consider the role of hostess. Imagine that you have spent weeks preparing a dinner party for your friends. The meal is to include wines chosen with the help of a local expert, several appetizers of your own invention, a meat sauce made from a recipe wangled from the chef at your favorite restaurant, a vegetable souffle, and a Japanese dessert which you have never tried but which comes highly recommended by a friend just back from Tokyo. One of your guests is a pianist who has agreed to play Chopin before and after dinner.

You have carefully pruned the guest list of all troublemakers and worked out a seating arrangement designed to maximize interesting conversation.

Your anxiety begins arising several days before the dinner party. You are aware of a faster heart beat, sweaty palms, a tightness in your throat, and an increased irritability. Your concentration is disturbed by fantasies of guests not showing up, souffles falling, jellied appetizers not jelling, tough meat, vinegary wine, spongy dessert, heavy drinking, arguments at the table, and guests leaving in disgust. To make things worse, the weather forecast is for several inches of snow.

At breakfast the day of the dinner your husband comments on how anxious you seem, an observation that predictably heightens your anxiety by making you concerned that it will show at the party. Later, when you are alone, the thought arises that agency may be implicated in what you are feeling. Having already committed yourself to a deterministic world view, you see this as a chance to take your belief deeper, while simultaneously reducing your level of anxiety. You explore the possibility of making some translations. At first, it is not apparent what needs translating. If you start with "The party may not be a success," nothing seems to follow. While it is true that the party may not be a success, that possibility in and of itself implies nothing about agency. To see if agency is distorting your perception of the party, it is necessary to couch your original statement in terms of a personal pronoun (at least when talking about yourself). Instead of "The party may not be a success," your starting point should be "I may not be successful as a hostess." When you translate that into "Success as a hostess may not arise here," you are in a position to interpret any reduction in anxiety as a sign that agency has influenced your original feelings. To be certain, you try a few more versions of the same idea: "I may not please my guests" becomes "Pleasing my guests may not arise here." "I may make mistakes" becomes "Mistakes may arise here."

Translating events into non-agency terms returns them to the stream of cause and effect where they belong. It makes clear that whatever happens will be determined by other factors in the stream rather than by some mysterious entity standing outside that stream. If reinterpreting the party from a deterministic perspective leads to a decrease in anxiety, it is reasonable to conclude that you have been viewing the situation in terms of agency. Assuming that to be the case, you can use this present situation to expand your understanding of non-agency. Sitting there at the table after breakfast, you start to think. "If all events are determined by circumstance, that includes tonight's events as well. While my choices in food and decor as well as my behavior toward my guests are certain to play a causal role in shaping the party's outcome, they are themselves a function of antecedent conditions. Both my efforts to make the party a success and my guests' responses to those efforts will unfold spontaneously out of what has gone before. There is no causally autonomous entity inside of me or any of them that can alter what is going to happen."

You can already feel a slight reduction in anxiety. You continue. "If my guests praise me, they will be addressing their comments to an agent I am convinced does not exist. But their evaluation will not be without meaning because of that fact. I can still enjoy their praise as a comment not on me as causal agent but on the behavior which arises here spontaneously. If they are pleased with the evening, they will show it in their smiles, in their conversation with each other, as well as in expressions of warmth and appreciation directed to me personally, all of which I can enjoy without drawing any inferences about my efficacy as a causal agent."

"Conversely, if they are not pleased, I will have to bear the brunt of their displeasure. But what is it precisely that I stand to lose by their not being pleased with me as a *person*? Will they stop caring for me? Unlikely. Will they stop inviting me to their homes for dinner? Equally improbable. They may, however, leave early and do less exclaiming about the meal as they say goodbye. They may also tell others about the evening, thereby compromising my reputation as cook and hostess. As a result, I may receive less attention when I meet friends and acquaintances in town. While that attention is not critical to my well-being, I have come to expect and enjoy it. I do have something to lose, then, if the party should fail and the possibility of that loss is disturbing enough to put me on edge. I am not alarmed, however, because I know that any loss of attention implies nothing about my worthiness as a causal agent."

You are now in a position to summarize your thoughts. "Giving up my belief in agency does not mean becoming indifferent to how other people react to me. It does mean, however, learning to interpret their thoughts and actions as a response to my behavior rather than as a response to me as author of that behavior. Once I see their judgments in that light, the prospect of being evaluated does not seem so threatening. I continue to prefer positive reactions to negative ones, but, without the assumption that they are evaluating me as a causal agent, I am less concerned about their verdict. I realize that all failures and successes arising *here* are determined by genes and environment; there is no secret agency inside of this body/mind with the power to influence what I think and do."

Reinterpreting anxiety-producing events in terms of non-agency represents one of the most effective means of dispelling the illusion of agency. An important by-product of that shift in thinking is a gradual reduction in the intensity and frequency of the anxiety itself. For someone suffering from chronic anxiety, the promise of relief from pain may, in fact, become the primary motive in learning to see the world in terms of non-agency. Although the strategy outlined here for giving up agency is not designed as a therapy, it can be used for that purpose by anyone suffering from evaluation anxiety.

In this regard, non-agency shares certain assumptions and strategies with cognitive therapy, especially as the latter has been applied to the treatment of what Beck and Emery call social anxiety.

> The central fear in the so-called social anxieties is that of negative evaluation by another person or persons, a fear that separates the social and the performance anxieties from agoraphobia. In the latter syndrome, a person may be afraid of wide-open squares, fields, or beaches where there are no people as well as closed-in groups or crowds of people. In agoraphobia, the fear of social disapproval appears to be secondary to the fear of losing control, fainting, going crazy, and so on. In contrast, in the social anxieties the central fear is of being the center of attention, of having one's "weaknesses" exposed, and consequently of being judged adversely by one or more people.

> There is a symbolic confrontation in the social anxieties whether the individual is calling a stranger on the telephone, trying to initiate a conversation in a social setting, or performing before a group. When the socially anxious person is engaged in a one-to-one encounter with another person or group of people, he believes that he is being scrutinized, tested, and judged. Under observation are his performance, fluency of speech, self-assurance, and freedom from anxiety.[2]

In treating social anxiety, the cognitive therapist typically starts by assuming that, somewhere in his or her life, the patient is "misconstruing innocuous situations as posing a threat."[3] The strategy, then, is to identify those specific distortions in the patient's thinking that have led to the perception of danger in what most people would consider a neutral or only mildly noxious situation. In the case of performance anxiety, for example, patients often equate mistakes with failure and failure with disaster, thereby making performance a far more dangerous activity than it really is. Cognitive therapy can help to reduce that fear by making the patient more realistic about audience reaction and what that reaction implies for success or failure.

Cognitive therapy rests on the assumption that what we believe affects what we feel, the same assumption that underlies our own strategy of using emotions to dispel the illusion of agency. In both approaches, beliefs are thought to affect feelings by changing the meaning of those stimuli to which the feelings represent a response. Both approaches assume that the most direct way to change the meaning of a situation and thereby reduce the anxiety accompanying that perception is to identify and correct any distortions in thinking.

The strategy being described here differs from that of cognitive therapy in several important respects. Unlike cognitive therapy, which is applicable to all forms of anxiety including phobias, generalized anxiety disorder, hysteria, and agoraphobia, non-agency is relevant only for those forms of anxiety involving evaluation. Secondly, cognitive therapists are interested in any form of cognitive distortion that contributes to anxiety, while the focus here is on one distortion in particular, that of free agency. Like most of us, cognitive therapists take the assumption of agency for granted.

Thirdly, cognitive therapy is a conventional therapy suitable to anyone seeking symptom relief, while non-agency, if used therapeutically, is appropriate for that much smaller population of sufferers whose fear of evaluation is too deeply rooted to benefit from minor, cognitive adjustments. Most people who suffer from performance anxiety simply want to be able to sing or talk before an audience without experiencing unusual fear. Adopting a more realistic assessment of their abilities and a more realistic perception of how audiences react to mistakes may be sufficient to achieve that end. For the true anxiety neurotic, however, a more intense, structurally-oriented remedy is required. There are many such remedies available. What makes non-agency unique among treatment approaches to anxiety is that it works not by shoring up the agent/self, or even by helping patients become more realistic about how others evaluate that self, but by making it clear that all causally autonomous selves are illusory. The person most likely to respond to that kind of treatment is someone who has failed to find relief through conventional therapy and who is willing to consider a radically different approach.

SADNESS

Sadness is another emotion we can use for the purpose of identifying situations in which agency continues to distort our thinking. Like anger and anxiety, sadness thrives on a belief in free will but can arise regardless of what we believe. At the core of sadness is the experience of loss: the loss of friend, of money, of health, hair, reputation, or anything else we either presently have or anticipate having. A belief in agency cannot by itself make us sad, but it can heighten or sustain our sad feelings by changing the meaning of what we have lost. From the perspective of causal autonomy, every loss carries a potential message about our worthiness as agents who are responsible for who we are and what we do. That message is clearest with losses that reflect on our skill, judgment, or attractiveness, for example, the loss of a job, the loss of a lover, or the loss of an elected position.

To see how sadness can be symptomatic of agency, imagine that you have just been laid off from a job you have held for many years. You spend your days looking through newspaper ads and sending your resumé to firms you think might be interested in someone with your background. You are finally invited to be interviewed by a firm that offers almost everything you want. Although the interview seems to go well, you receive a letter a week later explaining that the firm has hired someone else. You are overwhelmed with sadness. You feel weak, helpless, unwanted, and rejected.

As the day wears on, the thought arises that part of your sadness may be due to the way you are interpreting what happened. While the rejection is certainly real, your belief in agency may be making things worse than they need to be. To find out, you try translating the situation into non-agency terms. "I failed to get the job" immediately becomes "Getting the job failed to arise here." You feel a slight lift with that simple change of wording. You try several more ways of saying the same thing. "I wasn't good enough for the job" becomes "Being good enough for the job didn't arise here." "I still haven't gotten a job" becomes "Getting a job still hasn't arisen here."

Translating has the effect of taking some of the sting out of your failure to get the job. It makes it easier for you to view what happened as a spontaneous unfolding of events in which every thought, choice, and act was fully determined by previous conditions. While you must still take the consequences of what has arisen (you still don't have a job), the loss now has a different meaning. Without the burden of self-blame, your failure to get the job becomes easier to accept. Given all the circumstances involved, this is simply the way things worked out. All the steps in the process, including your decision to apply, your decision to write up your resumé the way you did, your decision to wear your blue suit rather than your gray one to the interview, and your choice of how to address the person interviewing you were determined by circumstance. At no point in the process was there any agent inside of you or inside any of the people who turned you down that could have altered the stream of events. While it is reasonable that you should continue to feel sad about the outcome, there is no reason to feel sad about your failure as a causal agent.

When sadness is extreme and sustained to the point where it affects sleeping and eating habits, interests, and energy, we call it depression. The basic problem remains that of loss, powerlessness, and inadequacy.

> It is relatively easy to detect the dominant theme in the statements of the moderately or severely depressed patient. *He regards himself as lacking some element or attribute that he considers essential for his happiness:* competence in attaining his goals, attractiveness to other people, closeness to family or friends, tangible possessions, good health, status or position.[4] (original italics)

While losses are real and must be dealt with, their felt significance depends very much on how we interpret them.

> Experiences just prior to the onset of depression are often no more severe than those reported by those who do not become depressed. The depression-prone differ in the way they construe a particular deprivation. They attach overgeneralized or extravagant meanings to the loss.[5]

One of the most common meanings the depressive gives to loss is that it occurred because of his own inadequacy. The patient regards himself as "a misfit, an inferior and inadequate being who is unable to meet his responsibilities and attain his goals."[6] A belief in agency has the power to strengthen that self-image by making the patient morally responsible for his inadequacy. If he is inadequate, it is because he has chosen to be that way, or, at the very least, because he has allowed himself to get that way. To the tangible loss of a business or friend, agency adds the implication that the person was free to choose otherwise, that he could have been wiser in his decisions or kinder in his behavior. The fact that he wasn't any wiser or kinder represents proof of his unworthiness as a free agent. For many Westerners, depression draws its power from a deep and abiding sense of causal or moral unworthiness.

Cognitive therapy approaches depression at the level of specific distortions in thinking. Typically, these distortions involve unrealistically low assessments of one's ability to cope and exaggerated estimates of what one has to cope with. The widespread success of cognitive therapy suggests that it is often possible to relieve depression without correcting the deeper error of agency. For most chronically depressed patients, in fact, any attempt to confront that more fundamental error is likely to evoke immediate resistance. It might appear at first that a message claiming that we do not cause our own behavior would be reassuring to someone who suffers from self-loathing. In my own experience as a therapist, I have found, on the contrary, that patients who feel depressed and ineffectual have no interest in learning how to accept their lack of causal autonomy. Although they express their goals in different ways, they almost always come to therapy to learn skills for enhancing their sense of adequacy as generators of thought and action.

For most of us, it is essential to learn how to feel good about our agent/I before entertaining the idea that it may be only a ghost (it is hard to become a nobody without being a somebody first). If our image of ourselves as causal agents is negative, our energy and aspirations are likely to be caught up in trying to change the content of that image. It is usually not until we have succeeded in making those changes that we can consider the possibility that we are not agents but constellations of experience and behavior.

There are a few of us, however, for whom the opposite is true. These are the depressives who never succeed in overcoming their sense of powerlessness through therapy but whose failure with conventional strategies has the effect of increasing their willingness to consider more radical solutions. Many of the conversion cases James describes in *The Varieties of Religious Experience* seem to be of this sort. Non-agency represents an equally radical non-religious alternative, one whose appeal is limited to those who are willing to reconsider their basic metaphysical assumptions. The dynamic in either case is that of surrendering the illusion of agent-power. Whether it be to God or to Circumstance, that surrender typically arises out of frustration with the conventional notion of self. Religion cultivates the acceptance of ultimate powerlessness by urging us to "let Thy, not my will be done." Non-agency attempts to achieve a similar end by exposing the illusory status of the agent/I as Uncaused Cause.

PRIDE

While anger, anxiety, and sadness are all possible without a belief in agency, pride is not. Whenever we congratulate ourselves for something we have thought or done, we are acting on the assumption that we are the causes of our own experience and behavior. For that reason, pride is an especially clear indicator of a continuing attachment to the illusion of an agent/I. Because it arises so frequently and can do so independently of outside stimulation, pride offers countless opportunities for dispelling that illusion. Unlike angry, sad, or anxious feelings, however, proud feelings are enjoyable, a fact which may affect our zeal in applying a strategy that is aimed at their elimination. In coping with that fact, it may help to remind ourselves that, in using pride to identify agency, we hasten the day when other agency-related feelings (anger, anxiety, sadness, and guilt) cease dominating our lives.

The strategy for using pride to locate a continuing belief in agency calls for the same steps described earlier: awareness, translation, and reinterpretation. Sometimes we cannot help but be aware of our pride, as in boasting, where we praise ourselves at the same time that we solicit credit from others. Translating those boasts into non-agency terms almost always leads to a change in feeling indicating that agency is implicated. In translation, for example, "I beat him two games out of three" becomes "Winning arose here two times out of three." To say that winning *arose* here takes most of the fun out of boasting. It is no longer our doing. It happened on its own. From this perspective, winning can be seen as a fully determined event, shaped by thousands of genetic, psychological, and social circumstances. Translating the boast into a language devoid of agency gives us a clearer idea of what it means to say that *all* accomplishments arise on their own out of circumstance.

Pride often arises in response to flattery. When someone tells us, "That was a brilliant report you wrote," we respond to the implied agent-evaluation with some internal agent-stroking of our own ("I'm really something great to have turned out such a brilliant report"). In translation, that act of self-congratulation becomes simply "A brilliant report arose here," which tells us what happened and where it happened, but which says nothing about its causal source. There is no pride, no moral credit in such a perspective. There may be reason for delight and gratitude, however, since being the body/mind where a brilliant report arose brings certain positional rewards, e.g., smiles, handshakes, and a higher probability of promotion with all the financial and supervisory advantages that implies.

Obvious expressions of pride such as boasting are the first to stop arising as non-agency begins to sink in. The more subtle ones take longer but eventually succumb to the same strategy. Imagine for a moment that, as you stroll down the street alone, an outrageous pun occurs to you. You cannot help breaking out into a huge grin. Almost immediately you begin congratulating yourself on how clever you are. While that may actually be true, it occurs to you a few blocks later that you might be taking more than positional credit for your sense of humor. To test yourself, you start translating. "I just made an outrageous pun" becomes "An outrageous pun just arose here." It is obvious to you that something gets lost in the translation, suggesting that the ghost of agency is still roaming the corridors of your psyche. As per instructions, you stop to dwell on exactly what this means.

If there is no entity inside of you that manufactured the pun, it must have come on its own out of previous experience, other thoughts, unconscious feelings, physiochemical processes, and so on. Despite its convoluted character, it is no less spontaneous than a belch. Because it arose in you and not someone else, you are the one who gets to experience it first hand. You are the one who also gets to enjoy any positional credit that goes with your status as the location in which it arose. Among other things, you are entitled to think of yourself as a funny *person*. What you are not entitled to is the credit that goes with having caused the pun to arise. If there is any causal credit to dispense, it must be awarded to Circumstance.

Try another example. You are returning from a book store where you have purchased several books, one on paleontology, another on modern French poetry, and a third on 14th century European history. As you walk down the street, you feel an extra spring in your step. You're standing a bit taller than usual, secretly pleased with life. At home in your living room, the thought arises that it may not be life that you are pleased with but yourself. It is clear that you enjoy thinking of yourself as an intellectually sophisticated person, interested in and knowledgeable about all kinds of things. But what does it mean to feel this way? Is your self-satisfaction anything more than thinly-veiled pride?

To find out, you try translating a statement about yourself into non-agency terms. "I have developed an interest in a wide variety of things" becomes "An interest in a wide variety of things has arisen here." If the latter sounds too "objective" or "impersonal," if it fails to take into consideration all that *you* have done to develop these interests, you are probably still clinging to the illusion of free agency. Perhaps you have forgotten that your interests have been determined by the circumstances of your education, your family life, your genetic inheritance, and your exposure to certain influential people. While coming to grips with that reality need not interfere with the delight you feel in pursuing intellectual interests, it makes taking pride in those interests meaningless. The next time you go shopping for books, there may be an extra spring to your step as you leave the store, but it is more apt to be from anticipating the pleasure of reading the books you have just purchased than from contemplating the sophistication of the agent/I that chose them.

GUILT

Ordinarily we think of guilt as a sign that we have violated an internalized rule or failed to live up to an internalized expectation. It seems strange to think of guilt as a sign of deluded thinking, but that is precisely what follows from the realization that experience and behavior are either random or determined by circumstance. It may seem even stranger to think of guilt as a sign of arrogance, but that also follows. Guilt and pride reflect an image of ourselves as divine entities that can move the world without being moved by other forces. Every time we feel either one of those emotions, we affirm our conviction that we cause our own thoughts, feelings, and behavioral choices.

Guilt differs from pride in that it represents one of the most painful human emotions, one which most of us would be only too happy to eliminate from our lives if that prospect itself did not make us feel guilty. It may make the concept of a world without agency or guilt more acceptable if we remember that when we break the law or violate community standards of right and wrong, we are still liable for the consequences. Without an internal agent, however, any punishment for our misdeeds must come at the hands of our neighbors and the police and not, as Freud put it, through the "superego's cruel whipping of the ego."

With the giving up of agency, guilt is replaced by regret. Although it no longer makes sense to punish ourselves for our behavior once we acknowledge its causal necessity, we may nevertheless regret that the offending behavior arose. The responsibility implied in regret is purely positional; we are blameable only in the sense that the behavior arose here and not somewhere else. We lament the fact that it arose here, not that we made it happen. Replacing guilt with regret is analogous to replacing pride with gratitude. Although we are no longer justified in taking credit for making our behavior happen, we can still feel grateful that it arose here.

The first requirement in using guilt to dispel agency is to be aware that you are feeling guilty. Let us assume that on your way home from a party you suddenly realize that your best friend could be hurt by confidential information that you let slip over a drink. That thought is followed by a sharp twinge of what you know from experience to be remorse. By the time you reach home, the feeling has found its way into every nook and cranny of your psyche. You are torn between calling your friend to apologize, confessing to your wife, and hoping that nothing will come of the whole affair. As you stretch out in bed, girding yourself for a sleepless night, the thought arises that your belief in agency may have something to do with what you are experiencing.

Translating your thoughts into non-agency terms produces a slight but immediate shift in feeling. Remorse over having broken a confidence begins to give way to regret that "A breach of confidence arose here." Once you adopt a causal viewpoint, it is not difficult to think of specific reasons why the breach occurred. Wanting to impress the people you just met may have had something to do with it, along with the fact that you drank too much. Envy of your friend may have also been involved. You realize that it is not essential to know all the exact causes. What matters is that you interpret what happened as a product of circumstance rather than an act of free will. In this light, given all the circumstances involved, your revealing something that could hurt your friend was causally necessary. However lamentable the slip, however much you now regret what arose, there is no causal *you* that could have kept it from arising.

The number of opportunities for using self-blame to detect a persisting belief in agency is legion. Many of them do not even involve harm to others. We commonly blame ourselves for buying things that we can't afford, for not speaking up to others, for eating or drinking too much, for having our hair cut too short, or for forgetting appointments and umbrellas. While such forms of self-harassment are rarely sufficient to depress us, they contribute significantly to our sustained mood of "quiet desperation." As a simple translation will show, they almost always involve the assumption that, as agents, we cause our own desires and choices. We not only regret that buying a new car has left us without next month's rent; we punish ourselves for having authored such a decision. When we forget our umbrella, we not only regret having to walk home in the rain; we blame ourselves for having allowed the forgetting to happen. An already unpleasant situation is made more painful by an error in thinking which holds that, as agents, we *make* our own mistakes. Given that assumption, it makes no sense to ask *how* or *why* we make mistakes, for to do so assumes that circumstances have played a part. If our will is truly free, even in part, our decisions must be, to that same degree, inexplicable. They must arise, like God's own creations, from nothingness.

All mistakes, oversights, acts of poor judgment, and failures to remember surface on their own. Because they are so common, they represent an inexhaustible source of data for locating distortions in our thinking. It is a simple matter to translate self-blame into non-agency terms. For example, "I made a mistake in buying such an expensive car" becomes "A mistake in buying such an expensive car arose here." While the purchase is no less foolish because it arose out of circumstance, it becomes easier to accept when we view it as a self-arising event. If a shift in feeling follows the translation, it means that the illusion of agency has been operating.

The same principle holds for translating "I shouldn't have been afraid to speak up at the conference" into "Being afraid to speak up at the conference arose here," or translating "I shouldn't have eaten so much last night" into "It is unfortunate that eating so much arose here last night." Translating our mistakes and failings into non-agency terms points the way to a reinterpretation of all behavior as an unfolding of events shaped by environment and heredity. Each time we perform that reinterpretation, we chip away at our belief in agency, hastening the day when guilt, remorse, and moral self-blaming of any kind stop arising.

CONCLUSION

Changing our beliefs about who we are requires being involved in the world. If we are to dispel the illusion of agency, it is essential that the illusion be aroused repeatedly, as it tends to be when we set goals, make decisions, and interact with others who are doing the same thing. Our belief in agency is so central to our thoughts and so deeply embedded in our perceptions that simply assenting to its illusoriness is unlikely to produce any observable change in our lives. To uproot that belief, we must become familiar with the whole mass of errors and distortions that have grown out of it. One of the best ways to identify those errors is through our emotional responses to other people. To do that requires getting involved in careers and relationships where we are constantly risking disapproval and rejection. While life in the cloister may facilitate some kinds of self-change, it is not the most effective site for dispelling the illusion of agency.

In the conventional world hardly a day goes by that we don't experience anger, anxiety, sadness, pride, and guilt. But even when we don't, we can work on reinterpreting the world in terms of non-agency by *imagining situations* in which these emotions seems likely to arise. We all have some idea of what can make us angry, anxious, sad, proud or guilty. If we know, for example, that giving speeches makes us anxious, we can construct an imaginary scene in which we are preparing to speak and are feeling tense about the prospect. In that fantasy, we treat the anxiety as if it were real, i.e., we identify it as a potential sign of agency and go on to translate the situation into non-agency terms to see if our anxiety diminishes. "I hope I give a good speech" becomes "Hopefully, a good speech will arise here," which serves to remind us that whether or not the speech is successful depends on the circumstances of our previous history, genes, and certain aspects of the present situation. The reduction in anxiety which follows when that thought arises can be taken as a sign that we are still clinging to a belief in agency. Although giving the speech remains no more than a fantasy, reinterpreting it in non-agency terms clarifies and deepens our belief that all events are self-arising.

While most of the work of uprooting agency is carried on internally, friends can accelerate the process by confronting us whenever we seem to be acting as if the illusion were real. Even when we have been working on agency for years, there are bound to be occasions when we fail to see that we are acting defensively, that we are bragging, straining, or judging others morally. Astute companions can change all of that by pointing out what they observe, either at the time a situation is unfolding or later in response to our description of the event. A group of like-minded people meeting regularly to share their experiences and observations of each other can do even more.

REFERENCES

1. Minsky, M., *The Society of Mind*, New York: Simon and Schuster, 1985, p. 307.
2. Beck, A., and Emery, G., *Anxiety Disorders and Phobias*, New York: Basic Books, 1985, pp. 151-152.
3. Beck, A., and Emery, G., *Anxiety Disorders and Phobias*, p. 30.
4. Beck, A., *Cognitive Therapy and The Emotional Disorders*, p. 105.
5. Beck, A., *Cognitive Therapy and The Emotional Disorders*, p. 109.
6. Beck, A., *Cognitive Therapy and The Emotional Disorders*, p. 106.

16

A Dignity We Never Had

Science does not dehumanize man, it de-homunculizes him.
B.F. Skinner, *Beyond Freedom and Dignity*

Dispelling the illusion that we are morally responsible for who we are promises to eliminate much of the pain of being human. Without the agency assumption there is less to brag about, less to feel guilty about, less to blame and praise others for, less to prove to the world. Our craving becomes less urgent, our clinging less tenacious. We protest less when things do not go our way, show less concern when others judge us adversely, and strain less when pursuing our goals. When we view ourselves as "that which is arising here," we experience more "ease of heart," more quiet joy, more stability and clarity of mind, greater acceptance of ourselves, greater acceptance of others, more patience, more honesty and openness, greater capacity for intimacy, and greater equanimity in the face of loss.

By this accounting, there would appear to be little to lose and much to gain from giving up our belief in free will. Why, then, do we resist the idea so passionately? Why are we willing to tolerate so much suffering when a far less painful life appears to be possible? The answer obviously lies in the accounting. In my list of what is to be gained and lost from giving up a belief in agency, I have omitted one of the most important considerations of all – the loss of dignity. We resist a view of ourselves as spontaneous expressions of circumstance and chance because that view leaves no room for the inner spirit that we take to be our true self. Eliminating that spirit appears to reduce us to organic machines. It robs us of our freedom, our power, and our dignity as God's or Nature's special creation.

If free agency is only an illusion, of course, we have no dignity to lose, at least no dignity of the kind we insist on having. Whatever special dignity we have appropriated for ourselves over the last 4000 years is as illusory as the belief in causal autonomy on which it is based. It is not as if we once enjoyed an exalted status and were now in danger of losing it; we never had such a status. The concept of ourselves as causally autonomous spirits is no more real and no more essential to our well-being than Ptolemy's concept of the earth as the center of the solar system. One of the reasons we hang onto such views long after they have been exposed as inconsistent with the facts is that they flatter us. We prefer to think of our planet not only as the center of the solar system but as the center of the universe itself. We prefer to think of ourselves not only as God's favorite creatures but as the raison d'etre for the whole of His creation. Free will is a highly flattering belief. It puts us in a category above and beyond everything else in nature. Like Ptolemaic astronomy and Creationist biology, it is inconsistent with the facts.

I propose the following hypothesis: we tolerate the psychic pain associated with a belief in agency for the sake of the (illusion of) dignity which that belief confers upon us. This generalization need not imply that we are aware of such a trade-off. Because of our cultural training, we tend to take both suffering and dignity for granted; they are simply part of the human condition. And therein lies a fatal error. From the fact of suffering we draw the conclusion that it is our lot to suffer, to live with anxiety and fear, to endure sadness and guilt, to bear the burdens of moral responsibility along with those of death, disease, starvation, and poverty. From the sensation that our thoughts and decisions are uncaused, we conclude that we are exempt from the laws of cause and effect that govern all other events in nature. What we rarely suspect is that both kinds of experience (psychic pain and the sensation of causal freedom) have been shaped by a particular belief we have about ourselves, a belief that happens to be untrue.

DIGNITY AND DIVINITY

What appeals to us about the concept of free agency is that it confers divine status upon each of us by positing an inner self with supernatural powers. That belief is basically religious in that it affirms the reality of a spiritual force capable of performing miracles. By a miracle I mean an event that violates the physical, chemical, biological or psychological laws of the natural world. A free agent performs a miracle every time it moves a muscle, creates a thought, or makes a decision. The essence of the agent's freedom lies in its ability to cause events without interference from "outside" forces. What makes an agent-caused event miraculous is that it cannot be traced to a previous genetic or environmental event. It must be traced, at least in part, to the Will or Soul. To say that a given act was caused by the Will or the Soul rather than by heredity or environment is tantamount to claiming that its "author" possesses the power of divine intervention. The only other being in the universe thought to possess that power, of course, is the Prime Mover himself. When we insist that we are free agents, then, we are making a religious statement and aligning ourselves with God.*

In the West, Man and God have shared the power to work miracles ever since the anti-Mesopotamians shattered the image of history as an impersonal, cyclical process in which neither the individual nor his deities counted for very much. In overturning the order of nature and reapportioning its power to God and Man, the rebel tribesmen laid claim to a causal freedom to which we, their heirs, have clung ever since. More than anything else, it is this claim to autonomy and divine status that lead us to resist non-agency so passionately. Adopting a view of ourselves as "that which is arising here" threatens our dignity by returning us to the order of nature. It severs our alliance with God and exposes our claim to divinity as pretense. Relinquishing that claim shows us to be animals, exceptionally intelligent ones to be sure, but animals nevertheless. Others would go further and say that giving up our souls reduces us to highly complex organic machines. Whether the demotion is to animals or to machines, giving up free will implies the loss of our status as minor gods. If we seem willing to accept the pain that goes with moral responsibility, it is because we are reluctant to give up that lofty status.

We accept without question that there is more dignity to be gained in being half-angel, half-beast than in being all beast. But have we ever taken the time to ask what that hybrid status implies for experience and behavior? The question of whether or not free will adds to our dignity cannot be answered simply by looking at the concept itself. We have to examine what it actually

---

* As Robert Nozick reminds us, the idea that man shares in God's contra-causal freedom was first articulated by Philo (20 B.C. - 50 A.D.). "In his view, God, in creating the world, reserved for himself the power to upset laws by working miracles, and gave to man a portion of that same power – although man's 'miracles' are not worked with respect to laws that he himself created." Nozick, R., *Philosophical Explanations*, Cambridge: Harvard University Press, 1981, p. 295.

implies for our thoughts, feelings, and behavior. A belief in free will enhances our self-importance by making us the authors and managers of our own lives, but does it lead us to behave more nobly? That same belief grants us the power to create thoughts and actions from nothingness – an ability that has all the earmarks of divinity – but does it make our behavior toward others more god-like? In assessing the relationship between free will and dignity, we must look at the full range of implications, including those that are not particularly flattering.

Consider for a moment how much it detracts from our dignity when we quarrel with a colleague over credit for an idea or when we bristle at a supervisor's suggestion that our work is inferior. Consider how it demeans us to boast about our accomplishments, to gloat over a rival's defeat, to respond peevishly to an imagined snub, or to be overwhelmed with anxiety at the thought of mispronouncing a word. Consider too how violently we react to heinous crimes and how quick we are to sacrifice our dignity – and that of our victims – to the pleasures of moral retribution. Free will erodes dignity in all of these situations by elevating our sensitivity to evaluation and by inflaming our desire to judge.

There are times, however, when our belief in free agency inspires us to behave in ways that give at least the appearance of dignity. For example, we sometimes make great sacrifices out of pride or guilt, as when we give up vacations or new cars in order to send our children to prestigious colleges. A belief in agency can also inspire us to make the prodigious effort necessary for victory in sports or battle. By creating the illusion of a causally autonomous Will, it can give us the strength to endure extreme physical hardship and sickness and even to postpone death.

More often than not, however, the belief that we are morally responsible for our behavior seems to invite defensiveness, bragging, pettiness, and self-love. By making us the authors of our own behavior, free will encourages us to be egocentric, hypersensitive to criticism, demanding of approval, and prone to self-pity. Whenever we interact with others, our dignity as agents is threatened by the vulnerability imposed by the illusion of causal freedom. We put ourselves (i.e., our agents) on the line every time we make a decision. To the degree that we are free to choose otherwise, we expose ourselves to judgment not simply for the decision itself but for our role as agents in creating it. Much of our most undignified behavior comes from the fear of being judged adversely, a fear rooted in the illusion of agency.

In clinging to the illusion of agency for the sake of the dignity it provides, we overlook all the small-mindedness which causal responsibility brings in its wake. The core of the problem lies with claiming to be only partly divine. The fact that we have god-like power (or at least think we do) to create choices out of nothingness does not guarantee that those choices will be wise. Nor does it make us immune to attacks on our authorship. Unlike God whose omniscience assures the wisdom of everything He does and whose omnipotence renders Him impervious to judgments about His creation, we must agonize over the consequences of our highly fallible choices. Whatever miraculous power free will is presumed to give us is compromised not only by its fallibility but by the fact that it is limited to the domain of our own personal experience. Much as we might like to, we do not will other people's thoughts into being or will their arms and legs into action. Ours is a local divinity at best, a private affair between soul and body/mind.

Because our divinity is only partial, the relationship between free will and dignity is two-sided. In some ways, our image of ourselves as free agents is ennobling; in other ways it is impoverishing. When we look at the whole range of human behavior, free will appears to undermine our dignity as often as it enhances it. If that is true, we may be suffering in vain. At the very least, it may be time to reexamine the trade-off between suffering and dignity that underlies our attachment to free will. That suggestion is not likely to win support, however, among those who take it for granted that dignity and free will go together – who assume, in fact, that without free will we would have no dignity at all.

Many contemporary philosophers have adopted such a position. Typically they begin with the assumption that free will is indispensable to our self-concept and go on from there to "examine" arguments for a premise to which they have committed themselves in advance. We are already familiar, for example, with Strawson's argument that the reactive attitudes we associate with a belief in free will are too desirable and deeply embedded in the human psyche for us to give them up, and Fischer's claim that any life worth living would be impossible without such attitudes. Harvard philosopher Robert Nozick reveals his own commitment to dignity when he writes:

> Without free will, we seem diminished, merely the playthings
> of external forces. *How, then, can we maintain an exalted view
> of ourselves?* Determinism seems to undercut human dignity,
> it seems to undermine our value. Our concern is to formulate
> a view of how we (sometimes) act so that if we act that way

our value is not threatened, our stature is not diminished.[1] (italics added)

Nozick's concern with maintaining "an exalted view of ourselves" precludes his being objective about whether we really have free will or not. That same apriori commitment to dignity discourages exploration of why an exalted view of ourselves is so crucial and whether, in light of post-Darwinian biology, it is even a reasonable view to have old. As anyone who has read the medieval scholastics knows, an argument that arises out of faith rather than curiosity (*fides querat intellectum*) runs the risk of becoming sophistic and turned in upon itself. Nozick's defense of free will, although of more recent vintage, attests to just how convoluted logic can become when faith precedes intellect.

> On the view we have presented, . . some actions are not causally determined, though they are, we correctly say in retrospect, caused by the reasons upon which the greater weight was bestowed in that very decision; so the causes may go back a long time, even to before birth, yet nonetheless the person still can originate actions. For which action she does, A or B, is under her originatory control, and though the occurrence of the reasons for each, Ra and Rb, are not under her control, the fact that one of them causes (though doesn't causally determine) her act – which one does so – *is* under her control. She can choose A or B; if she chooses A she makes it true that Ra caused A while if she chooses B she makes it true that Rb caused B. The existence of the cause is not under her control and doesn't originate with her but the fact the *it* causes her act is and does.[2] (original italics)

Daniel Dennett follows a path similar to Nozick's when he opens his defense of free will with a statement of personal values.

> The varieties of free will we deem worth wanting are those – if there are any – that will secure for us our dignity and responsibility.[3]

It is not simply that we want to be free to make our own decisions. More importantly, Dennett is saying, we want to be morally responsible for our behavior because dignity lies in being held accountable for what we do.

> It is interesting that when people hit upon this suggestion [that there is no foundation for moral responsibility], they do not as a rule view it as the prospect of a welcome holiday, a chance to do whatever they like without running the risk of feeling – or being – guilty. One might think that the supposition that responsibility was a baseless concept would be liberating, exhilarating, a breath of fresh air blowing away the gloomy old dogmas of guilt and sin. But strangely enough, it seems that we want to be held responsible. Why?[4]

Dennett's question can be answered most easily by pointing to the same desire for exalted status of which Nozick spoke. There is nothing arcane in any of this. Wanting to be held morally responsible is tantamount to wanting to be god-like. However commendable we might find the concept of moral responsibility, the claim to causal autonomy which underlies that concept remains a bid for supernatural power and status.

The desire for such status, of course, is itself shaped by the implanting of the agency illusion early in childhood. Our life-long quest for dignity begins with the birth of the agent/I. Without the fiction of free agency, we would be less interested in establishing our "exalted status" vis-à-vis the rest of nature or laying claim to a specifically moral kind of responsibility. As agent-less body/minds, we would probably be content with the dignity and responsibility that go with being unusual but fully natural organisms.

DIGNITY, FREEDOM, AND POWER

Dignity and freedom are inseparable. More than anything else, it is our freedom to choose that gives us our special place in the sun. This illusion of autonomy plays a dominant role, some might even say a sacred role, in Western culture. But what kind of freedom is it that we value so highly – and what does non-agency imply for that kind of freedom? If by having freedom we mean having options to choose from, we can be sure that the world will continue to offer abundant choices even after we have dispelled the illusion that it is we as agents who are doing the choosing. When we enter a supermarket, for example, we are likely to have the same feeling of freedom that we now enjoy, the only difference being that in a non-agency world we take it for granted that our choices are arising spontaneously out of genetic and environmental conditions rather than out of will. As we reach for the Spanish rather than the Bermuda onions, the choice is likely to feel as free as ever despite this new way of viewing the process. The choice continues to feel free because we are unaware of the many antecedent factors operating upon that choice at the moment it arises. In most of our choosing, the causal pathways linking past and present lie buried far below consciousness. One effect of this lack of awareness is to give both present and future choices the appearance that they could have turned out otherwise. There is little reason to believe that giving up the illusion of agency will alter the immediate sensation of freedom. What it is more likely to change is the emotional content of the experience. Once we recognize that our choices are determined by genetic and environmental conditions, we can go about choosing without the distraction of emotions like guilt and pride that spring from a belief in agency.

If the kind of freedom we want depends on our being able to cause our own choices, it follows from non-agency that we are not free and that we have never been free. As persons, we are not free to break the chain of causality linking choice to circumstance. If we are not free, however, it is equally clear that we are not unfree either. If agency is only an illusion, there is no entity inside of us that is either free and controlling on the one hand or captive and controlled on the other. Whether we as agents are free or not is a meaningless question; there are no such agents.

Dignity, freedom, and power are all related. The freedom to choose otherwise becomes, with a slight shift in perspective, the power to make things happen. One of the attractions of agency is the image of ourselves as powerful controllers of experience and behavior standing apart from a world in which all other events are causally determined. While non-agency certainly implies giving up that image, it would be erroneous to conclude that it also means giving up our ability to influence events. In our zeal to view ourselves as free agents, we forget that, as persons, we are already controllers of our environment. The response we get from others every time we interact testifies to the very significant influence we have on what people feel and do. As constellations of body/mind, we have already changed the face of the earth, altered the air we breathe, and threaten to do even more. As persons we are extremely powerful. We are not agents, however, who create our own power.

Giving up our pretensions to contra-causal freedom and power returns us to earth where we belong. Instead of lamenting that loss, we can remind ourselves that our very special place in the universe has never rested on our divinity but on our unique animal gifts. Paramount among those gifts is reason. While human history is already rich in the application of reason to art and science, even greater accomplishments may be yet to come. In our ability to shape our environment we have no peers. Our capacity for changing ourselves – culturally, psychologically, even physiologically – makes us even more unique. None of those gifts requires an exemption from the laws of cause and effect. None requires divine status. What they demand, if we are ever to take full advantage of them, is that we give up our pretensions and accept our place as fully participating members of the natural world.

IS NON-AGENCY DEHUMANIZING?

For some readers the danger in giving up free agency lies not in the loss of exalted status but in the loss of our humanity. That fear is spawned by the belief that a soulless human is simply an animal driven exclusively by concern for its own survival. Without a belief in agency, the argument continues, there would be no guilt or empathy to restrain us from using each other as means to our own selfish ends. It is our souls, according to this view, that make civilized life possible.

That argument, of course, fails to account for the very high degree of civilization found in non-Western cultures where the individual soul is either seen as illusory (Buddhism) or assimilated to the all-encompassing One (Hinduism). More to the point, it fails to consider the dehumanizing effects of agency in our own culture. I refer to all the inhumanities we inflict upon each other in the name of justice and desert, inhumanities ranging from humiliation and ridicule to character assassination and capital punishment. As Freud suggested in *Civilization and Its Discontents*, much of the malicious delight we take in exposing and punishing the sins of others come from the workings of our own conscience. Self-blaming leaves a residue of frustration and anger that flows quickly into the blaming of others. If we long to hang every thief, rapist, or murderer we can get our hands on, it is at least partly due to the struggle in ourselves between the agent/I and its watchdog, the superego.

Rather than dehumanizing man, non-agency makes it easier for us to be humane by defusing the moral wrath that intensifies our need to hurt each other. Learning to view ourselves as spontaneous expressions of circumstance rather than as free agents makes us more accepting of each other's mistakes. By de-spiritualizing our own choices, non-agency makes us more tolerant of the choices that govern the behavior of others. It makes us more patient, self-forgetful, forgiving, and at peace with the world – all of which contribute to making us more humane.

However convincing that argument might be, a human without a soul remains suspect. As Skinner puts it, "from the traditional point of view, he may not seem to be a man at all." This is the point of view that identifies that self not with the person but with the homunculus agent/I. Ultimately, of course, the issue we have to address is not whether a person without a soul no longer seems like a person or whether soulless humans are less free, powerful, or humane, but whether souls are real. How one goes about making that determination depends on one's philosophical starting point. From the naturalistic perspective I have adopted throughout this book, there is no reason to believe that the human soul is anything more than a flattering fiction. Granting this, the real task before us is spelling out what non-agency implies for our personal lives – and then learning to live with those implications. Skinner is among the few who have attempted to steer us in that direction.

> The picture which emerges from a scientific analysis is not of a body with a person inside, but of a body which *is* a person in the sense that it displays a complex repertoire of behavior. The picture is, of course, unfamiliar. The man thus portrayed is a stranger, and from the traditional point of view he may not seem to be a man at all . . .

> We are told that what is threatened is "man *qua* man," or "man in his humanity," or "man as Thou and not It," or "man as a person not a thing." These are not very helpful expressions, but they supply a clue. What is being abolished is autonomous man – the inner man, the homunculus, the possessing demon, the man defended by the literature of freedom and dignity.

> His abolition has long been overdue. Autonomous man is a device used to explain what we cannot explain in any other way. He has been constructed from our ignorance, and as our understanding increases, the very stuff of which he is composed vanishes. Science does not dehumanize man, it dehomunculizes him, and it must do so if it is to prevent the

abolition of the human species. To man *qua* man we readily say good riddance. Only by dispossessing him can we turn to the real causes of human behavior. Only then can we turn from the inferred to the observed, from the miraculous to the natural . . .[5]

Over the last three centuries science has gradually replaced religion as a theoretical model for explaining the workings of the empirical world. As the continuing appeal of Christian theology, creationism, and astrology attest, however, the victory of science is far from complete. Of all the forms of animistic-spiritualistic thinking that persist in Western culture, free will represents one of the most subtle. Because it is so deeply rooted in our secular thinking, it has succeeded in eluding the scrutiny of science longer than those overtly religious concepts like heaven and hell, creation, immortality, and absolute good and evil. Our cultural commitment to science is too strong, however, to allow us to postpone indefinitely the discovery that the agent/I is also an illusion. Once we dispel that illusion, we can, as Skinner suggests, "turn from the miraculous to the natural." And get on with the task of learning to live with who we really are.

References

1. Nozick, R., *Philosophical Explanations*, Cambridge: Harvard University Press, 1981, p. 291.
2. Nozick, R., *Philosophical Explanations*, p. 315.
3. Dennett, D., *Elbow Room*, Cambridge: MIT Press, 1984, p. 153.
4. Dennett, D., *Elbow Room*, p. 153.
5. Skinner, B.F., *Beyond Freedom and Dignity*, New York: Ballantine Books, 1971, pp. 190-191.

BIBLIOGRAPHY

Augustine, *Confessions*, VII, 3, quoted in Adler, M., and Van Doren, C., *Great Treasury of Western Thought*, New York: R.R. Bowker, 1977.

Augustine, *City of God*, XXII, 24, quoted in Adler, M. and Van Doren, C., *Great Treasury of Western Thought*.

Ayer, A., *The Concept of a Person*, New York: St. Martin's Press, 1963.

Barrett, W., *Death of the Soul*, Garden City: Anchor Press, 1987.

Bateson, G., *Steps To an Ecology of Mind*, New York: Ballantine Books, 1972.

Beardsley, M. (ed.), *The European Philosophers from Descartes to Nietzsche*, New York: Modern Library, 1960.

Beck, A., *Cognitive Therapy and The Emotional Disorders*, New York: New American Library, 1976.

Beck, A., and Emery, G., *Anxiety Disorders and Phobias*, New York: Basic Books, 1985.

Becker, C., *The Heavenly City of the Eighteenth-Century Philosophers*, New Haven: Yale University Press, 1932.

Brandt, R., "Determinism and The Justifiability of Moral Blame," in S. Hook (ed.), *Determinism and Freedom*, New York: Collier Books, 1958.

Breer, P., and Locke, E., *Task Experience as a Source of Attitudes*, Homewood: Dorsey Press, 1965.

Campbell, J., *Occidental Mythology*, New York: Penguin Books, 1964.

Campbell, J., *Myths To Live By*, New York: Bantam Books, 1972.

Cannon, W.B., *The Wisdom of The Body*, New York: Norton, 1932.

Cassirer, E., *The Philosophy of the Enlightenment*, Princeton: Princeton University Press, 1951.

Clark, T., "Why We Want Free Will," unpublished MS, 1988.

Dennett, Daniel, *Elbow Room*, Cambridge: The MIT Press, 1984.

The Dhammapada, trans. Thomas Byrom, New York: Vintage Books, 1976.

Dinesen, I., *Out of Africa*, New York: Random House, 1937.

Engler, J., "Therapeutic Aims in Psychotherapy and Meditation," in *Transformations of Consciousness* by Ken Wilber, Jack Engler and Daniel P. Brown, Boston: Shambhala, 1986.

Epicurus, "Letter to Menoeceus," in Bailey, C., *Epicurus*, Oxford: Clarendon Press, 1926.

Erikson, E., *Identity: Youth and Crisis*, New York: W.W. Norton, 1968.

Fischer, J., *Moral Responsibility*, Ithaca: Cornell University Press, 1986.

Franklin, J., *Molecules of the Mind*, New York: Dell Publishing Co., 1987.

Freud, S., *The Ego and the Id*, New York: W.W. Norton, 1960.

Freud, S., *The Future of An Illusion*, New York: W.W. Norton, 1961.

Freud, S., *Civilization and Its Discontents*, New York: W.W. Norton, 1961.

Freud S., *Moses and Monotheism*, III, II, 9, quoted in Adler, M., and Van Doren, C., *Great Treasury of Western Thought*, New York: R.R. Bowker, 1977.

Glover, J., *I: The Philosophy and Psychology of Personal Identity*, London: The Penguin Press, 1988.

Hesse, H., *Demian*, quoted in Kaufmann, W., *Discovering the Mind*, New York: McGraw-Hill, 1980, vol. II.

Hofstadter, D., and Dennett, D., *The Mind's I*, New York: Basic Books, 1981.

Hume, D., *A Treatise of Human Nature*, Middlesex: Penguin Books, 1969. First published in 1739-40.

James, W., *The Varieties of Religious Experience*, New York: Penguin, 1982.

James, W., *The Principles of Psychology*, Cambridge: Harvard University Press. First published in 1890.

Kallen, H., *The Philosophy of William James*, New York: The Modern Library, 1925.

Kaufmann, W., *Nietzsche*, Princeton: Princeton University Press, 1974.

Kaufmann, W., *Goethe, Kant, and Hegel*, Vol. 1 of *Discovering the Mind*, New York: McGraw-Hill, 1980.

Kegan, R., *The Evolving Self*, Cambridge: Harvard University Press, 1982.

Kubler-Ross, E., *On Death and Dying*, New York: Macmillan, 1969.

Laing, R.D., *The Divided Self*, New York: Pantheon Books, 1960.

Lao-tsu, *Tao Te Ching*, translated by Gia-Fu Feng and Jane English, New York: Vintage Books, 1972.

Locke, J., *Some Thoughts Concerning Education*, 56, quoted in Adler, M., and Van Doren, C., *Great Treasury of Western Thought*, New York: R.R. Bowker, 1977.

Luther, *On the Enslaved Will*, quoted in Cassirer, E., *The Philosophy of the Enlightenment*, Princeton: Princeton University Press, 1951.

Mannheim, K., *Ideology and Utopia*, New York: Harcourt, Brace & Co., 1936.

Minsky, M., *The Society of Mind*, New York: Simon and Schuster, 1985.

Nagel, T., "Brain Bisection and The Unity of Consciousness," in Perry, J. (ed.) *Personal Identity*, Berkeley: University of California Press, 1975.

Nagel, T., *Mortal Questions*, Cambridge: Cambridge University Press, 1979.

Nietzsche, F., *The Will To Power*, New York: Vintage Books, 1968.

Nietzsche, F., *Ecce Homo*, New York: Vintage Books, 1969.

Nietzsche, F., *On the Genealogy of Morals*, New York: Vintage, 1969.

Nozick, R., *Philosophical Explanations*, Cambridge: Harvard University Press, 1981.

Parfit, D., *Reasons and Persons*, Oxford: Clarendon Press, 1984.

Parsons, T., Unpublished lectures, Harvard University, 1955.

Perls, F., *The Gestalt Approach*, Palo Alto: Science and Behavior Books, 1973.

Riesmann, D., *The Lonely Crowd*, New Haven: Yale University Press, 1950.

Rorty, A., "Fearing Death," *Philosophy*, 58, 1983.

Rougemont, D. de, *Love in the Western World*, New York: Pantheon, 1940.

Sacks, O., *The Man Who Mistook His Wife for a Hat*, New York: Harper and Row, 1970.

Sartre, J., "Existentialism Is A Humanism," in Kaufmann, W. (ed.), *Existentialism from Dostoevsky to Sartre*, New York: Meridian Books, 1975.

Schopenhauer, A., *The World As Will and Representation*, vol. II, tr. By E.F.J. Payne, New York: Dover Publications, 1966.

Searle. J., *Minds, Brains and Science*, Cambridge: Harvard University Press, 1984.

Skinner, B.f., *Beyond Freedom and Dignity*, New York: Ballantine Books, 1971.

Skinner, B.F., "The Origins of Cognitive Thought," *American Psychologist*, 1989, vol. 44., No. 1.

Strawson, P., *Freedom and Resentment*, London: Methuen & Co., 1974.

Thomas, D., *Collected Poems*, New York: New Directions, 1971.

Turkle, S., *Psychoanalytic Politics*, London: Burnett, 1979.

Turkle, S., *The Second Self*, New York: Simon and Schuster, 1984.

Vaihinger, H., *The Philosophy of As If*, London: Routledge and Kegan Paul, 1935. First published in 1911.

Watts, A., *The Wisdom of Insecurity*, New York: Vintage, 1951.

Watts, A., *The Way of Zen*, New York: Vintage Books, 1957.

Watts, A., *The Book*, New York: Vintage, 1966.

Watts, A., *The Essence of Alan Watts*, Millbrae: Celestial Arts, 1974.

Watts, A., *Tao: The Watercourse Way*, New York: Pantheon, Books, 1975.

INDEX

CPSIA information can be obtained at www.ICGtesting.com
Printed in the USA
BVOW081142061112

304805BV00001B/130/P